Praise for *Microsoft Certified Azure Developer Associate (AZ-204) Study Guide*

A must-have guide for aspiring and experienced Azure developers alike, Adora Nwodo's *Microsoft Certified Azure Developer Associate (AZ-204) Study Guide* makes Azure approachable, actionable, and inspiring. This book not only equips readers with the hands-on skills and strategies needed for certification and real-world cloud success, but also lights the way for cultivating true mastery and confidence in modern cloud development.

—*Sanyam Jain, senior cloud and compliance security engineer, Domo, Inc.*

Adora Nwodo has created a rare and valuable resource that bridges the world of certification prep with the demands of enterprise-grade cloud solutions. It's a guide that enables aspiring cloud leaders to think with precision and build with purpose.

—*Vishrut Trivedi, senior product leader, data and AI*

This book will teach you how to design, build, and secure Azure solutions. It covers the Azure tools you need to run your solutions, store your data, and secure it all. It gives you practical code samples showing exactly how to build your Azure projects. After reading this book, you will be ready to pass the AZ-204 certification exam and to succeed in building valuable projects with Azure.

—*Eric Potter, director of IT Education*

Microsoft Certified Azure Developer Associate (AZ-204) Study Guide

In-Depth Guidance and Practice

Adora Nwodo

Microsoft Certified Azure Developer Associate (AZ-204) Study Guide
by Adora Nwodo

Published by O'Reilly Media, Inc., 141 Stony Circle, Suite 195, Santa Rosa, CA 95401.

O'Reilly books may be purchased for educational, business, or sales promotional use. Online editions are also available for most titles (*http://oreilly.com*). For more information, contact our corporate/institutional sales department: 800-998-9938 or *corporate@oreilly.com*.

Acquisitions Editor: Megan Laddusaw
Development Editor: Jill Leonard
Production Editor: Aleeya Rahman
Copyeditor: nSight, Inc.
Proofreader: Heather Walley
Indexer: BIM Creatives, LLC
Cover Designer: Karen Montgomery
Cover Illustrator: José Marzan Jr.
Interior Designer: David Futato
Interior Illustrator: Kate Dullea

August 2025: First Edition

Revision History for the First Edition
2025-08-07: First Release

See *http://oreilly.com/catalog/errata.csp?isbn=9781098173494* for release details.

978-1-098-17349-4

[LSI]

Table of Contents

Preface

There's never been a more exciting time to be building in the cloud. Every day, developers are shipping faster, scaling further, and solving bigger problems. That's largely because of the flexibility and power of platforms like Microsoft Azure. What makes it even more exciting is how Azure has evolved. It's no longer just a platform for large enterprises or specialized teams. It's a place where anyone, regardless of their background, can build reliable, production-grade applications.

I've always been drawn to Azure. Not just because I worked at Microsoft, but because I've seen how much of a difference it makes when developers understand how to use it well. You can experiment freely, manage resources with precision, and build systems that actually support your users in real life. That's powerful.

If you're preparing for the AZ-204 exam, you're not just chasing a certification. You're building the kind of knowledge that helps you create things that matter. I'm glad you picked up this book.

Who Should Read This Book

This book is for developers who want to take their Azure skills to the next level. Maybe you're already building web apps, working with APIs, or deploying resources to the cloud, and now you're ready to do it with more structure, confidence, and depth. Maybe you're moving from another cloud platform and want to understand how things work in Azure. Or maybe you're just starting to take on more cloud responsibilities in your role and need a clear path forward.

If you're preparing for the AZ-204 exam, this book is built for you. But even beyond the exam, it's written to help working professionals understand what it really means to build, deploy, secure, and monitor applications on Azure. Whether you work at a startup or a large company, the skills covered here are relevant and practical.

To get the most out of this book, you should already be comfortable writing code in at least one programming language, preferably C#, JavaScript, or Python. You should also understand the basics of HTTP APIs and general application development. You don't need to be an Azure expert before you start, but by the time you finish, you'll think like one.

Why I Wrote This Book

When I first started working with Azure, I was impressed by how much was possible. The platform had solid documentation, rich tools, and support for building almost anything you could imagine. But even with all that, it wasn't always easy to connect the dots, especially when trying to figure out what skills really mattered for day-to-day development or how to prioritize learning in a way that made sense.

Many years later, that's why I wrote this book. I've spent a good part of my career building on Azure, as a consultant, as an engineer at Microsoft in global-scale engineering teams, and now as a platform engineering leader. I've seen what developers struggle with, what teams need to deliver faster, and what kinds of knowledge actually move the needle when you're working in production.

This book is meant to bring clarity to all of that. It's about helping you grow into the kind of developer who builds systems that scale, who understands how Azure services work together, and who can make smart decisions under pressure. If that's what you're aiming for, you're in the right place.

Navigating This Book

This book is organized as follows:

- Chapter 1, "Introduction to the Azure Developer Associate Exam", introduces the AZ-204 certification, explaining the exam structure, study tips, and what it means to be an Azure developer associate.
- Chapter 2, "Azure App Service", and Chapter 3, "Azure Function Apps", cover web and serverless application development using Azure App Service and Azure Functions, including continuous integration and continuous deployment (CI/CD) and deployment strategies.
- Chapter 4, "Infrastructure as Code with Azure Bicep", dives into infrastructure as code using Azure Bicep, teaching you how to define, deploy, and manage cloud resources through code.
- Chapter 5, "Managing Data in Azure", focuses on managing structured, semi-structured, and unstructured data using Azure's storage and database solutions.
- Chapter 6, "Building Containerized Solutions on Azure", teaches you how to build, deploy, and manage containerized applications with Azure Kubernetes Service and Azure Container Registry.

- Chapter 7, "Implementing Azure Security", explores Azure security practices, including identity, access, network protection, and threat detection.
- Chapter 8, "API Management in Azure", covers API Management, from securing and publishing APIs to monitoring and scaling them effectively.
- Chapter 9, "Event-Driven Architecture with Azure", introduces event-driven architecture with services like Event Grid, Event Hubs, and Service Bus for building reactive systems.
- Chapter 10, "Monitoring and Observability on Azure", explains monitoring and observability tools in Azure, helping you keep applications healthy and cost-effective.
- Chapter 11, "Caching Strategies in Azure", focuses on caching strategies, patterns, and services like Azure Cache for Redis and Azure CDN.
- Chapter 12, "Networking in Azure", covers networking fundamentals in Azure, including VNets, subnets, private endpoints, and load balancing.
- Chapter 13, "Developer Practices in Azure", explores essential developer tools and practices, using a fictional app to bring everything together.
- Chapter 14, "Putting It All Together", helps you apply everything you've learned, with strategies for tackling the exam and thinking like a real-world cloud developer.

Conventions Used in This Book

The following typographical conventions are used in this book:

Italic
: Indicates new terms, URLs, email addresses, filenames, and file extensions.

`Constant width`
: Used for program listings, as well as within paragraphs to refer to program elements such as variable or function names, databases, data types, environment variables, statements, and keywords.

`< >`
: Shows text that should be replaced with user-supplied values or by values determined by context.

This element signifies a general note.

O'Reilly Online Learning

O'REILLY®

For more than 40 years, *O'Reilly Media* has provided technology and business training, knowledge, and insight to help companies succeed.

Our unique network of experts and innovators share their knowledge and expertise through books, articles, and our online learning platform. O'Reilly's online learning platform gives you on-demand access to live training courses, in-depth learning paths, interactive coding environments, and a vast collection of text and video from O'Reilly and 200+ other publishers. For more information, visit *https://oreilly.com*.

How to Contact Us

Please address comments and questions concerning this book to the publisher:

O'Reilly Media, Inc.
141 Stony Circle, Suite 195
Santa Rosa, CA 95401
800-889-8969 (in the United States or Canada)
707-827-7019 (international or local)
707-829-0104 (fax)
support@oreilly.com
https://oreilly.com/about/contact.html

We have a web page for this book, where we list errata, examples, and any additional information. You can access this page at *https://oreil.ly/microsoft-certified-azure*.

For news and information about our books and courses, visit *https://oreilly.com*.

Find us on LinkedIn: *https://linkedin.com/company/oreilly-media*.

Watch us on YouTube: *https://youtube.com/oreillymedia*.

Acknowledgments

Writing a book is never a solo effort, and I'm incredibly grateful to the people who made this possible.

First, I thank God, for the wisdom, strength, and peace that carried me through every part of this process. His grace has been my foundation from start to finish.

To Jill, my editor, thank you deeply for your thoughtfulness, patience, and encouragement. You made this book better in every way, and I'm so thankful I got to work with you. I'm also grateful to Megan, John, and the rest of the wonderful O'Reilly team for your support, feedback, and belief in this project from the start.

To my friends and family, thank you for being a constant source of strength, laughter, and perspective. Your love created the space I needed to stay grounded.

To my team, thank you for holding it down. Because of you, I could focus on writing while continuing to lead, educate, and grow. I deeply appreciate the way you've kept things moving across NexaScale, my nonprofit work, and everything else under the Adora brand umbrella. This book exists because you made the space for it.

Thank you, all of you, for being part of this journey.

CHAPTER 1

Introduction to the Azure Developer Associate Exam

The beginning is the most important part of any work, especially in the case of a young and tender thing, for that is the time at which the character is being formed and the desired impression is more readily taken.

—Plato

Becoming Azure certified provides many benefits. In this chapter, you will learn about the role of an Azure developer, as well as the benefits of becoming Microsoft certified. I'll also share what's required of you and walk through how the exam is structured. Additionally, this chapter will share tips on how you can create a study plan to further set yourself up for success. Beginnings lay the foundation for exceptional work. Understanding the fundamentals of the Azure Developer Associate Exam is crucial for anyone looking to take this exam to make the best of it.

By the end of this chapter, you will be equipped with a clear understanding of what lies ahead and how to approach your study journey. The road to certification may be challenging, but with the right preparation and mindset, it is entirely achievable. Let's get started on your path to becoming a certified Azure developer associate!

The State of Azure in the Cloud Market

Learning Azure is increasingly important due to its substantial market share and the expanding role it plays in cloud computing. Azure is one of the most popular cloud computing platforms right now. As of 2024, Azure holds a significant position in the global cloud infrastructure market, capturing approximately 25% of the market share. This places Azure firmly in second place, just behind Amazon Web Services (AWS), which has a market share of around 31%. Google Cloud follows with about 11% of the market share. In addition to market share, it's also important to consider Azure's extensive customer base, which has grown in recent years. As of early 2024, Azure served nearly 350,000 businesses globally, reflecting a 14.2% increase in its customer base from the previous year.

Learning Azure gives you the knowledge to take full advantage of its global network, and this can enhance your ability to support and drive growth for businesses of different sizes through effective cloud strategies. With increasing reliance on the cloud, this is a timely skill to develop.

Understanding the Role of an Azure Developer

The role of an Azure developer is important in the modern cloud ecosystem. As businesses increasingly migrate to the cloud, the demand for skilled Azure developers who can design, build, and maintain cloud-based applications and services continues to grow significantly. As you read this section, it's important to think of yourself as an *Azure developer in training* and know that these skills are about to become yours as you continue to develop your knowledge in this area.

Azure developers are responsible for various tasks, including designing applications that run on cloud solutions, making sure those applications are compliant with specified security standards, and optimizing performance. They work with services like Azure Functions, Azure Kubernetes Service (AKS), virtual private network (VPNs), Azure security services, and more to create and maintain secure applications.

Let's examine the skills of an Azure developer:

Technical proficiency
: Developers should have a blend of cloud-specific skills and programming knowledge. This means understanding programming languages like C#, TypeScript, or Python, and also understanding Azure software development kits (SDKs), APIs, and development tools like Visual Studio and Azure DevOps.

Collaboration
: Azure developers work across multidisciplinary teams and collaborate with product managers, security professionals, data analysts, other software engineers, and more. As a result, it's important to effectively communicate and also be a good team player so that projects meet technical requirements and business objectives.

Continuous improvement
: The Azure organization within Microsoft is constantly innovating and creating new cloud services for different things, as well as improvements to their already existing services. As a result, you should be committed to continuous learning and improvement so you consistently have up-to-date knowledge.

Developing for scalability
: Most of our daily interactions are currently influenced by distributed applications, and this shows how important they are in technology today. Working in this discipline involves understanding networking and using load balancing, autoscaling, and microservices architecture to ensure that applications can handle increased traffic and remain available under various conditions.

Monitoring and support
: In some cases, and depending on how your team is structured, you may also be tasked with monitoring, troubleshooting, and optimization. Here, you may be required to use tools like Azure Monitor and Azure Log Analytics to track application performance and identify issues.

Now that you're clear on some of the priorities of an Azure developer, let's talk about the benefits you get from being Microsoft certified.

Benefits of Becoming a Microsoft Certified Azure Developer

Becoming Microsoft certified can have different benefits that may add long-term value to your cloud engineering career. Let's explore a few:

Certifications are a formal validation of your skills and knowledge.
: It shows that you have the ability to design, build, test, and maintain cloud applications and services using Azure. This formal validation can separate you from your peers who are noncertified, which gives you an edge when recruiters are assessing candidates.

Earning this certification gives you professional recognition from both your peers and industry leaders.
: It highlights your dedication to professional growth and shows that you are committed to maintaining high standards in your work. This acknowledgment can enhance the respect and trust you receive within your organization and your broader professional network.

Getting certified takes work.
: It requires a lot of commitment and involves rigorous study and practical application of your skills. This contributes to personal growth and increased confidence in your abilities. As you overcome the challenges of certification, you build resilience and a deeper understanding of Azure, which can be applied to different disciplines.

Certifications give you a comprehensive understanding of Azure that extends beyond the scope of typical project work.
: As you build projects, you may only use a limited subset of Azure's offerings. Certifications, on the other hand, expose you to the full range of Azure services and capabilities. This broad knowledge can enhance your ability to innovate and solve diverse challenges in your cloud engineering career.

Certifications can make you more attractive to employers, especially those looking to meet Microsoft partner status requirements.
: With a certification, recruiters and hiring managers can quickly see your expertise, which can lead to more interview opportunities and potential job offers. This is particularly beneficial in highly competitive fields where employers are looking for candidates who have proven their capabilities through recognized credentials. This demand can increase your job prospects and make you a valuable candidate for many companies.

Ultimately, the decision to pursue certification is personal, but the rewards in career advancement, recognition, and personal development make it a worthwhile endeavor.

Prerequisites

Here are some of the prerequisites you'll need as you get ready to take the exam. Having these foundations will also be very helpful as you continue reading this book.

Cloud Fundamentals

Before diving into Azure-specific skills, it's important to have a solid understanding of fundamental cloud computing concepts. This includes knowledge of different cloud service models such as infrastructure as a service (IaaS), platform as a service (PaaS), and software as a service (SaaS). It's also important to understand cloud deployment models—public, private, and hybrid clouds. Let's do a quick review.

Cloud service models

Cloud service models are frameworks that define how cloud services are delivered and utilized. Here are the three main cloud service models:

Infrastructure as a service
: IaaS provides businesses with virtualized computing resources over the internet. It allows businesses to have on-demand access to cloud infrastructure such as servers, storage, and networking.

Platform as a service
: PaaS provides businesses with tools, or platforms, over the internet. These tools are designed to help businesses with building, testing, deploying, and managing cloud applications.

Software as a service
: SaaS provides everyone with software applications over the internet on a subscription basis.

Cloud deployment models

Cloud deployment models specify the configuration of a cloud infrastructure. These models define how cloud services are made available to users and how resources are allocated and managed. The five main cloud deployment models are:

Public cloud
: With this model, services are delivered publicly over the internet and shared across multiple organizations. These services are usually owned by third-party cloud providers.

Private cloud
: With the private cloud, an organization has access to a cloud computing environment that is dedicated exclusively to its use. This setup can be hosted on premises in the organization's own data center or by a third-party service provider.

Hybrid cloud
: In the hybrid cloud, an organization combines public and private clouds, allowing data and applications to be shared between them. This model combines the scalability and cost-efficiency of public cloud services with the control and security of a private cloud.

Multicloud
: In a multicloud model, organizations use multiple cloud computing services from different providers simultaneously. This allows them to distribute workloads across various cloud environments, optimizing for performance, cost, and specific service features. Unlike hybrid cloud, which integrates public and private clouds to create a unified environment, multicloud does not necessarily connect these clouds; instead, it focuses on using the best services from each provider independently. This approach helps businesses avoid vendor lock-in, enhance reliability by diversifying their cloud strategy, and take advantage of the unique strengths and pricing options of each provider.

Community cloud
: A community cloud is shared by a group of organizations with similar needs, like security, compliance, or business goals. It provides a cloud environment tailored to these shared needs, allowing the organizations to work together while keeping control over their data and resources.

Knowing these deployment models helps you choose the right one for your needs. Each model has its benefits and can be customized to fit what you require. I assume you have this knowledge if you're preparing for the Azure developer certification. If these topics are unfamiliar to you, I recommend you take time to familiarize yourself with them prior to continuing with this book so you're able to get the most out of this publication. To learn more about the fundamentals of the cloud, you can read my third book, called *Confident Cloud* (*https://oreil.ly/ccloud*). You also can read *Essentials of Cloud Computing* by K. Chandrasekaran, *Cloud Computing* by A. Srinivasan, or *Cloud Computing Basics: A Non-Technical Introduction* by Anders Lisdorf.

An Azure Account

Having an active Azure account is important for hands-on practice and learning. Microsoft gives free Azure accounts with a limited number of credits to get started. You can create a free account by visiting *https://portal.azure.com*. It's important to note that while you do need to enter your credit card details to sign up, you won't be charged unless you choose to upgrade or exceed the free tier limits. Microsoft provides clear alerts before any charges are incurred, ensuring you stay within your budget and avoid unexpected costs. An active Azure account allows you to:

- Explore the Azure portal.
- Deploy resources like web apps, databases, storage accounts, virtual machines, and more.
- Use Azure's monitoring tools to track resource usage and performance.

Azure CLI

The Azure CLI is a set of commands you can use to create and manage Azure resources. This CLI allows you to interact with Azure services through the command line. With the Azure CLI, you can:

- Write command-line scripts to automate tasks on Azure.
- Perform actions that help you manage your Azure resources.
- Retrieve information about your Azure resources and troubleshoot issues.

You can get the Azure CLI on Microsoft's website (*https://oreil.ly/azcli*). It's available for Windows, macOS, and Linux, and you can also run it in your Docker container.

Azure PowerShell

Azure PowerShell is another command-line tool that allows you to manage your Azure resources using PowerShell cmdlets. It provides an alternative to the Azure CLI and is particularly useful for people who are already familiar with PowerShell scripting. With Azure PowerShell, you can:

- Automate tasks on Azure and manage your Azure resources.
- Add more complex scripts to your continuous integration and continuous deployment (CI/CD) pipeline to make it more dynamic.
- Retrieve information about your Azure resources and troubleshoot issues.

You can download Azure PowerShell (*https://oreil.ly/tn_qE*) on Windows, Linux, macOS, or your Docker container.

PowerShell, the underlying framework, is a cross-platform command-line shell and scripting language used for automating tasks and managing configurations. It passes objects between commands for efficient data handling and supports a wide range of extensions through modules, such as Azure PowerShell. This makes it a versatile tool for managing systems across different environments, integrating with other Microsoft products, and enhancing automation workflows. For more information or to download PowerShell for your machine, visit the Microsoft PowerShell page (*https://oreil.ly/uSrv0*).

Eligibility Criteria

In addition to the prerequisites, here are some eligibility criteria for taking the Azure certification exam:

- Candidates should have at least one to two years of professional experience in developing cloud applications with Azure.
- Candidates should also be able to program in an Azure-supported language such as Python, C#, JavaScript, or Java.
- Candidates should be proficient in Azure because this is the knowledge assessed by the certification exam. Specifically, candidates should be proficient in Azure SDKs, data storage options, data connections, APIs, security features (authentication and authorization), container services, and debugging.
- Candidates should also be proficient in Azure CLI, PowerShell, and CI/CD. This familiarity is important for implementing and managing Azure DevOps pipelines.

Additionally, the skills measured for this certification cover several critical areas. These include developing Azure compute solutions, which involve creating and managing virtual machines and containerized applications. Candidates must also know how to develop for Azure storage using services like Azure Blob Storage and databases. Implementing Azure security is another key area, focusing on safeguarding data and applications using tools such as Microsoft Entra ID and role-based access control. Additionally, the certification covers monitoring, troubleshooting, and optimizing Azure solutions to maintain and enhance performance.

All of these areas will be covered in this book.

Overview of the Exam Structure

The Microsoft Certified: Azure Developer Associate certification (Exam AZ-204) (*https://oreil.ly/dmf4l*) validates essential skills for developing applications and services on Microsoft Azure. The following is an overview of its structure.

Exam Format

The AZ-204 exam is an online, monitored exam. It typically lasts 100 minutes and includes a variety of question types. Candidates should allocate approximately two hours for the entire process, which includes reviewing instructions, signing the nondisclosure agreement, and providing feedback.

Exam Registration and Policies

Candidates can register for the exam through the Microsoft Certification Dashboard. The exam fee varies by location but is generally around USD 165. The exam may contain interactive components, is supervised, and isn't a closed-book assessment. If a candidate fails, a 24-hour wait is required before retaking the exam.

Candidates can also take unscheduled breaks during the exam, but the exam clock will continue to run, so it's important to note this and schedule your time accordingly.

Preparing a Study Plan

Preparing for the AZ-204 exam requires a structured study plan to help you cover the exam objectives so you are ready. Here's how you can create an effective study plan:

Understand the subject areas the exam covers
: We've talked about this in this chapter, so you should now have an idea of the skills measured and topics covered. This will help you to focus your studying on the important things you really need to know.

Study

Reading this book is a great first step because this study guide will cover all the key areas needed for the exam. You'll find detailed explanations, practical examples, and tips to help you understand and apply the concepts. This book, combined with hands-on practice, will prepare you thoroughly for the certification exam.

Set a study schedule and track your goals

Break down your study sessions into manageable chunks and allocate time to each exam objective. For example, you can do something like this:

- Weeks 1–2: Developing Azure compute solutions
- Weeks 3–4: Developing for Azure storage
- Week 5: Implementing Azure security
- Week 6: Monitoring and optimizing solutions
- Week 7: API management
- Weeks 8–10: Review and practice exams

Note that the number of weeks you allocate to each exam objective and how you break down your learning should be based on:

- Your current knowledge: Spend more time on areas where you have less experience.
- Learning style: Adjust the pace and methods to suit your personal learning preferences.
- Schedule flexibility: Consider your availability and other commitments you might have and account for this when creating your study plan so it's sustainable.

Practice

Theoretical knowledge is necessary, but practicing on Azure is how you verify that you know what you've read about. Create case studies for problems you're passionate about and implement solutions using various Azure services. Experiment with deploying applications, setting up storage, configuring security, and integrating third-party services. This hands-on practice not only reinforces your learning but also helps you build a portfolio of real-world projects that demonstrate your skills to potential employers. Beyond practicing for your certification, these portfolio projects may also help you get jobs.

Join communities
: If there are Azure user groups, or other communities around you, you could join them to meet people currently building on Azure, too. These communities can provide support and tips from fellow learners, certified professionals, and other builders in the ecosystem.

Take mock exams
: Regularly review what you've learned to reinforce your knowledge. Take mock exams to test your understanding and adjust your study plan based on your performance. As you iterate, you should also identify weak areas and focus more on those topics.

Final revision
: In the final weeks leading up to the exam, you should focus on revision (as opposed to learning something new). Go over all the exam objectives, ensure you understand key concepts, and take several full-length practice exams to build confidence.

With a structured plan and consistent effort, you'll be well prepared to pass the AZ-204 exam and advance your career in Azure and the cloud.

Summary

Effective preparation is essential for understanding the exam objectives and structure. Achieving the Azure Developer Associate certification not only validates your skills but also opens up numerous career opportunities, making you a valuable asset in the tech industry. With dedication and the right preparation strategy, you are well on your way to becoming a certified Azure Developer Associate. The following chapters will focus on the core concepts of Azure. Good luck on your journey!

CHAPTER 2
Azure App Service

Azure App Service makes it easy to deploy, manage, and scale your web apps. It's a fantastic platform for developers to leverage so they can focus on what they do best: building great applications. Azure App Service supports multiple programming languages including .NET, Java, Node.js, PHP, or Python, and provides a managed platform (PaaS) that abstracts away the underlying infrastructure. This means that developers can deploy their applications without worrying about server management, patching, or networking. Additionally, Azure App Service automatically handles scaling, load balancing, and high availability, ensuring that applications remain responsive and resilient under varying loads.

In this chapter, you will see how to use Azure App Service for your web application development and deployment processes. First, you will be introduced to the features and benefits of Azure App Service, providing a solid foundation for understanding its capabilities. Next, you will go through the process of building and deploying web applications using this platform, highlighting best practices and tips for optimal performance. You'll also see how you can use Azure DevOps and GitHub Actions to deploy an app to Azure App Service. Finally, you will learn about advanced deployment techniques such as blue-green deployments using deployment slots.

Introduction to Azure App Service

Azure App Service is a comprehensive cloud offering from Microsoft Azure that allows developers to build, deploy, and scale web applications, mobile backends, and RESTful APIs quickly and efficiently. As a fully managed PaaS, it abstracts away the underlying infrastructure, enabling developers to focus solely on application development.

Another significant advantage of Azure App Service is its managed production environment. This platform automatically handles the patching and maintenance of the operating system and language frameworks, freeing developers from routine administrative tasks. This allows them to focus on writing great applications while Azure takes care of the underlying platform maintenance. Additionally, Azure App Service supports containerization and Docker, enabling developers to dockerize their applications and host custom Windows or Linux containers. This feature also supports running sidecar containers, making it easier to migrate Docker-based applications to Azure.

Azure App Service is optimized for DevOps practices, and it is fairly straightforward to use it with continuous integration and deployment tools like Azure DevOps, GitHub, Bitbucket, Docker Hub, and Azure Container Registry (ACR). App Service also supports scaling applications globally with high availability, allowing developers to host their apps anywhere within Microsoft's extensive data center infrastructure. Azure's global reach and the App Service SLA (service-level agreement) ensure that applications remain highly available and performant.

Security and compliance are top priorities for Azure App Service, which is ISO, SOC, and PCI compliant. These standards are important for keeping data safe and ensuring that cloud services are secure and reliable:

ISO compliance
: This refers to standards set by the International Organization for Standardization, which ensures best practices for security management.

SOC compliance
: SOC stands for Service Organization Controls, which are reports that verify if a service's controls, like security and data handling, are effective.

PCI compliance
: This refers to the Payment Card Industry standards that ensure secure handling of credit card information.

Azure App Service also provides robust security features, including IP address restrictions, managed service identities, and protection against subdomain takeovers. Now that you've been introduced to Azure App Services and their advantages, the next section will cover how to build and deploy web apps.

What Is a Service-Level Agreement?

An SLA is an agreement from a cloud provider (e.g., Microsoft) that defines the expected level of service, such as uptime and performance. It's essentially a promise that the service will be available a certain percentage of the time, like 99.99%, and outlines what happens if the provider fails to meet these expectations. This helps you understand the reliability you can expect for your applications.

Building and Deploying to Azure App Service

Building and deploying web apps to Azure App Service involves several steps.

Minimally, you'll need:

- The Azure CLI: The Azure Command-Line Interface (CLI) is a set of commands used to create and manage Azure resources. You can download it from Microsoft (*https://oreil.ly/Gt-Rg*).
- Azure PowerShell: Azure PowerShell has a set of commands used to create and manage Azure resources. You can download it from Microsoft (*https://oreil.ly/Hd_Bu*).
- An Azure account: You'll be creating an Azure service and also deploying your code to Azure. If you don't have an Azure account, sign up through Microsoft (*https://oreil.ly/wj8lt*).

Next, I'll walk through how to create your Azure App Service infrastructure and deploy your web app to it using the Azure CLI, Azure PowerShell, and the Azure portal.

Using Azure App Service in the Azure CLI

To get access to Azure through the CLI, you need to run:

```
$ az login
```

This command allows you to access your Azure account through the Azure CLI. When you run this command, it will open a web page where you can sign in with your Azure credentials. After signing in, the CLI will have access to your Azure resources and you can start executing various Azure commands to manage your services and infrastructure.

To create an App Service, you will need to create a resource group first. In Azure, a resource group is a logical container that holds related resources for an Azure solution. You can manage and organize resources like databases, storage accounts, and web apps within a resource group. When creating resources in Azure, it's important to understand the concept of scopes. Scopes in Azure define the boundaries within which permissions are granted. The main levels of scope are:

Tenant
: A tenant is a dedicated instance of Microsoft Entra ID (previously known as Active Directory) that an organization receives when it signs up for a Microsoft cloud service such as Azure. A tenant can contain one or more subscriptions. It's the highest level of organization in Azure, and it manages users, groups, and applications across all subscriptions within the tenant.

Management group
: This is the second-highest level of scope. Management groups help you organize your subscriptions, making it easier to manage access, policies, and compliance for multiple subscriptions. You can apply policies and access controls to a management group, and they will be inherited by all subscriptions and resources within that group.

Subscription
: Each subscription can have multiple resource groups and is associated with billing. Subscriptions help you separate resources for different projects, environments, or teams. They also act as a security boundary for resources.

Resource group
: Within a subscription, resource groups help you organize and manage related resources. A resource group acts as a container for resources that share the same lifecycle, allowing you to deploy, update, and delete them together. You can apply policies, permissions, and monitoring at the resource group level.

Resource
: This is the smallest scope. A resource could be any service instance you create, such as a virtual machine, storage account, or web app. Resources inherit permissions and policies from their parent resource group, subscription, and management group.

Now that you know what scopes are and the different scopes in Azure, run the following command to create an Azure resource group that will hold the Azure App Service resource:

```
$ az group create --name SampleRg --location eastus
```

The previous code snippet creates a resource group named `SampleRg` in the `eastus` region. In Azure, regions are specific geographic locations where data centers are situated. Choosing a region is important because it determines where your resources are physically located, which can affect performance, compliance, and availability. For example, you might choose a region close to your users for faster access or select a region that meets specific regulatory requirements.

Now that you've created your resource group, you can create the App Service plan.

What Is an App Service Plan?

An App Service plan in Azure provides the resources for your web apps to run. When you create an App Service plan, you select the region, pricing tier, and instance size(s) that determine the compute resources available for your web applications. Essentially, the App Service plan acts as a container for your web apps and defines the resources and features available to them. It supports different tiers such as Free, Shared, Basic, Standard, Premium, and Isolated. Each of these tiers offer different levels of performance, scalability, and features.

The following command is used to create an App Service plan:

```
$ az appservice plan create --name
                             --resource-group
                            [--app-service-environment]
                            [--hyper-v]
                            [--is-linux]
                            [--location]
                            [--no-wait]
                            [--number-of-workers]
                            [--per-site-scaling]
                            [--sku {B1, B2, B3, D1, F1, FREE, I1, I1MV2,
                                    I1V2, I2, I2MV2, I2V2, I3, I3MV2, I3V2,
                                    I4MV2, I4V2, I5MV2, I5V2, I6V2, P0V3, P1MV3,
                                    P1V2, P1V3, P2MV3, P2V2, P2V3, P3MV3, P3V2,
                                    P3V3, P4MV3, P5MV3, S1, S2, S3, SHARED, WS1,
                                    WS2, WS3}]
                            [--tags]
                            [--zone-redundant]
```

The parameters in the square brackets [ ] are optional, so if you create an App Service plan with only its name and resource group, it defaults to the basic tier. When using optional parameters, make sure to remove the brackets and just include the parameter and its value. For example, to specify the region, you would use `--location eastus` without brackets.

To create an App Service plan with the name `SamplePlan`, in the `sampleRg` resource group, and with the `P1V2` SKU (stock-keeping unit), the command would look like this:

```
$ az appservice plan create --name SamplePlan
                             --resource-group SampleRg
                             --sku P1V2
```

For detailed information on all parameters and options, please refer to the official Azure CLI documentation for `az appservice plan create` (*https://oreil.ly/v_ZMx*). To understand and differentiate between the various SKUs available, you can check the App Service pricing details (*https://oreil.ly/ohz_E*), which provides a comprehensive comparison of features, costs, and use cases for each SKU.

Once the App Service plan is created, you can now create the app service that will use that plan. This happens with the `az webapp` command. The following code snippet will create an app service (also known as a web app):

```
$  az webapp create --resource-group SampleRg
                    --plan SamplePlan
                    --name sampleApp
```

Please note that running this (and future resource creation commands) may start to use your Azure credits or incur expenses. Make sure to monitor your Azure usage and understand the pricing details for the resources you create.

Azure supports various deployment methods. Here, we'll cover ZIP deployment using the Azure CLI. This method involves zipping your build artifacts and deploying them directly to Azure. To run a ZIP deployment, run the following command:

```
$ az webapp deploy
     --resource-group SampleRg
     --name sampleApp
     --src-path ./path/to/file.zip
     --type zip
     --async true
```

In this code snippet, the `az webapp deploy` command deploys the artifact to Azure Web Apps. For this to work, you will need to pass in the name of the resource group where the app service is deployed, the name of the app service, and the path to the built artifacts. In this command, `./path/to/file.zip` refers to the path where your ZIP file is located on your local machine. This ZIP file should include all the components of your web application you want to deploy. The path should be adjusted to point to the actual location of your ZIP file. For example, if your ZIP file is named *myapp.zip* and is located in your current directory, you would use `--src-path ./myapp.zip`. Make sure your ZIP file is structured correctly and includes everything needed for your app to run properly.

Using Azure App Service in the Azure Portal

You can also carry out the same steps in the Azure portal. First, check that you are logged in. As shown in the previous section, you will need to create a resource group first. To do this, search for "Resource groups" in the search bar at the top and click on the result under Services (Figure 2-1). This will launch a page with the list of already existing resource groups in the current directory (Tenant).

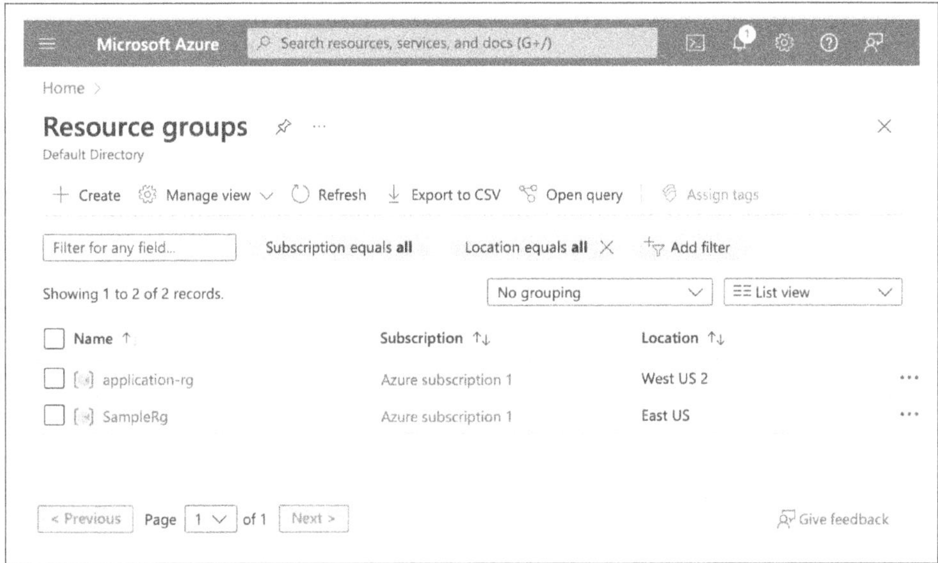

Figure 2-1. List of resource groups in the current directory

Click Create. This will launch the window where you will enter all the information required to create the resource group. Follow the wizard and specify all the necessary details. Once this step is completed, you can review changes; if there are no errors, go ahead to create your resource group. This process might take a few seconds (or minutes) depending on your internet connection and other factors. Figure 2-2 shows what the Azure portal looks like when you attempt to create a resource group.

Once the resource group is successfully created, you will be able to see it in the list of resource groups available to you, and you will be able to add more resources there. If you were successful creating your resource group, the next step will be for you to create your App Service plan (also known as hosting plan).

To create your App Service plan, search for "App Service plans" in the search bar at the top of the window and click on the result under Services. This will launch a page with the list of already existing App Service plans in the current directory (Tenant). Click Create to launch the window where you will enter all the information required to create the App Service plans. Follow the wizard and specify all the necessary details. Once this step is completed, you can review changes; if there are no errors, go ahead to create your App Service plan.

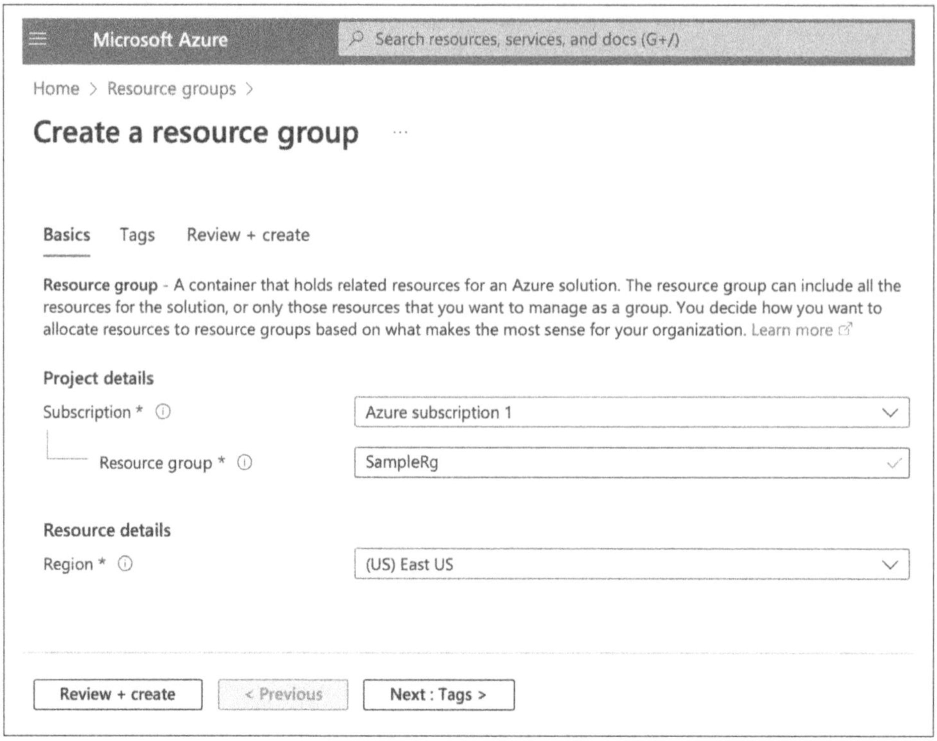

Figure 2-2. Creating a resource group in Azure

Once the App Service plan is successfully created, you will be able to see it in the list of App Service plans available to you, and you will be able to add more resources there. If you were successful in creating your App Service plan, the next step will be for you to create your app service (also known as web app).

To create your app service, search for "App Services" in the search bar at the top and click on the result under Services. This will launch a page with the list of already existing app services in the current directory (Tenant). Click Create to launch the window where you will enter all the information required to create the app service. Follow the wizard and specify all the necessary details. Once this step is completed, you can review changes; if there are no errors, go ahead to create your app service.

Using Azure App Service in Azure PowerShell

Here, you'll see how to create an Azure App Service using PowerShell. First, you need to authenticate to Azure. Figure 2-3 shows how to log in using `Connect-AzAccount` in PowerShell.

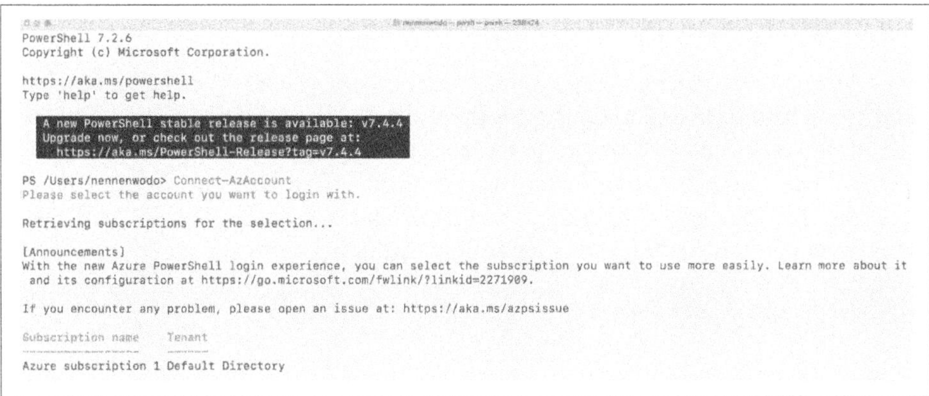

Figure 2-3. Log in using Connect-AzAccount

Once you are logged into Azure on the terminal using the `Connect-AzAccount` command, you can run the following PowerShell command to create a resource group:

```
$ New-AzResourceGroup -Name SampleRg -Location EastUS
```

The previous code snippet creates a resource group named `SampleRg` in the `EastUS` region. As mentioned earlier in the chapter, there are multiple regions available; in practice/production you'll want to select the most appropriate for your application. Now that you've created your resource group, you can create the App Service plan.

```
$ New-AzAppServicePlan
    -Name SamplePlan
    -ResourceGroupName SampleRg
    -Tier Premium
```

Once the App Service plan is created, you can now create the app service that will use that plan. The following command will create an app service:

```
$ New-AzWebApp
    -Name sampleApp
    -ResourceGroupName SampleRg
    -AppServicePlan SamplePlan
```

After running all the commands to create your infrastructure, you can verify the creation of your app service by navigating to the Azure portal or using the following command to get details about the app service:

```
$ Get-AzWebApp -ResourceGroupName SampleRg -Name sampleApp
```

These commands give you an alternative way to interact with Azure beyond the portal and the Azure CLI. But it doesn't stop here; there's more you can do in App Services.

Configuring and Scaling App Services

When you created your web app infrastructure, you probably set it to have one instance, which might be sufficient for a small app. However, in production, you may need more instances to accommodate the scale your application demands. This is where configuring and scaling Azure App Services becomes crucial. Proper configuration ensures your app is optimized for performance, security, and cost efficiency. Azure gives you tools and features for scaling, including vertical scaling (scaling up) to increase resource capacity and horizontal scaling (scaling out) to add more instances to handle increased loads.

Configuring App Services

When you create infrastructure for the applications you want to put on the cloud, you need to consider deployment. Your applications could be deployed to different regions and may require unique settings, such as database connection settings, app settings, or other parameters that vary between environments (e.g., development, testing, and production). These settings are often managed using environment variables—commonly stored in a file known as an ENV file—rather than being hardcoded into the application. These configurations ensure that each deployment environment operates with the correct parameters and things are not hardcoded. They make your applications dynamic. Azure App Services offer various tools to manage these settings efficiently, and this section will cover that.

Configuring your Azure App Service involves setting up the environment to meet the specific needs of your application. This includes defining application settings, configuring connection strings, and setting up deployment slots.

Application settings

Application settings (also known as environment variables) include configuration keys and values that your application needs to run. They can be set directly in the Azure portal or through configuration files. For instance, you might set API keys, feature flags, or any other environment-specific settings.

To add an app setting using Azure CLI, use the following command:

```
$ az webapp config appsettings set
    --resource-group <ResourceGroupName>
    --name <AppName>
    --settings <SettingName>=<SettingValue>
```

For example:

```
$ az webapp config appsettings set
    --resource-group SampleRg
    --name sampleApp
    --settings Environment=Production
```

This command sets an application setting named `Environment` with the value `Production` for the web app `sampleApp` in the resource group `SampleRg`.

You can also add an app setting using Azure PowerShell using the following command:

```
$ settings = @{"MySetting" = "MyValue"}
  Set-AzWebApp
   -ResourceGroupName <ResourceGroupName>
   -Name <AppName>
   -AppSettings $settings
```

For example:

```
$ settings = @{"Environment" = "Production"}
  Set-AzWebApp
   -ResourceGroupName <ResourceGroupName>
   -Name <AppName>
   -AppSettings $settings
```

There are other ways to include app settings in your application. You can use infrastructure as code (*https://oreil.ly/aj-29*) to add the different configurations or add them directly in the Azure portal as shown in Figure 2-4.

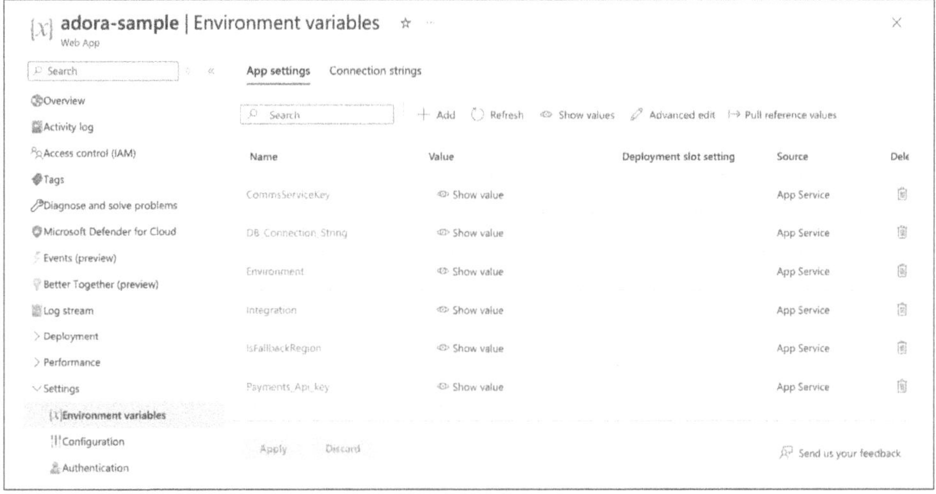

Figure 2-4. Environment variable in Azure

Deployment slots

Deployment slots provide isolated environments for testing new versions of your application. For example, you can have a staging slot where you deploy and test new features before swapping them into production to ensure your main application remains unaffected by any potential issues during deployment. I'll cover deployment slots in the blue-green deployments section of this chapter.

Connection strings

Connection strings are secure values used to connect your app to databases or other services. To add a connection string using Azure CLI, use the following command:

```
$ az webapp config connection-string set
    --resource-group <ResourceGroupName>
    --name <AppName>
    --settings MyConnectionString="Server=myServer;Database=myDB;User
      Id=myUser;Password=myPassword;"
    --connection-string-type SQLAzure
```

Note that the only accepted values for connection string type are `ApiHub`, `Custom`, `DocDb`, `EventHub`, `MySql`, `NotificationHub`, `PostgreSQL`, `RedisCache`, `SQLAzure`, `SQLServer`, and `ServiceBus`. This means that if you have an external service or API key you'd like to add as a connection string, you need to do it as an application setting.

When defining connection strings using PowerShell, you can use the following command:

```
$   $connectionStrings = @{"MyConnectionString" =
@{Value="Server=myServer;Database=myDB;User Id=myUser;Password=myPassword;";
    Type="SQLAzure"}}

Set-AzWebApp
     -ResourceGroupName <ResourceGroupName>
     -Name <AppName>
     -ConnectionStrings $connectionStrings
```

These commands give you alternative ways to add settings to your web app infrastructure as you build dynamic applications.

Scaling Your App Services Vertically

Vertical scaling involves upgrading the service plan to a higher tier with more resources, such as CPU, memory, and additional features like custom domains and Secure Sockets Layer (SSL) support. This type of scaling is beneficial for applications that need more power per instance rather than adding more instances (which is known as horizontal scaling and will be covered next). For instance, moving from a Standard to a Premium plan can provide enhanced performance and features that are crucial for high-demand applications.

To scale up your App Service through the Azure portal, navigate to your App Service and select "Scale up (App Service plan)" from the left menu. Choose the desired pricing tier (*https://oreil.ly/PFM2i*) and click Apply to upgrade your service plan (Figure 2-5).

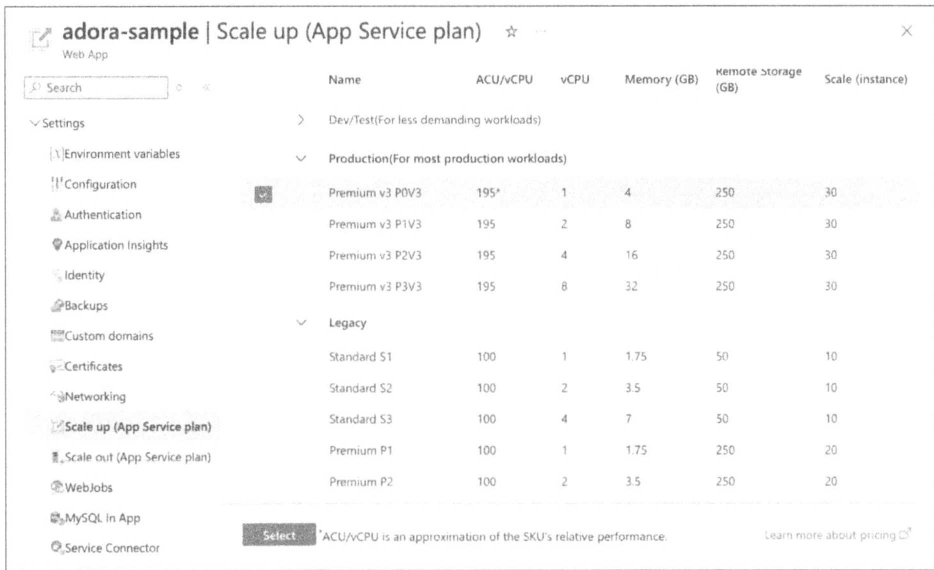

Figure 2-5. Scaling up an App Service plan in the Azure portal

To scale up your App Service using the Azure CLI, you can update the App Service plan resource using the following command:

```
$ az appservice plan update
    --name <AppServicePlanName>
    --resource-group <ResourceGroupName>
    --sku <SkuToScaleTo>
```

The value of `SkuToScaleTo` could be `P1v3` or any other tier that fits your needs.

To scale up your App Service using Azure PowerShell, you can update the App Service plan resource using the following command:

```
$ Set-AzAppServicePlan
    -ResourceGroupName <ResourceGroupName>
    -Name <AppServicePlanName>
    -Tier <SkuToScaleTo>
    -WorkerSize Large
```

The value of `SkuToScaleTo` could be `PremiumV3` or any other tier that fits your needs.

Scaling Your App Services Horizontally

Horizontal scaling, or scaling out, adds more instances of your app to distribute the load. Azure App Services support autoscaling, which automatically adjusts the number of instances based on predefined rules and real-time metrics like CPU usage, memory usage, or HTTP queue length. This ensures your application can handle different traffic patterns efficiently without manual intervention.

Creating the autoscale settings

The following Azure CLI command creates the autoscale settings to scale between two and nine instances, leaving four as the default.

```
$  az monitor autoscale create   ❶
      --resource-group {resource-group-name} ❷
      --resource {resource-id} ❸
      --min-count 2 ❹
      --max-count 9 ❺
      --count 4 ❻
```

❶ This command is used to establish autoscale settings for an Azure resource.

❷ This parameter denotes the resource group where these settings will be applied, which you replace with your actual resource group name.

❸ Identifies the specific resource, such as an App Service, that the autoscale setting will govern, using its unique resource ID.

❹ Ensures there will always be a minimum of two instances running, providing a baseline capacity to handle basic traffic.

❺ Sets an upper limit of nine instances, preventing excessive scaling that could lead to high operational costs.

❻ This parameter sets the default number of instances to start with, meaning that under typical conditions, the application will operate with four instances.

Creating the scale-out rule

The following Azure CLI command creates a scale-out rule:

```
$  az monitor autoscale rule create
      --resource-group {resource-group-name}
      --autoscale-name {resource-name} ❶
      --scale out 1 ❷
      --condition "Percentage CPU > 75 avg 5m" ❸
```

❶ This parameter indicates the name of the autoscale setting that will use this rule.

❷ This parameter defines the action to be taken when the condition is met, which in this case is to add one instance.

❸ This parameter specifies the condition that triggers this scaling action. This rule states that if the average CPU usage exceeds 75% over a five-minute period, an additional instance will be added to handle the increased load.

In this example, the condition `Percentage CPU > 75 avg 5m` represents a scaling rule based on CPU usage. Azure's autoscaling feature allows you to define such rules using a flexible syntax, which means you can create scaling conditions tailored to your specific needs. These rules govern when and how scaling events occur by monitoring various metrics, such as CPU load, memory, or other application-specific performance indicators.

There are two main types of rules you can configure:

Metric-based rules
: These trigger scaling actions based on performance metrics. For instance, if a certain resource, like CPU or memory, exceeds a set threshold, the system can automatically scale out to handle increased demand.

Time-based rules
: These allow you to scale your resources based on a predefined schedule. For example, you could set a rule to scale out during peak hours, like weekday afternoons, when traffic to your app is typically higher.

You can also define multiple scaling rules in an autoscale profile to address different conditions. Azure supports combining up to 10 rules, and when scaling out, if any of the conditions in your rules are met, the system will automatically add more instances. However, for scaling in (reducing resources), all conditions across your rules must be met, making scaling in more controlled. This flexibility allows you to ensure your application responds dynamically to varying workloads, improving performance while controlling costs.

Creating the scale-in rule

The Azure CLI command below creates a scale-in rule:

```
$  az monitor autoscale rule create
     --resource-group {resource-group-name}
     --autoscale-name {resource-name}
     --scale in 1
     --condition "Percentage CPU < 25 avg 5m"
```

This command follows the same structure as the scale-out rule, starting with the creation directive and specifying the resource group with `--resource-group {resource-group-name}`. The `--autoscale-name {resource-name}` parameter again indicates which autoscale setting will use this rule. The `--scale in 1` parameter defines the action to be taken, which in this case is to remove one instance. The condition for this action, specified by `--condition "Percentage CPU < 25 avg 5m"`, means that if the average CPU usage drops below 25% over a five-minute period, one instance will be removed to reduce resource usage and cost.

Autoscaling in the Azure portal

In the Azure portal, you can also specify rules-based or automatic scaling. Click the "Scale out (App Service plan)" tab on the sidebar, and you will see the option to either select automatic scaling or rules-based scaling (Figure 2-6). If you choose automatic scaling, you have two required parameters to set:

Maximum burst
: Number of instances your App Service plan can scale out under load. Its value should be greater than or equal to current instances for the plan.

Always ready instances
: Number of instances that are always ready for the web app to use by default.

You can also choose to enforce a scale-out limit and have that limit specified so your web app will never scale beyond that specific number of instances.

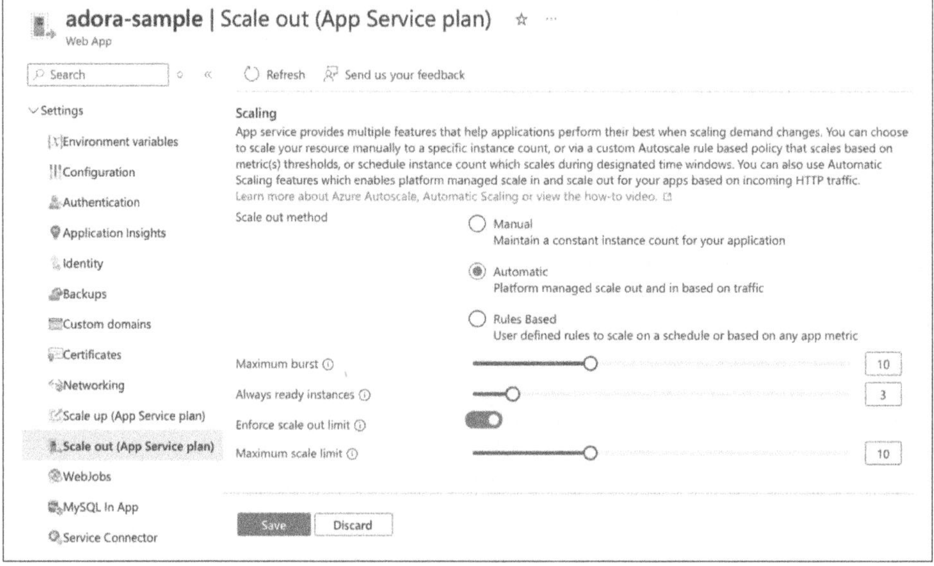

Figure 2-6. Automatic scaling (App Service plan)

For rules-based scaling (Figure 2-7), you will need to configure the scaling rules. Bear in mind that if you have automatic scaling enabled, rules-based scaling will be ignored. Once you click configure, it will take you to a different page to complete the process. Select "Custom autoscale" to define a new profile. Within this profile, you can set the minimum, maximum, and default instance counts to control the range of scaling. Add scaling rules to specify the conditions under which scaling occurs. For example, you can create rules based on metrics such as CPU utilization or memory usage. Define whether the action should increase or decrease instances and set the threshold values that will trigger these actions. Additionally, configure the cooldown period, which is the time Azure waits before applying additional scaling actions after a previous action.

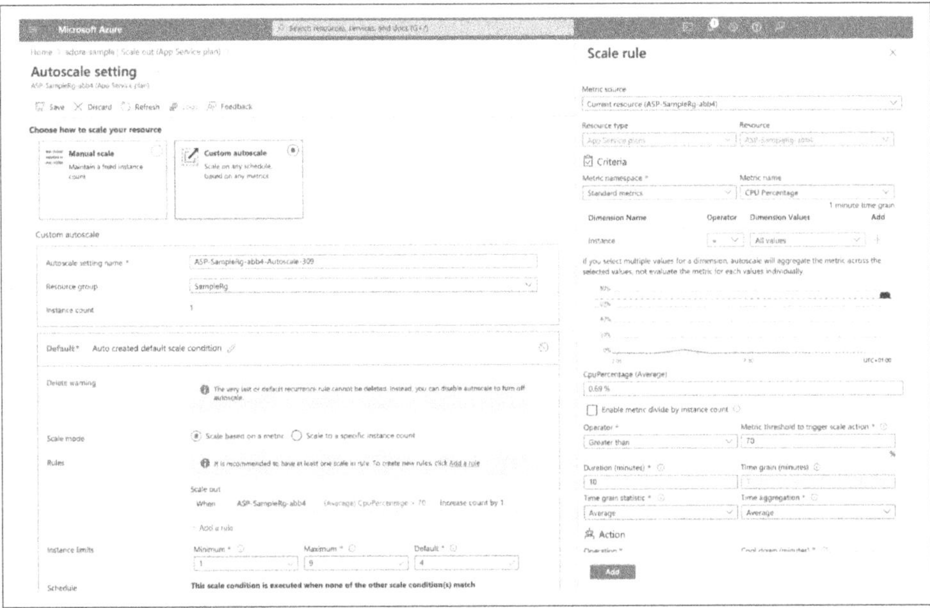

Figure 2-7. Rules-based autoscaling

Blue-Green Deployment with Slots

Now that you know how to create an app service, deploy code to it, add app settings to make it dynamic, and configure autoscaling, let's talk about deploying apps and reducing negative customer impact. There are several strategies for achieving smooth and reliable deployments, and one of the most effective is blue-green deployments.

Blue-green deployment is a technique that reduces downtime and risk by running two identical production environments, known as blue and green. At any time, only one of these environments is live, serving all production traffic. For example, blue is the current live environment while green is the environment where the new version of the application is deployed. After thorough testing in the green environment, traffic is switched from blue to green, making green the live environment. If any issues are detected, you can quickly roll back to the blue environment.

In Azure App Service, blue-green deployments can be implemented using deployment slots. Deployment slots are live apps with their own hostnames. You can deploy your application to a nonproduction slot, test it, then swap it with the production slot to complete the deployment with minimal downtime.

Here's how you can set up blue-green deployments using deployment slots with both Azure CLI and Azure PowerShell.

First, create a new deployment slot named `staging` for an App Service named `SampleApp` in the resource group `SampleRg`. I've provided examples for both Azure CLI and Azure PowerShell:

Azure CLI:

```
$ az webapp deployment slot create
      --name sampleApp
      --resource-group SampleRg
      --slot staging
```

Azure PowerShell:

```
$  New-AzWebAppSlot
      -ResourceGroupName "SampleRg"
      -Name "sampleApp"
      -Slot "staging"
```

After successfully creating your staging slot, deploy your new application to the staging slot.

Azure CLI:

```
$  az webapp deploy
      --resource-group SampleRg
      --name sampleApp
      --src-path "./path/to/file.zip"
      --slot "staging"
      --type zip
      --async true
```

Azure PowerShell:

```
$  Publish-AzWebApp
      -ResourceGroupName SampleRg
      -Name sampleApp
      -Slot staging
      -ArchivePath "./path/to/file.zip"
```

Once your app has been deployed to the slot, you may run all your tests there until they pass or you get a satisfactory result. Once the tests pass and it's validated the code works and the slot is healthy, you can swap the staging slot with the production slot (the main app service).

Azure CLI:

```
$  az webapp deployment slot swap
     --resource-group SampleRg
     --name sampleApp
     --slot staging
```

Azure PowerShell:

```
$ Swap-AzWebAppSlot
    -ResourceGroupName "SampleRg"
    -Name "sampleApp"
    -SourceSlotName "staging"
    -DestinationSlotName "production"
```

If any issues arise with the new version as you test, you can quickly swap the slots back.

Beyond using Azure CLI and PowerShell, you can also create and manage slots directly from the dashboard from the "Deployment slots" tab on the sidebar as shown in Figure 2-8.

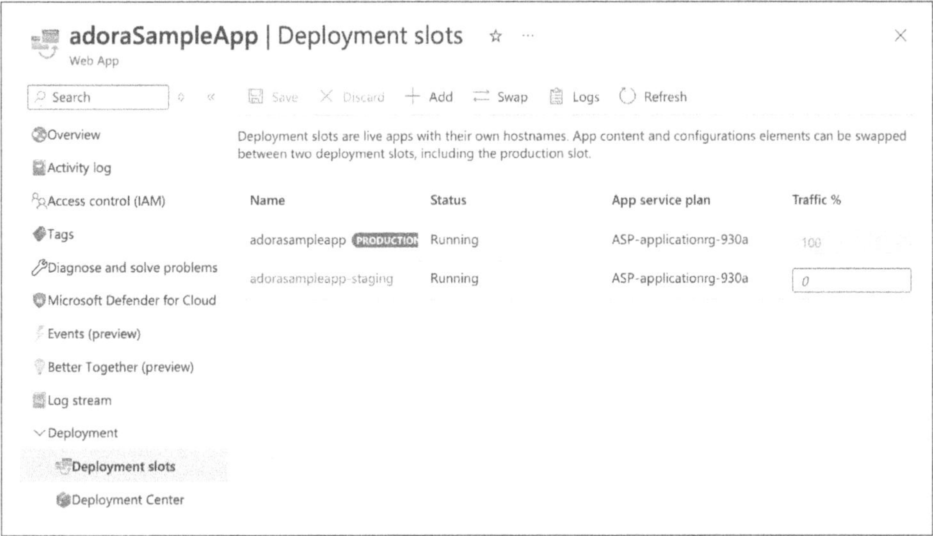

Figure 2-8. Dashboard showing deployment slots

Automating App Service Deployments

In a real project, you will not run CLI commands from your local computer to deploy to production. Changes will be automated, and things will flow through a CI/CD pipeline to ensure consistency, reliability, and efficiency. Automating deployments for Azure App Service can be achieved using different CI/CD tools, but this section will introduce you to how you can do it using Azure DevOps and GitHub Actions.

Using Azure DevOps

When you create a pipeline in Azure DevOps, you define your build and release process using a YAML file. Here's an example pipeline definition:

```
trigger:
  branches:
    include:
      - main

pool:
  vmImage: 'ubuntu-latest'

steps:
- task: UseDotNet@2
  inputs:
    packageType: 'sdk'
    version: '5.x'
    installationPath: $(Agent.ToolsDirectory)/dotnet

- script: dotnet build --configuration Release
  displayName: 'Build project'

- task: ArchiveFiles@2
  inputs:
    rootFolderOrFile: $(System.DefaultWorkingDirectory)
    includeRootFolder: false
    archiveType: 'zip'
    archiveFile: $(Build.ArtifactStagingDirectory)/$(Build.BuildId).zip
    replaceExistingArchive: true

- task: PublishBuildArtifacts@1
  inputs:
    pathToPublish: $(Build.ArtifactStagingDirectory)
    artifactName: drop
    publishLocation: 'Container'

- task: AzureWebApp@1
  inputs:
    azureSubscription: 'your-service-connection'
    appName: 'MyAppService'
    package: $(Build.ArtifactStagingDirectory)/$(Build.BuildId).zip
```

This YAML file defines a pipeline that triggers on changes to the main branch. It sets up the .NET SDK, builds the project, creates a ZIP archive of the build artifacts, and deploys the application to an Azure App Service. The `AzureWebApp` task uses a service connection to authenticate with Azure and deploy the package to the specified App Service.

In Azure, a service connection allows you to securely connect and authenticate with Azure resources from external tools or services, such as Azure DevOps, GitHub Actions, or other CI/CD pipelines. It serves as a bridge, enabling these external systems to perform various operations on your Azure resources without requiring direct user credentials each time an action is performed.

To set up a service connection using the Azure CLI, you typically create a service principal and assign it a role with the required permissions. For example, to create a service principal with Contributor permissions for a specific resource group, you would use the following commands:

```
# Create a service principal
$  az ad sp create-for-rbac
    --name http://my-service-connection
    --role contributor
    --scopes /subscriptions/{subscription-id}/resourceGroups/{rg-name}
```

The `az ad sp create-for-rbac` command creates a new service principal and assigns it the Contributor role for the specified resource group. The `scopes` parameter defines the scope of permissions.

Using GitHub Actions

When you create a workflow in GitHub Actions, you define the steps for your CI/CD process directly in your GitHub repository using a YAML file. Here's an example workflow:

```
name: Build and Deploy to Azure Web App

on:
  push:
    branches:
      - main

jobs:
  build-and-deploy:
    runs-on: ubuntu-latest

    steps:
    - name: Checkout code
      uses: actions/checkout@v2

    - name: Set up .NET
      uses: actions/setup-dotnet@v2
      with:
        dotnet-version: '5.x'

    - name: Build project
      run: dotnet build --configuration Release

    - name: Publish artifact
      run: dotnet publish -c Release -o ./publish

    - name: Deploy to Azure Web App
      uses: azure/webapps-deploy@v2
      with:
        app-name: 'MyAppService'
        slot-name: 'production'
        publish-profile: ${{ secrets.AZURE_WEBAPP_PUBLISH_PROFILE }}
        package: './publish'
```

This workflow triggers pushes to the main branch. It checks out the code, sets up the .NET environment, builds and publishes the project, and then deploys the application to an Azure Web App using the `azure/webapps-deploy` action. The deployment uses a publish profile stored as a secret in the GitHub repository for authentication.

Cleaning Up: Deleting App Service Resources and Resource Groups

Once you've finished working with the resources and resource groups created in this chapter, it's essential to clean them up to avoid unnecessary charges. In Azure, resources left running will continue to incur costs, so it's a good practice to delete any resources and resource groups you're no longer using. Here are the steps to delete both individual resources and entire resource groups using Azure CLI and PowerShell:

1. To delete specific resources, such as an App Service, you can use the following command:

   ```
   $ az webapp delete
         --name <app-name>
         --resource-group <resource-group-name>
   ```

   This command will remove the specified web app from your resource group. However, if you've created other resources like databases or storage accounts, you'll need to delete them individually or delete the entire resource group. To delete the entire resource group (and all resources within it), use this command:

   ```
   $ az group delete
         --name <resource-group-name>
         --yes
         --no-wait
   ```

   This will permanently delete the resource group and all associated resources in one step. The `--yes` flag skips the confirmation prompt, and `--no-wait` allows the deletion to proceed asynchronously.

2. If you're using PowerShell, you can delete an individual app service with the following command:

   ```
   Remove-AzWebApp
         -Name <app-name>
         -ResourceGroupName <resource-group-name>
   ```

   To delete the entire resource group, including all its resources, use:

   ```
   Remove-AzResourceGroup
         -Name <resource-group-name>
         -Force
   ```

The `-Force` parameter skips the confirmation, ensuring the command runs immediately.

Cleanup is important because leaving unused resources in your Azure account can lead to unexpected billing, even if those resources are not actively being used. Azure charges for various services based on consumption, so keeping your account clean by regularly deleting unused resources and resource groups helps avoid unnecessary costs. Always review your resources after completing your work to ensure you're not incurring charges for resources you no longer need. By following these steps, you can easily manage your Azure resources and ensure that your account stays organized and cost effective.

Summary

This chapter covered Azure App Service. Here, you learned about the fundamentals of Azure App Service, including how to configure and scale App Services to ensure optimal performance and reliability. You were also introduced to blue-green deployments using deployment slots, demonstrating how to minimize downtime and risk during application updates by using two identical production environments. Additionally, the chapter explored the automation of App Service deployments using Azure DevOps and GitHub Actions, showing how to implement CI/CD pipelines. In the next chapter, you will learn about serverless computing using Azure Functions.

CHAPTER 3
Azure Function Apps

Azure Functions makes it easy to create apps that can have event-driven execution and scale dynamically based on demand. As a PaaS, this serverless compute service allows developers to run code on demand without having to explicitly provision or manage the underlying infrastructure. PaaS offerings like Azure Functions abstract the complexity of infrastructure management, enabling developers to focus solely on writing and deploying their applications. In this chapter, you will see how to use Azure Function Apps for your serverless application development and deployment processes.

First, you will be introduced to the features and benefits of Azure Function Apps, and this will give you a solid foundation so you can understand their capabilities. Next, you will go through the process of building and deploying serverless applications. This will include creating a simple function, setting up triggers, and configuring bindings to connect your function to other services and resources. You'll also see how you can use Azure DevOps and GitHub Actions to deploy an Azure Function App, advanced deployment techniques such as blue-green deployments using deployment slots, monitoring and debugging Azure Functions, and advanced concepts like Durable Functions.

By the end of this chapter, you will have a comprehensive understanding of Azure Functions, from basic concepts to advanced deployment strategies, and this will empower you to use this service to deploy your serverless applications.

Introduction to Serverless Computing

In a regular web API, you typically have a server or a set of servers running all the time, listening for requests. These servers need to be maintained, scaled, and monitored, and they consume resources even when there are no incoming requests. The infrastructure setup requires you to provision the right amount of resources to handle peak loads, which can lead to underutilization during off-peak times or resource constraints during unexpected traffic spikes.

However, when it comes to the serverless architecture, you don't have to worry about managing servers. Instead, you write your application code in small, discrete units called functions. These functions are deployed to a cloud service like Azure Functions, which focuses on running individual pieces of code in response to specific events. Unlike an app service, which deploys entire web applications typically written in a framework like ASP.NET or Django and listens for incoming web requests, functions are more lightweight. They are designed to run specific tasks or pieces of logic with minimal knowledge of how they are triggered.

Functions are event-driven, meaning they execute only when triggered by an event such as an HTTP request, a message in a queue, a database change, or a scheduled timer. This allows your application to scale dynamically, as the cloud service provisions resources only when your functions are running. When no requests are being made, no resources are being consumed, leading to cost savings. Additionally, the cloud service ensures high availability and fault tolerance, so you can focus on writing your application logic without worrying about the underlying infrastructure.

Creating Azure Function Apps

There are different ways to create an Azure Function App infrastructure. Like other Azure resources, you can either create it using the Azure CLI, Azure PowerShell, the Azure portal, or infrastructure as code (IaC) tools like Terraform and Azure Bicep. Let's start by looking at how you can use the Azure CLI to create an Azure Function App.

To create an Azure Function App with the Azure CLI, you begin by opening your terminal or command prompt. First, make sure you are logged into your Azure account using the following command:

```
$ az login
```

After logging in, you need to create a resource group to hold your function app by using the command:

```
$ az group create --name <resource-group-name> --location <location>
```

Once the resource group is created, you can then create a storage account, which is required for the function app, with the command:

```
$  az storage account create
     --name <storage-account-name>
     --location <location>
     --resource-group <resource-group-name>
     --sku <sku>
```

With the storage account in place, the next step is to create the actual function app by running:

```
$  az functionapp create
     --resource-group <resource-group-name>
     --consumption-plan-location <location>
     --name <app-name>
     --storage-account <storage-account-name>
     --runtime <runtime>
     --os-type <os-type>
     --functions-version <functions-version>
```

Replace the properties with their respective values. This command sets up your function app on a consumption plan, which means it scales automatically based on demand.

Why Do Function Apps Need Storage Accounts?

A storage account is needed to support the underlying infrastructure and function of an Azure Function App, so an Azure Function App uses storage accounts for a few things. First, it is used for file storage (to store files such as function code, binaries, and dependencies). Second, storage accounts provide a way for Azure Functions to manage state, allowing the storing and retrieving of data between function executions. Additionally, storage accounts help in logging and diagnostics, as they store logs, traces, and other diagnostic data for Azure Functions. The Azure Functions runtime also uses storage accounts to store runtime data, including function metadata and configuration.

Next, let's explore how to create the same infrastructure using Azure PowerShell. Start by opening your PowerShell terminal and logging into your Azure account with the following command:

```
$  Connect-AzAccount
```

After successfully logging in, you need to create a resource group using the command:

```
$  New-AzResourceGroup
     -Name <resource-group-name>
     -Location <location>
```

Following that, you create a storage account required by the function app with the following command:

```
$ New-AzStorageAccount
    -ResourceGroupName <resource-group-name>
    -Name <storage-account-name>
    -Location <location>
    -SkuName <sku>
```

Once the storage account is set up, you proceed to create the function app itself using the command:

```
$ New-AzFunctionApp
    -ResourceGroupName <resource-group-name>
    -Name <app-name>
    -StorageAccountName <storage-account-name>
    -Location <location>
    -Runtime <runtime>
    -FunctionsVersion <functions-version>
```

This command not only creates the function app but also specifies the runtime and version you want to use.

Finally, let's also create an Azure Function App using the Azure portal. To start, navigate to the Azure portal and sign in with your Azure account. Once logged in, click the "Create a resource" button found on the top left corner of the portal.

In the new page, type "Function App" in the search box and select the Function App result that appears. Click the Create button to begin the process. You will be prompted to fill in several fields, including selecting a subscription, creating or selecting a resource group, providing a unique name for your function app, and choosing a region (Figure 3-1).

You'll also need to create a storage account if you don't already have one. After filling in all the required details, click the "Review + create" button, and then the Create button to deploy your function app. The Azure portal will handle the creation of the necessary resources, and you can monitor the deployment progress from the notifications area.

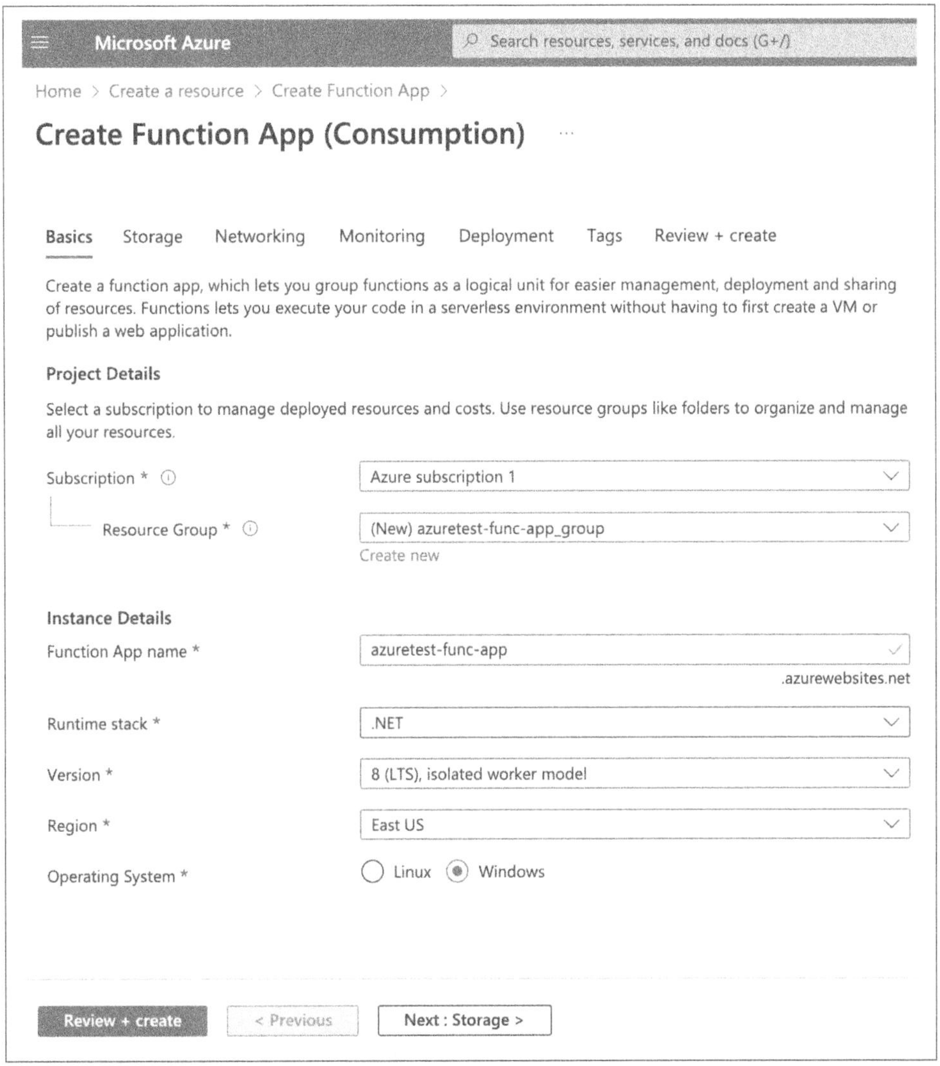

Microsoft Azure

Search resources, services, and docs (G+/)

Home > Create a resource > Create Function App >

Create Function App (Consumption) ...

Basics Storage Networking Monitoring Deployment Tags Review + create

Create a function app, which lets you group functions as a logical unit for easier management, deployment and sharing of resources. Functions lets you execute your code in a serverless environment without having to first create a VM or publish a web application.

Project Details

Select a subscription to manage deployed resources and costs. Use resource groups like folders to organize and manage all your resources.

Subscription * Azure subscription 1

Resource Group * (New) azuretest-func-app_group

Create new

Instance Details

Function App name * azuretest-func-app

.azurewebsites.net

Runtime stack * .NET

Version * 8 (LTS), isolated worker model

Region * East US

Operating System * Linux Windows

Review + create < Previous Next : Storage >

Figure 3-1. Creating an Azure Function App

Deploying Azure Function Apps

Once you've successfully created your app, you can now deploy code to it. First, ensure your function app code is packaged correctly. Azure Functions supports various deployment formats such as ZIP, JAR, WAR, and folder-based deployment. This example will focus on deploying a ZIP package.

Deploying with the Azure CLI

To deploy your function app package using the Azure CLI, use the `az functionapp deployment source config-zip` command like this:

```
$  az functionapp deployment source config-zip
       --resource-group MyResourceGroup
       --name MyFunctionApp
       --src functionapp.zip
```

This command uploads the ZIP file to your function app. In this command, `--resource-group MyResourceGroup` specifies the resource group containing your function app, `--name MyFunctionApp` is the name of your function app, and `--src functionapp.zip` is the path to the ZIP file containing your function app code.

Deploying with Azure PowerShell

To deploy your function app package using Azure PowerShell, use the `Publish-AzWebApp` cmdlet like this:

```
$resourceGroup = "MyResourceGroup"
$functionAppName = "MyFunctionApp"
$packagePath = "./functionapp.zip"

Publish-AzWebApp
    -ResourceGroupName $resourceGroup
    -Name $functionAppName
    -ArchivePath $packagePath
```

This cmdlet uploads the ZIP file to your function app. In this command, `-ResourceGroupName $resourceGroup` specifies the resource group containing your function app, `-Name $functionAppName` is the name of your function app, and `-ArchivePath $packagePath` is the path to the ZIP file containing your function app code.

Hosting Options for Azure Function Apps

Azure has multiple hosting options for functions, and each one is designed to meet different needs and use cases. One of the most popular options is the Consumption plan. It allows your functions to scale automatically based on demand, meaning you only pay for the compute resources used during execution. This plan is cost-effective for applications with unpredictable or infrequent workloads, as it scales down to zero when not in use, helping you save costs by not consuming resources when idle.

Azure also has the Flex Consumption plan, which is suitable for complex serverless applications. It is currently in preview and builds on the Consumption plan by offering more flexibility and customizability without compromising on existing capabilities. This plan provides event-driven scaling decisions per function. It also supports advanced features such as private networking and instance memory size selection.

The Premium plan offers additional features like VNET integration, increased memory, and longer execution times. It provides always-ready instances to avoid cold starts, and this means that functions using this plan respond quickly to incoming events. This plan is ideal for applications requiring high performance and consistent response times, as it maintains warm instances ready to handle requests immediately.

For applications with more predictable workloads or those that require continuous execution, the Dedicated plan is a good fit. This plan runs your functions on dedicated virtual machines (VMs) within an App Service plan, which means you pay for the underlying compute resources rather than paying per function execution. It is beneficial for scenarios where you have existing underutilized VMs or need to run custom containers.

Last, Azure Functions can also be hosted on Azure Container Apps, which allows you to deploy function apps in Linux containers. This hosting option provides the flexibility to run serverless functions alongside other containerized applications. This is great for teams using Kubernetes or looking for hybrid and multicloud solutions.

Triggers and Bindings

There are different kinds of function triggers and bindings. This way you are able to respond to multiple events and build flexible applications. A trigger is a specific type of event that initiates the execution of an Azure Function. It can be an HTTP request, a new message in a queue, a timer event, or even a new file in a storage blob. On the other hand, bindings are used to connect the function to other resources or services, allowing it to read or write data without needing additional code to handle these interactions.

For instance, an HTTP trigger allows a function to be executed via an HTTP request. This is useful for building web APIs or responding to webhooks. The function is triggered whenever an HTTP request is sent to it. Here's an example in C#:

```
public static async Task<IActionResult> Run([
HttpTrigger(AuthorizationLevel.Function,
"get",
"post",
Route = null)] HttpRequest req, ILogger log)
{
```

```
        log.LogInformation("C# HTTP trigger function was called.");

        string name = req.Query["name"];
        return name != null
            ? (ActionResult)new OkObjectResult($"Hello, {name}")
            : new BadRequestObjectResult("Please add a name");
    }
```

In this code, the function is triggered by an HTTP GET or POST request. It reads a `name` parameter from the query string or the request body and returns a greeting message. If the `name` parameter is not provided, it returns a bad request response.

Another common trigger is the Timer trigger, which lets you execute functions on a schedule, similar to cron jobs. This is particularly useful for periodic tasks such as data cleanup or sending notifications:

```
public static void Run([TimerTrigger("0 */5 * * * *")] TimerInfo myTimer, ILogger log)
{
    log.LogInformation($Function executed at: {DateTime.Now}");
}
```

In this example, the function is triggered every five minutes, as specified by the cron expression `0 */5 * * * *`. The function logs the current time each time it runs.

The Blob Storage trigger is activated when a new file is uploaded or an existing file is updated in Azure Blob Storage. This trigger is ideal for processing files as they arrive, such as image resizing or format conversion:

```
public static void Run([BlobTrigger("samples-workitems/{name}",
    Connection = "AzureWebJobsStorage")]
    Stream myBlob, string name, ILogger log)
{
    log.LogInformation($"Blob trigger function Processed blob\n Name:{name} \n
        Size: {myBlob.Length} Bytes");
}
```

Here, the function is triggered whenever a blob is added or updated in the `samples-workitems` container. It logs the name and size of the blob.

The Queue Storage trigger is useful for background processing. It triggers a function whenever a new message is added to an Azure Storage Queue:

```
public static void Run([QueueTrigger("myqueue-items", Connection = "AzureWebJobsStorage")]
      string myQueueItem, ILogger log)
{
    log.LogInformation($"C# Queue trigger function processed: {myQueueItem}");
}
```

This function is triggered by new messages in the `myqueue-items` queue. It logs the content of each message it processes.

Similarly, the Service Bus trigger is used to process messages from an Azure Service Bus queue or topic. This is useful for building scalable, decoupled applications where different parts of the system communicate via messages:

```
public static void Run([ServiceBusTrigger("myqueue", Connection = "AzureWebJobsServiceBus")]
    string myQueueItem, ILogger log)
{
    log.LogInformation($"C# ServiceBus queue trigger function processed message:
        {myQueueItem}");
}
```

In this code, the function is triggered by messages in the `myqueue` Service Bus queue. It logs the content of each message it processes.

The Cosmos DB trigger allows a function to be executed in response to changes in a Cosmos DB collection. This is particularly useful for real-time processing of data changes, such as updating materialized views or triggering workflows:

```
public static void Run([CosmosDBTrigger(
    databaseName: "ToDoList",
    collectionName: "Items",
    ConnectionStringSetting = "CosmosDBConnection",
    LeaseCollectionName = "leases")] IReadOnlyList<Document> input, ILogger log)
{
    if (input != null && input.Count > 0)
    {
        log.LogInformation("Documents modified " + input.Count);
        log.LogInformation("First document Id " + input[0].Id);
    }
}
```

In this example, the function is triggered whenever documents in the `Items` collection of the `ToDoList` database are modified. It logs the number of modified documents and the ID of the first document.

Bindings in Azure Functions make it easier to work with various services without writing boilerplate code. For example, an output binding can write data to a blob storage directly from a function:

```
public static async Task<IActionResult> Run(
    [HttpTrigger(AuthorizationLevel.Function, "get", "post", Route = null)] HttpRequest req,
    [Blob("output-container/{rand-guid}.txt", FileAccess.Write)]
    Stream outputBlob,
    ILogger log)
{
    string requestBody = await new StreamReader(req.Body).ReadToEndAsync();
    byte[] byteArray = Encoding.UTF8.GetBytes(requestBody);
    outputBlob.Write(byteArray, 0, byteArray.Length);

    return new OkObjectResult("Data written to blob");
}
```

In this example, the function reads the body of an HTTP request and writes it to a new blob in the `output-container`. The blob name includes a random GUID (Globally Unique Identifier) to ensure it is unique.

Another example is an input binding from Cosmos DB, which allows a function to read data directly from a Cosmos DB collection:

```
public static IActionResult Run(
    [HttpTrigger(AuthorizationLevel.Function, "get", "post", Route = null)]
      HttpRequest req,
    [CosmosDB(
        databaseName: "ToDoList",
        collectionName: "Items",
        ConnectionStringSetting = "CosmosDBConnection",
        Id = "{Query.id}",
        PartitionKey = "{Query.partitionKey}")] ToDoItem todoItem,
    ILogger log)
{
    if (todoItem != null)
    {
        return new OkObjectResult(todoItem);
    }
    else
    {
        return new NotFoundResult();
    }
}
```

This function reads a `ToDoItem` from a Cosmos DB collection based on an ID provided in the query string. It returns the item if found, or a `not found` response if the item does not exist.

Beyond the triggers and bindings previously mentioned, Azure Functions supports many others for various services, including Event Hubs, IoT Hub, SignalR, Table Storage, SendGrid, RabbitMQ, and Twilio.

Blue-Green Deployment with Slots

You've seen blue-green deployments in the previous chapter, and the concept is the same fundamentally. However, the commands to swap slots and manage deployments are slightly different when working with Azure Functions compared with Azure App Services. Let's see how to set up blue-green deployments using deployment slots for Azure Functions.

First, create a new deployment slot named `staging` for a function app named `SampleFunctionApp` in the resource group `SampleRg`.

Azure CLI:

```
$  az functionapp deployment slot create
    --name SampleFunctionApp
    --resource-group SampleRg
    --slot staging
```

Azure PowerShell:

```
$  New-AzFunctionAppSlot
     -ResourceGroupName "SampleRg"
     -Name "SampleFunctionApp"
     -Slot "staging"
```

After successfully creating your staging slot, deploy your new application to the staging slot.

Azure CLI:

```
$  az functionapp deployment source config-zip
     --resource-group SampleRg
     --name SampleFunctionApp
     --src ./path/to/file.zip
     --slot staging
```

Azure PowerShell:

```
$  Publish-AzWebApp
      -ResourceGroupName SampleRg
      -Name SampleFunctionApp
      -Slot staging
      -ArchivePath "./path/to/file.zip"
```

Once your function app has been deployed to the staging slot, you may run all your tests there until they pass or you get a satisfactory result. Once the tests pass and it's validated the code works and the slot is healthy, you can swap the staging slot with the production slot (the main function app).

Azure CLI:

```
$  az functionapp deployment slot swap
      --resource-group SampleRg
      --name SampleFunctionApp
      --slot staging
```

Azure PowerShell:

```
$  Swap-AzWebAppSlot
      -ResourceGroupName "SampleRg"
      -Name "SampleFunctionApp"
      -SourceSlotName "staging"
```

If any issues arise with the new version, you can quickly swap the slots back. Beyond using Azure CLI and PowerShell, you can also create and manage slots directly from the Azure portal dashboard from the Deployment slots tab on the sidebar (Figure 3-2).

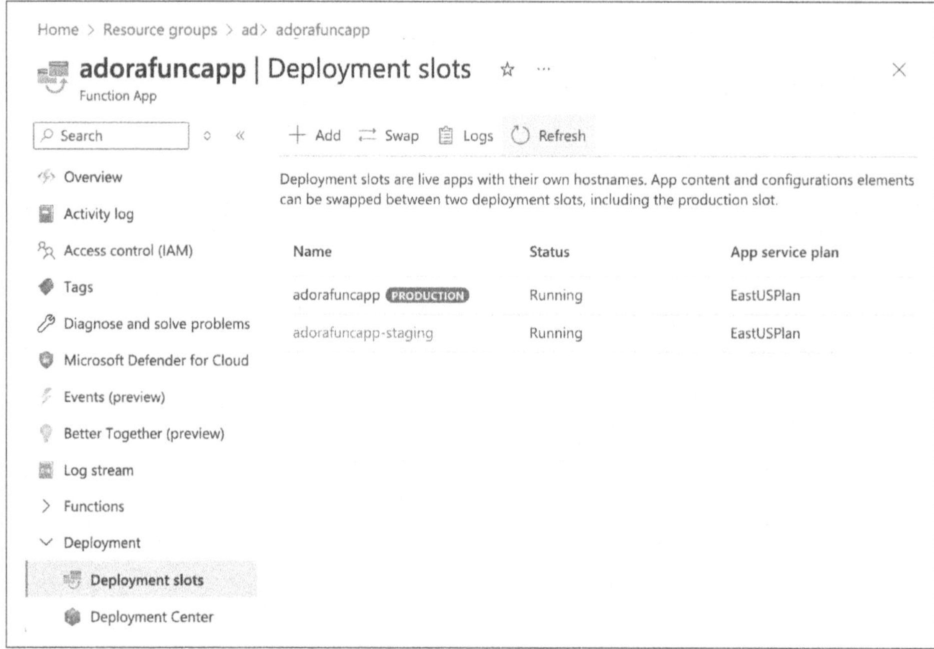

Figure 3-2. Dashboard showing deployment slots

Automating Azure Function Deployments

We've also previously discussed how to automate web app deployments, and the steps are fundamentally the same for Azure Functions. However, there are a few key differences when deploying Azure Function Apps, especially in terms of the deployment task within the YAML files.

For Azure DevOps, the deployment task specifically for Azure Functions would look like this:

```
- task: AzureFunctionApp@1
  inputs:
    azureSubscription: 'your-service-connection'
    appName: 'MyFunctionApp'
    package: $(Build.ArtifactStagingDirectory)/$(Build.BuildId).zip
```

This task uses the `AzureFunctionApp@1` task instead of the `AzureWebApp@1` task. The parameters, including the Azure subscription service connection, the name of the function app, and the path to the package to be deployed, remain similar.

For GitHub Actions, the deployment step for an Azure Function App would be:

```
- name: Deploy to Azure Function App
  uses: azure/functions-action@v1
  with:
    app-name: 'MyFunctionApp'
    publish-profile: ${{ secrets.AZURE_FUNCTIONAPP_PUBLISH_PROFILE }}
    package: './publish'
```

Here, we use the `azure/functions-action@v1` action instead of `azure/webapps-deploy@v2`. Again, the parameters include the name of the function app and the publish profile stored as a secret in the GitHub repository, along with the package path.

In both scenarios, the rest of the steps, including setting up the environment, building the project, and creating the package, remain consistent with what we discussed for Azure App Service deployments.

Writing Custom Logs in Your Code

When you deploy an Azure Function App infrastructure through your pipeline or your CLI, you will see logs. However, deployment logs are not the only logs required for monitoring and troubleshooting your application. For you to be able to see application logs in Azure Functions monitoring tools, you have to emit the logs. With Azure Functions, different programming languages have different logging interfaces, but the core concept remains the same: you log messages at various levels (e.g., Information, Error) to understand your application's behavior and troubleshoot issues effectively.

C#

In C#, Azure Functions use the `ILogger` interface for logging. This interface provides methods for logging messages at different levels such as `LogInformation`, `LogError`, and `LogWarning`. Here's an example:

```
using Microsoft.Azure.WebJobs;
using Microsoft.Extensions.Logging;

public static class LogExampleFunction
{
    [FunctionName("LogExampleFunction")]
    public static void Run([QueueTrigger("queue-items",
Connection = "AzureWebJobsStorage")] string item,
ILogger log)
    {
        log.LogInformation($"Function processed: {item}");

        // ... more code here
    }
}
```

JavaScript/TypeScript

In JavaScript and TypeScript, Azure Functions use the `context.log` method for logging. Here's an example:

```
const { app } = require('@azure/functions');

app.http('sayHello', {
    methods: ['POST', 'GET'],
    handler: async (request, context) => {
        context.log('Http function was triggered.');
        return { body: 'Hello, good morning!' };
    }
});
```

Python

In Python, Azure Functions use the `logging` module for logging. Here's an example:

```
import azure.functions as func
import logging

app = func.FunctionApp(http_auth_level=func.AuthLevel.ANONYMOUS)

@app.route(route="HttpExample")
@app.queue_output(arg_name="msg", queue_name="outqueue", connection="AzureWebJobsStorage")
def HttpExample(req: func.HttpRequest,
                msg: func.Out [func.QueueMessage]) -> func.HttpResponse:
    logging.info('HTTP trigger function processed a request.')
```

Java

In Java, Azure Functions use the `java.util.logging.Logger` class for logging. Here's an example:

```
import com.microsoft.azure.functions.annotation.*;
import com.microsoft.azure.functions.*;

import java.util.logging.Level;
import java.util.logging.Logger;

public class Function {
    Private static final String className = Function.class.getName();
    private static final Logger logger = Logger.getLogger(className);

    @FunctionName("Function1")
    public void run(
        @QueueTrigger(name = "message",
queueName = "myqueue-items",
connection = "AzureWebJobsStorage") String myQueueItem,
        final ExecutionContext context
    ) {
        logger.log(Level.INFO, "Function processed a request.");
    }
}
```

Monitoring and Debugging Azure Functions

Beyond building and deploying the app, maintenance is very important. As someone in a team maintaining a live product, monitoring and debugging are crucial for ensuring the health, performance, and reliability of your Azure Functions. There are different tools on Azure that help you monitor and debug your functions effectively. These tools are Application Insights and Azure Monitor, Azure Functions runtime logs, Kudu, Visual Studio and Visual Studio Code (VS Code), and various diagnostics and troubleshooting tools.

Application Insights and Azure Monitor

Application Insights and Azure Monitor provide comprehensive monitoring capabilities for your Azure Functions. These tools integrate tightly and will be discussed extensively in a later chapter. They enable you to collect telemetry data, set up alerts, and create dashboards for monitoring the performance and usage of your functions. With Application Insights, you can track requests, dependencies, exceptions, and custom metrics, while Azure Monitor offers log analytics, alerts, and detailed insights into your function apps.

Azure Functions Runtime Logs

Runtime logs are essential for debugging and understanding the behavior of your Azure Functions. These logs provide detailed information about function executions, errors, and performance metrics. Let's now see how you can configure and access these logs.

Configuring logging in host.json

The *host.json* file is used to configure the logging behavior for your Azure Functions. You can set different log levels to control the verbosity of the logs generated. Here's an example of how to configure logging in *host.json*:

```
{
    "version": "2.0",
    "logging": {
        "logLevel": {
          "Function.MyFunction": "Information"
        },
        "applicationInsights": {
            "samplingSettings": {
              "isEnabled": true
            }
        }
    }
}
```

In the preceding configuration, `applicationInsights.samplingSettings.isEnabled` controls whether sampling is enabled to limit the volume of telemetry data, and `logLevel` specifies the log levels for different categories. You can set it to Trace, Debug, Information, Warning, Error, or Critical. Trace logs the most detailed information for troubleshooting, while Debug is used for development-related diagnostics. Information captures the regular flow of application activity, and Warning indicates potential issues that are not yet errors. Error logs serious issues that affect functionality, and Critical logs the most severe problems that cause the application to fail.

Accessing logs with Azure CLI

You can stream logs in real time using the Azure CLI, which is useful for monitoring your functions during development and troubleshooting.

To stream logs for a function app:

```
$ az webapp log tail
    --resource-group <resource-group-name>
    --name <function-app-name>
```

This command will stream the logs to your terminal, allowing you to see log entries as they are generated.

Accessing logs with Azure PowerShell

You can also use Azure PowerShell to manage and view logs for your function app. Here's how you can enable streaming logs:

```
$ Set-AzWebApp
    -RequestTracingEnabled $True
    -HttpLoggingEnabled $True
    -DetailedErrorLoggingEnabled $True
    -ResourceGroupName $ResourceGroupName
    -Name $AppName
```

Accessing logs from the Azure portal

From the Azure portal (Figure 3-3), you can view file system logs and app insights log streams. To stream logs in the portal, navigate to the Log stream section through the sidebar of your Azure Function App dashboard.

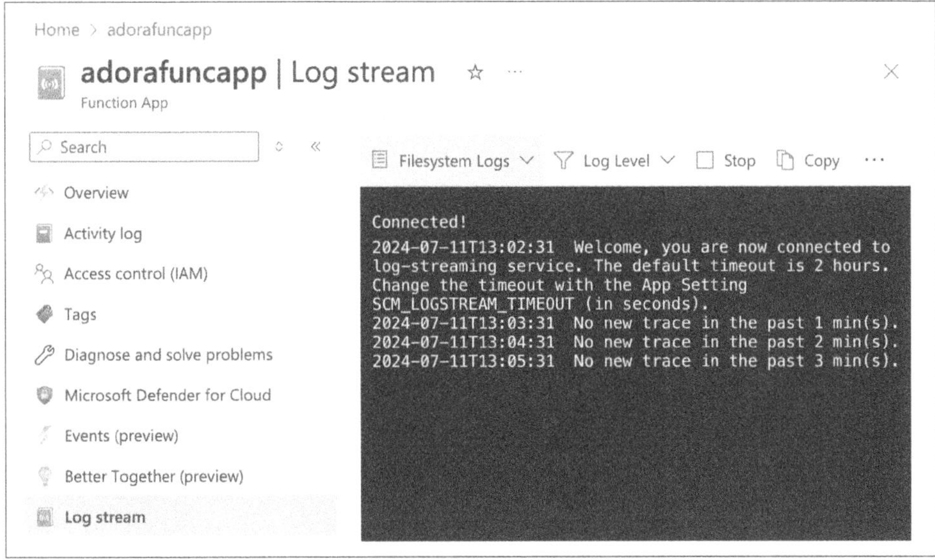

Figure 3-3. Viewing log streams from the Azure portal

Kudu (Advanced Tools)

With Kudu, you have access to a set of advanced tools for managing and debugging your function app. It has a web-based debug console, process explorer, and detailed diagnostics and logs. You can access Kudu by navigating to the Advanced Tools section in the Azure portal for your function app (Figure 3-4).

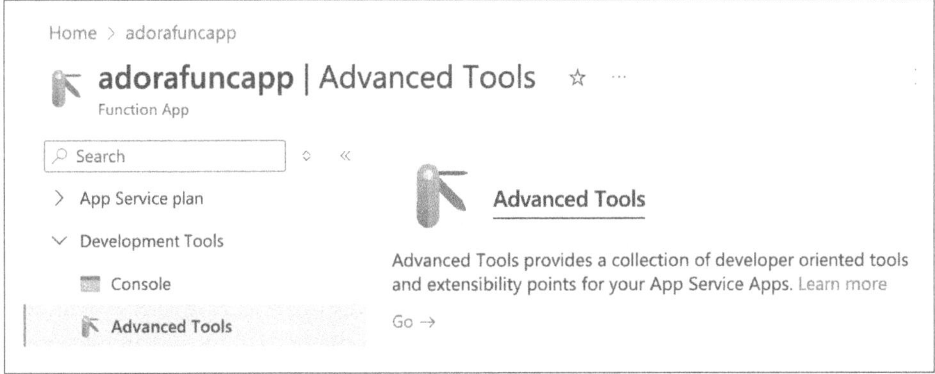

Figure 3-4. Navigating to Kudu

Once you launch Kudu, you get a dashboard that looks similar to what you see in Figure 3-5.

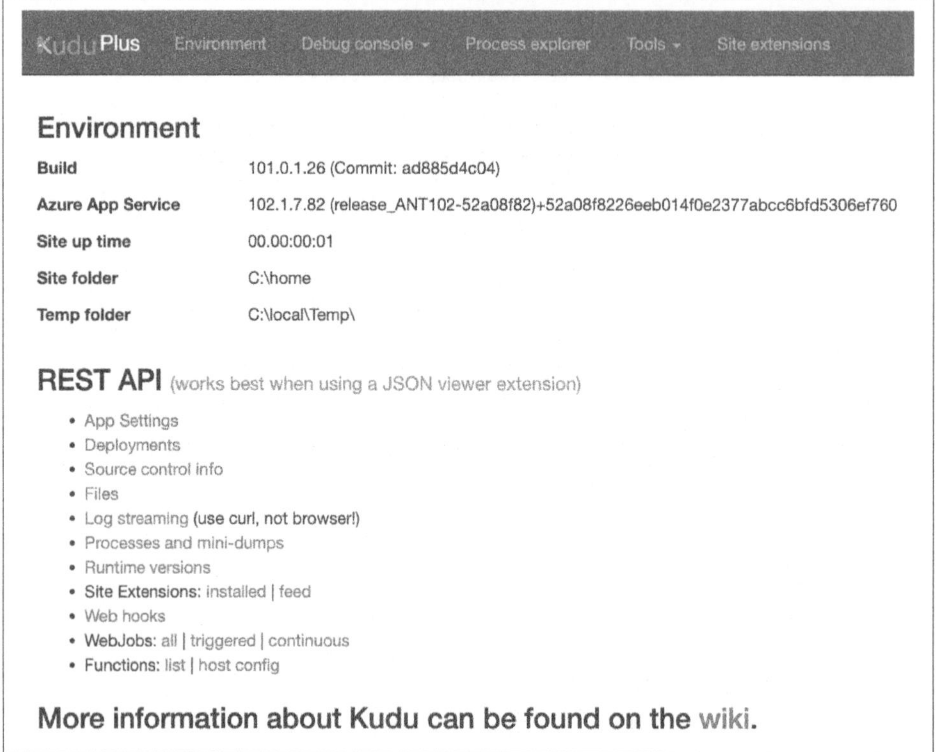

Figure 3-5. Kudu dashboard

From here, you can access the Debug console, a web-based CLI that provides access to execute commands directly on the server, manage files, and explore your application's directory structure. This allows you to work in CMD or PowerShell consoles as needed, so you will be able to run diagnostic commands and interact with the file system in ways that are already familiar.

Kudu also has a Process explorer, which allows you see what processes are running in your function app environment. You can see detailed process information including ID and CPU and memory usage. This is useful for identifying and troubleshooting performance issues or unresponsive processes so you can maintain the health and efficiency of your Azure Functions.

Kudu offers much more than the Debug console and Process explorer. The Tools section displays diagnostic information and logs, including deployment logs, which can help you understand what happened during a deployment. You can also access the Site extensions feature, where you can install extensions to add extra functionality to your function app environment. The Environment tab in Kudu also provides detailed information about the environment variables, paths, and settings, which is good for troubleshooting configuration issues and understanding the runtime environment of your application.

Advanced Functions Concepts and Optimizations

To get the most out of Azure Functions, it's important to understand advanced concepts and optimizations that can improve performance and ensure your applications scale effectively. Following are some advanced techniques and optimizations.

Durable Functions

By default, Azure Functions are stateless. This means function execution is independent, which can be beneficial in scenarios that need to handle executions that don't need to manage state. Statelessness makes it easy to scale Azure Functions, and executions are more flexible. However, there are scenarios where you might need to maintain state between executions. Imagine you are building an ecommerce application that requires processing a series of steps in order, such as placing an order, processing payment, and shipping the product. That's where Durable Functions come in. This is because these processes can be individual functions that *depend* on each other. So the function to place an order is called first and once that is successfully executed, the function to process payment is triggered with data/state from the previous state (and so on).

Durable Functions are an extension of Azure Functions that allow you to write stateful workflows in a serverless environment. This capability is built on the Durable Task Framework and enables you to define complex workflows using orchestrator functions, which can call activity functions and manage state efficiently.

The following sections outline the key concepts of Durable Functions, which enable you to manage state and complex workflows effectively.

Orchestrator functions

These functions define the workflow and can call other functions, manage their outputs, and handle retries and error handling. Orchestrator functions maintain their state between calls, allowing them to resume from where they left off after each awaited operation. Here's an example of an orchestrator function in C#:

```
[FunctionName("DurableOrchestrationFunction")]
public static async Task RunOrchestrator(
    [OrchestrationTrigger] IDurableOrchestrationContext context)
{
    var output1 = await context.CallActivityAsync<string>(
        "ActivityFunction1", null);
    var output2 = await context.CallActivityAsync<string>(
```

```
            "ActivityFunction2", output1);
        var output3 = await context.CallActivityAsync<string>(
            "ActivityFunction3", output2);

        return output3;
    }
```

Activity functions

These functions perform the actual work and are called by the orchestrator functions. They are stateless and can be executed multiple times if needed (e.g., in case of retries). Here's an example of an activity function in C#:

```
[FunctionName("ActivityFunction1")]
public static string RunActivity1([ActivityTrigger] string input, ILogger log)
{
    log.LogInformation($"Processing input: {input}");
    return $"Processed {input}";
}
```

Entity functions

These functions manage state directly. They are useful for scenarios requiring explicit control over state operations. Unlike regular functions, entity functions can be invoked explicitly by sending messages to them. They are not automatically triggered when the state is mutated. Instead, you must call them directly, usually through a durable client in the context of Durable Functions. Here's an example of an entity function in C#:

```
[FunctionName("EntityFunction")]
public static void EntityFunction([EntityTrigger] IDurableEntityContext ctx)
{
    switch (ctx.OperationName.ToLowerInvariant())
    {
        case "add":
            ctx.SetState(ctx.GetState<int>() + ctx.GetInput<int>());
            break;
        case "reset":
            ctx.SetState(0);
            break;
        case "get":
            ctx.Return(ctx.GetState<int>());
            break;
    }
}
```

Durable Functions allow you to build workflows that can resume from the last checkpoint; this helps when optimizing systems for reliability. By using Durable Functions, you can ensure that even if there are interruptions, your workflows can continue from where they left off without losing any progress or state.

One of the key benefits of Durable Functions is simplified state management. Durable Functions handle the complexity of state management, making it easier to build complex workflows without worrying about state persistence. This capability is crucial for applications that require maintaining state across multiple steps or over extended periods. Another significant advantage is the ability to orchestrate and chain multiple functions seamlessly. With Durable Functions, you can easily orchestrate multiple functions and chain them together, making sure each step is executed in order and handling any retries or failures.

Durable Functions are also well suited for long-running operations. They can run for extended periods, which means they are suitable for tasks that require waiting for external events or long processing times. This feature is beneficial for scenarios where processes may take hours, days, or even longer to complete, so your application remains responsive and efficient throughout the entire duration.

Binding Expressions

You can use binding expressions to dynamically bind parameters to functions based on runtime data. This feature makes it possible to have more flexible and powerful bindings:

```
public static void Run([QueueTrigger("samples-workitems",
Connection = "AzureWebJobsStorage")] string myQueueItem,
     [Blob("samples-workitems/{queueTrigger}", FileAccess.Read,
Connection = "AzureWebJobsStorage")] Stream myBlob,
      ILogger log)
{
    log.LogInformation($"Function processed: {myQueueItem}");
}
```

Summary

This chapter covered Azure Functions. Here, you learned about the fundamentals of Azure Functions, including how to create and deploy to Azure Functions. We explored various methods to deploy code to Azure Functions, such as using the Azure CLI, Azure PowerShell, and the Azure portal. You were also introduced to the different hosting options for Azure Function Apps, such as the Consumption plan, Premium plan, and Dedicated plan, each offering distinct features tailored to specific use cases.

In this chapter, you also learned about triggers and bindings, fundamental concepts that enable Azure Functions to respond to various events and interact with other Azure services. We examined common triggers like HTTP, Timer, Blob Storage, and Queue Storage and discussed how bindings simplify the connection to data sources and services without additional code. This knowledge allows you to build flexible, event-driven applications. We also covered blue-green deployments using deployment slots, demonstrating how to minimize downtime and risk during application updates by using two identical production environments.

Additionally, the chapter explored the automation of Azure Function deployments using Azure DevOps and GitHub Actions. You also learned how to write custom logs in Azure Functions using different programming languages and how to view and stream those logs for monitoring and debugging purposes.

Finally, this chapter covered advanced concepts like Durable Functions and binding expressions. Durable Functions enable you to create stateful workflows, manage complex operations, and maintain state across multiple executions, making them ideal for long-running tasks and orchestrations. Binding expressions provide a dynamic way to bind parameters, enhancing the flexibility and power of your functions. In the next chapter, you will learn about infrastructure as code with Azure Bicep.

CHAPTER 4

Infrastructure as Code with Azure Bicep

In the previous chapters, we've been provisioning resources using the Azure CLI, Azure PowerShell, or directly on the Azure portal. However, these are not the only ways to create and manage Azure services. There's the concept of infrastructure as code (IaC), which helps automate the deployment, management, and configuration of infrastructure. Deployments can be made more consistently and repeatedly by using IaC to specify your infrastructure using code.

This chapter will explore the topic of IaC using Azure Bicep, a declarative domain-specific language (DSL) for delivering Azure resources. Azure Bicep offers the same functionality as conventional JSON templates, but makes Azure Resource Manager (ARM) template development easier by having a more legible and manageable syntax. We will begin by discussing IaC, its advantages, and the reasons it is turning into an essential approach for modern cloud deployments. Then, we'll go over the syntax, organization, and fundamental elements of the Azure Bicep language. You'll discover how to create Bicep files to define and deploy resources to Azure.

After that, we'll talk about how to keep your infrastructure updated and maintained so your deployments remain consistent. Last, we'll talk about Azure's best practices for IaC. These best practices will help you manage configurations efficiently, writing clean, secure, and effective Bicep code and integrating IaC into your CI/CD pipelines for automated deployments.

By the end of this chapter, you will have a solid understanding on how to use Azure Bicep to define, deploy, and manage your Azure infrastructure as code, giving you complete control over your cloud environments.

Understanding IaC

There are many ways to provision infrastructure for your Azure services. Prior to this chapter, we've been using the Azure CLI, Azure PowerShell, and the Azure portal. But there are also declarative IaC tools like Azure Bicep. The major problem IaC helps solve is the inconsistency and potential errors that can arise from manual configuration. When deploying infrastructure manually, it's easy to miss a step or misconfigure a setting, leading to issues that can be hard to trace and replicate.

IaC addresses this problem by allowing you to define your infrastructure in code. This code acts as a blueprint for your resources, ensuring that the same configuration is applied every time it is executed. With IaC, infrastructure configurations are stored in source control, making them versioned, trackable, and auditable. This approach brings the principles of software development, such as version control, testing, and continuous integration, to infrastructure management. Some organizations may call this approach infrastructure as software.

Using IaC tools like Azure Bicep, you can define the desired state of your infrastructure declaratively. This means you describe what you want rather than how to achieve it. For example, you can specify that you need a virtual network with certain properties, and the IaC tool will handle the creation and configuration of that network. This abstraction simplifies the process and reduces the need for deep technical knowledge about the underlying infrastructure.

One of the significant benefits of IaC is its ability to automate the deployment of infrastructure. This automation reduces the time and effort required to set up environments, which is particularly valuable in Agile and DevOps practices where speed and repeatability are crucial. Automated deployments also ensure that environments are set up consistently, minimizing the risk of configuration drift where environments deviate from their intended configuration over time.

What Is Configuration Drift?

In a traditional setting without IaC, when software developers want to update infrastructure across multiple regions or environments, they often make these changes manually in each location. Over time, these manual changes can lead to differences between what was originally planned and what actually exists in each region or environment. This difference is called "configuration drift." Configuration drift happens because manual updates are not always consistently applied or tracked, leading to mismatched settings and potential issues.

Scalability is another critical advantage of IaC. As organizations grow, the complexity of their infrastructure tends to increase. Managing this complexity manually becomes impractical. IaC allows organizations to scale their infrastructure efficiently by automating the provisioning and configuration processes. This scalability extends not just to the number of resources but also to the complexity and diversity of configurations.

Another important aspect of IaC is its role in disaster recovery and backup strategies. By having infrastructure configurations codified, you can quickly redeploy environments in the case of failures or disasters. This capability significantly reduces downtime and ensures business continuity. It also allows for testing disaster recovery plans regularly, as the same code used for production can be used to create test environments.

Now that you know a bit about IaC and its advantages, it's time to learn about Azure Bicep, an IaC tool used to provision resources in a more efficient and manageable way.

Azure Bicep Language Essentials

Azure Bicep is a DSL that helps you to create infrastructure for Azure. It is designed to simplify the deployment of Azure resources. It serves as an abstraction layer over ARM templates, making it easier to define, deploy, and manage your cloud infrastructure. Unlike ARM templates, which use JSON and can become quite lengthy and complex, Azure Bicep provides a more concise and readable syntax, which reduces the amount of code needed to describe infrastructure configurations.

One of the good things about Bicep is its simplicity. Bicep syntax is designed to be more intuitive and less error prone than ARM templates. For instance, creating a storage account in Bicep requires fewer lines of code and avoids the extensive nested structures common in JSON-based ARM templates.

Here's a basic comparison between ARM JSON and Bicep.

ARM template JSON:

```
{
  "$schema": "https://schema.management.azure.com/schemas/2019-04-01/
            "deploymentTemplate.json#",
  "contentVersion": "1.0.0.0",
  "resources": [
    {
      "type": "Microsoft.Storage/storageAccounts",
      "apiVersion": "2019-04-01",
      "name": "teststorage",
      "location": "eastus",
      "sku": {
        "name": "Standard_LRS"
      },
      "kind": "StorageV2",
      "properties": {}
    }
  ]
}
```

Bicep:

```
resource myStorageAccount 'Microsoft.Storage/storageAccounts@2021-04-01' = {
  name: 'teststorage'
  location: 'eastus'
  sku: {
    name: 'Standard_LRS'
  }
  kind: 'StorageV2'
}
```

In the Bicep example, the same storage account is defined with significantly less code and more straightforward syntax.

Setting Up Azure Bicep on Your Computer

To try some of the code snippets you will see in this chapter, you'll need to have Azure Bicep installed. If you have Azure CLI version 2.20.0 or later installed, Bicep can be easily used because it is integrated with the Azure CLI. However, if you don't have this version of Azure CLI installed, you can follow these steps to get set up:

1. Install Azure CLI: If Azure CLI is not installed, you can download and install it from the official Azure CLI installation page (*https://oreil.ly/CudN3*).
2. Update Azure CLI: Ensure you have the latest version of Azure CLI by running the command `az upgrade` in your terminal.

What Makes Up a Bicep File?

Each Bicep file is composed of various elements that work together to describe the desired state of your infrastructure. Understanding these components is important because it helps you effectively use Bicep in your cloud projects. In this section, we'll run through some of the components that make up a Bicep template.

Resource declarations

At the core of a Bicep file are *resource declarations*, which define the Azure resources you want to deploy. A resource declaration includes a symbolic name, the type of resource, the API version, and a block of properties specific to that resource type. For instance, when declaring a storage account, you specify details like the account name, location, SKU, and other configuration settings. This clear structure helps in organizing and managing different resources within your infrastructure.

Here's an example:

```
resource myStorageAccount 'Microsoft.Storage/storageAccounts@2021-04-01' = {
  name: 'teststorage'
  location: 'eastus'
  sku: {
    name: 'Standard_LRS'
  }
  kind: 'StorageV2'
}
```

In the preceding code, a storage account is declared with the name `teststorage`, located in `eastus`. The `sku` block specifies the type of storage (Standard_LRS), and the `kind` property indicates the type of account (StorageV2).

Parameters

Parameters allow you to pass values into a Bicep file at the time of deployment, making it possible to use the same template in different environments with different configurations. For example, you can use parameters to define the location of resources, the names of services, or other environment-specific settings.

In Bicep, you can also assign *default values* to parameters. This means if no value is provided during deployment (via a parameter file or command-line argument), the default value will be used. However, the default value can be overridden when necessary. Here's an example:

```
param deploymentRegion string = 'eastus'

resource myStorageAccount 'Microsoft.Storage/storageAccounts@2021-04-01' = {
  name: 'teststorage'
  location: deploymentRegion
  sku: {
    name: 'Standard_LRS'
  }
  kind: 'StorageV2'
}
```

In the preceding code snippet, the location parameter is defined with a default value of `eastus`. This parameter is then used in the resource declaration for the storage account, specifying that the resource will be created in the `eastus` region. Parameters make the template versatile; you can easily override the location parameter's default value for different deployments or environments.

To override the parameter values during deployment, you can use parameter files or command-line arguments. This approach allows for consistent templates across different environments while providing the necessary customization through parameterization.

Overriding parameter values using parameter files. Parameter files are JSON files that store parameter values separately from the main Bicep file. This separation of parameters from the template can help you organize your configurations better.

Here's a parameter file example (*parameters.json*):

```
{
  "$schema":
      "https://schema.management.azure.com/schemas/2019-04-01/deploymentParameters.json#",
  "contentVersion": "1.0.0.0",
  "parameters": {
    "location": {
      "value": "westus"
    }
  }
}
```

In this example, the *parameters.json* file specifies that the location should be set to `westus`. During deployment, this file can be used to override the default parameter values defined in the Bicep file. To deploy using the parameter file, you can use the Azure CLI with the following command:

```
$ az deployment group create
    --resource-group sample-resource-group
    --template-file main.bicep
    --parameters @parameters.json
```

This command specifies the resource group (`sample-resource-group`), the main Bicep template (`main.bicep`), and the parameter file (`@parameters.json`). The `@` symbol is used to indicate the file is being passed as input.

Overriding parameter values using the CLI. Parameters can also be provided directly via the command line for quick changes or testing purposes. This method is useful for simple overrides or when parameter files are not necessary:

```
$ az deployment group create
    --resource-group sample-resource-group
    --template-file main.bicep
    --parameters location='centralus'
```

In this example, the location parameter is overridden to `centralus` during the deployment process.

Conditionals

Conditionals in Bicep help us include or exclude resources and configurations based on specific conditions. This feature is useful for managing different deployment scenarios within a single template. For example, you can use conditionals to deploy certain resources only if a specific parameter is set to a particular value:

```
param deployStorage bool = true

resource myStorageAccount 'Microsoft.Storage/storageAccounts@2021-04-01' =
if (deployStorage) {
  name: 'mystorageaccount'
  location: 'eastus'
  sku: {
    name: 'Standard_LRS'
  }
  kind: 'StorageV2'
}
```

Loops

Loops allow you to deploy multiple instances of a resource based on a set of input values. Loops are useful when you need to create a series of similar resources, such as multiple VMs or network subnets, without duplicating the code for each instance. Loops are created using the `for` keyword:

```
param numberOfInstances int = 3

resource myStorageAccounts 'Microsoft.Storage/storageAccounts@2021-04-01' =
[for i in range(0, numberOfInstances): {
  name: 'mystorageaccount${i}'
  location: 'eastus'
  sku: {
    name: 'Standard_LRS'
  }
  kind: 'StorageV2'
}]
```

In this example, the loop creates three storage accounts, which are named `mystorageaccount0`, `mystorageaccount1`, and `mystorageaccount2`, based on the loop index value. This is achieved using *string interpolation*, where the index value `i` is dynamically inserted into the name property of the resource. The syntax `mystorageaccount${i}` allows the `i` value to be substituted within the string, producing unique names for each storage account. String interpolation in Bicep lets you combine static text with dynamic values, making your templates more adaptable and reusable across different deployments.

Variables

Variables also exist in Bicep. Unlike parameters, which are provided by the user or deployment environment, variables are used within the Bicep file to store intermediate values or results of calculations. They help simplify complex expressions, make templates easier to read, and reduce repetition by allowing the same value or calculation to be reused multiple times. Variables are defined using the `var` keyword and can hold any type of data, such as strings, numbers, arrays, or objects.

The following code snippet illustrates ways to use variables in Bicep:

```
param baseName string = 'app'
param numberOfInstances int = 3
param baseResourceGroupId string = '/subscriptions/12345678/resourceGroups/base-rg'

var storageAccountNames = [for i in range(0, numberOfInstances): '${baseName}storage${i}']
var resourceGroupId = '${baseResourceGroupId}/subGroups/${environment}'

resource storageAccounts 'Microsoft.Storage/storageAccounts@2021-04-01' =
[for i in range(0, numberOfInstances): {
  name: storageAccountNames[i]
  location: 'eastus'
  sku: {
    name: 'Standard_LRS'
  }
  kind: 'StorageV2'
}]
```

In the previous code snippet, we are using variables to store two things:

storageAccountNames
: An array of storage account names is generated by looping over a range of numbers (from `0` to `numberOfInstances`) and appending the loop index into the base name `appstorage`.

resourceGroupId
: This variable constructs a new resource group ID by appending a subgroup path to the base resource group ID, incorporating the environment.

Outputs

Bicep also supports *output declarations*, which allow you to export values from a deployment for use in other operations or subsequent deployments. Outputs can include information like resource IDs, connection strings, or any other data generated during the deployment process.

This code snippet shows how to declare outputs in Bicep:

```
output storageAccountId string = myStorageAccount.id
```

In this example, the `output` keyword is used to declare an output named `storageAccountId`, which exports the ID of the created storage account.

Outputs can also be useful when chaining deployments or integrating with other systems and services.

Let's imagine we have a deployment that creates a storage account and a second deployment that creates a storage container (among other things) and we want to be able to pass in the storage account name from the first deployment to the second one. This will be possible because of outputs. Using Figure 4-1, let's see how this would work.

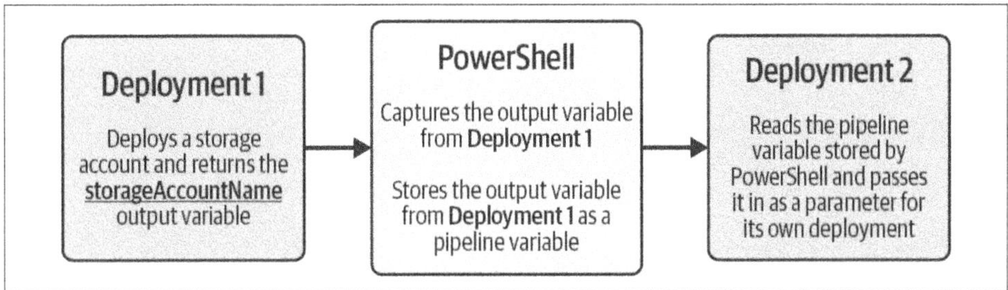

Figure 4-1. Chaining deployments

Let's consider how this will look in code. The following code example shows the two Bicep templates and the Azure Pipeline YAML that stores the output variable as a pipeline variable. If you don't understand Azure Pipeline or CI/CD, we will cover that in Chapter 13.

First Bicep template (*main.bicep*):

```
param location string

resource storageAccount 'Microsoft.Storage/storageAccounts@2023-04-02' = {
  name: 'storageaccount${uniqueString(resourceGroup().id)}'
  location: location
  sku: {
    name: 'Standard_LRS'
  }
  kind: 'StorageV2'
}

output storageAccountName string = storageAccount.name
```

Second Bicep template (*dependent.bicep*):

```
param storageAccountName string

resource storageAccount 'Microsoft.Storage/storageAccounts@2021-04-01' existing = {
    name: storageAccountName
}

resource storageContainer 'Microsoft.Storage/storageAccounts/blobServices/
containers@2023-04-02' = {
  name: 'mycontainer'
  parent: storageAccount
}
```

Azure Pipeline:

```
trigger:
  - main

pool:
  vmImage: 'ubuntu-latest'

steps:
- task: AzureCLI@2
```

```
      inputs:
        azureSubscription: 'YourSubscriptionName'
        scriptType: 'bash'
        script: |
          az deployment group create \
            --name myResourceGroup \
            --template-file main.bicep \
            --parameters location=westus

    - task: PowerShell@2
      inputs:
        targetType: 'inline'
        script: |
          $deployment = az deployment group show --name myResourceGroup --output json
          $storageAccountName = $deployment.properties.outputs.storageAccountName.value
          Write-Host "##vso[task.setvariable variable=storageAccountName]$storageAccountName"

    - task: AzureCLI@2
      inputs:
        azureSubscription: 'YourSubscriptionName'
        scriptType: 'bash'
        script: |
          az deployment group create \
            --name myResourceGroup \
            --template-file dependent.bicep \
            --parameters storageAccountName=$(storageAccountName)
```

The preceding code snippet is executed in the following steps:

- The first Bicep template creates a storage account and outputs its name.
- The second Bicep template creates a container in a storage account based on the provided name.
- The pipeline deploys the first template.
- It extracts the output variable `storageAccountName` from the deployment and sets it as a pipeline variable.
- The pipeline deploys the second template, passing the `storageAccountName` as a parameter.

With this, we can see how Azure Pipelines orchestrate multitemplate deployments by capturing outputs from one deployment and using them as inputs for subsequent ones, creating a seamless chain of infrastructure provisioning.

Modules

Modules in Bicep allow you to encapsulate and reuse infrastructure code. A module is a separate Bicep file that defines a set of resources. This modularity helps keep your IaC organized and promotes reuse so it's easier to manage and maintain large and complex deployments.

To illustrate the use of modules, let's look at an example where we have a module named `website` that includes the definition of only the resources needed to build websites across our organization (App Service Plan, an App Service, and Application Insights). This module can then be referenced in other Bicep files, and we can have consistent deployments of web application environments across different projects or environments.

Defining the website module. The `website` module defines the infrastructure for a web application. Here is a simplified version of what the *website.bicep* file might look like, including the creation of an App Service plan, an App Service, and an Application Insights resource:

```
param appServicePlanName string
param appName string
param location string

resource appServicePlan 'Microsoft.Web/serverfarms@2021-02-01' = {
  name: appServicePlanName
  location: location
  sku: {
    name: 'P1v2'
    tier: 'PremiumV2'
  }
}

resource webApp 'Microsoft.Web/sites@2021-02-01' = {
  name: appName
  location: location
  properties: {
    serverFarmId: appServicePlan.id
    httpsOnly: true
  }
}

resource appInsights 'Microsoft.Insights/components@2020-02-02' = {
  name: '${appName}-ai'
  location: location
  properties: {
    Application_Type: 'web'
  }
}

output appInsightsInstrumentationKey string = appInsights.properties.InstrumentationKey
```

In the preceding module, three Azure resources were created. `appServicePlan` defines an App Service plan, which determines the pricing tier and the amount of resources allocated to your web app. `webApp` defines the app service (web app) itself, specifying the `appServicePlan.id` to link it with the App Service plan. `appInsights` sets up Application Insights for monitoring and logging.

Using the website module. To use the `website` module in another Bicep file, you would reference the module and pass in the necessary parameters:

```
param location string = 'eastus'
param environmentName string = 'production'

module websiteModule 'website.bicep' = {
  name: 'websiteDeployment'
  params: {
    appServicePlanName: '${environmentName}-plan'
    appName: '${environmentName}-app'
    location: location
  }
}

output instrumentationKey string = websiteModule.outputs.appInsightsInstrumentationKey
```

Here, the `module` keyword is used to include the website module, referencing the *website.bicep* file. Parameters like `appServicePlanName`, `appName`, and `location` are passed to customize the deployment for a specific environment.

Deploying Resources with Azure Bicep

Now, it's time to deploy resources using Bicep. Azure Bicep allows you to deploy Azure resources declaratively, specifying the desired state in a Bicep file. This approach ensures resources are consistently created and configured, aligning with IaC principles. Bicep supports deploying resources across four scopes: resource group, subscription, management group, and tenant. Each scope has specific use cases and is suitable for different levels of resource management.

Resource Group Scope

The most common deployment scope is the resource group. This scope is used to manage resources that share the same lifecycle, such as a web application, its database, and related networking components. Most of the Azure deployments you do will be to resource groups, so you can use this scope. You can set the scope to resource group using the `targetScope` command:

```
targetScope = 'resourceGroup'

resource myCosmosDB 'Microsoft.DocumentDB/databaseAccounts@2021-06-15' = {
  name: 'mycosmosdb'
  location: 'eastus'
  properties: {
    databaseAccountOfferType: 'Standard'
    consistencyPolicy: {
      defaultConsistencyLevel: 'Session'
    }
  }
}
```

In this example, a Cosmos DB account is deployed in the `eastus` region. The `targetScope` is set to `resourceGroup`, indicating that the deployment will be within a specific resource group.

Subscription Scope

Deploying resources at the subscription scope is useful for resources that should be shared across multiple resource groups, such as policies or role assignments. Additionally, this scope can be used to create new resource groups themselves. You cannot deploy *regular* Azure resources like databases, key vaults, app services, etc. to a subscription directly. They need to be deployed to a resource group within the subscription.

The following code snippet creates a resource group and a policy assignment at the subscription level:

```
targetScope = 'subscription'

resource newResourceGroup 'Microsoft.Resources/resourceGroups@2021-04-01' = {
  name: 'MyNewResourceGroup'
  location: 'westus'
}

resource policyAssignment 'Microsoft.Authorization/policyAssignments@2020-09-01' = {
  name: 'enforceTaggingPolicy'
  properties: {
    displayName: 'Enforce Tagging Policy'
    policyDefinitionId: '/subscriptions/{subscription-id}/providers/Microsoft.Authorization/
      policyDefinitions/{policy-definition-id}'
    scope: newResourceGroup.id
    parameters: {
      tagName: {
        value: 'Environment'
      }
    }
  }
}
```

Management Group Scope

Deploying at the management group scope is ideal for organizations that have multiple subscriptions grouped under a management hierarchy. This scope allows for the application of policies, access controls, and compliance measures across multiple subscriptions.

Here's a code snippet you can use to deploy at the management group scope:

```
targetScope = 'managementGroup'

resource policyDefinition 'Microsoft.Authorization/policyDefinitions@2020-09-01' = {
  name: 'requireTaggingPolicy'
  properties: {
    displayName: 'Require Tagging'
```

```
      description: 'Ensures all resources are tagged with "Environment"'
      policyRule: {
        if: {
          field: 'tags'
          exists: 'false'
        }
        then: {
          effect: 'audit'
        }
      }
    }
  }
```

In this example, a policy definition is created at the management group level, which can be used to enforce tagging across multiple subscriptions within the management group.

Tenant Scope

The tenant scope is the highest level of deployment scope in Azure, encompassing the entire Microsoft Entra ID tenant. This scope is generally used for Microsoft Entra-specific resources like `tenantConfigurations`, `billingProfiles`, `policies`, or more.

```
targetScope = 'tenant'

resource billingProfile 'Microsoft.Billing/billingAccounts/billingProfiles@2020-05-01' = {
  name: 'myBillingProfile'
  properties: {
    displayName: 'My Billing Profile'
    ...
  }
}
```

Deploying with the Azure CLI

To deploy a Bicep file using the Azure CLI, you can use the `az deployment` commands. The command varies depending on the target scope:

Resource group scope:

```
$ az deployment group create
    --resource-group <resource-group>
    --template-file <template-file>
    --parameters <parameters>
```

Subscription scope:

```
$ az deployment sub create
    --location <location>
    --template-file <template-file>
    --parameters <parameters>
```

Management group scope:

```
$ az deployment mg create
    --management-group-id <management-group-id>
```

```
    --location <location>
    --template-file <template-file>
    --parameters <parameters>
```

Tenant scope:

```
$ az deployment tenant create
    --location <location>
    --template-file <template-file>
    --parameters <parameters>
```

Deploying with the Azure PowerShell

Azure PowerShell can also be used to deploy Bicep files. The `New-AzDeployment` command supports similar parameters for specifying the deployment scope.

Resource group scope:

```
$ New-AzResourceGroupDeployment
    -ResourceGroupName <ResourceGroupName>
    -TemplateFile <TemplateFile>
```

Subscription scope:

```
$ New-AzDeployment
    -Location <Location>
    -TemplateFile <TemplateFile>
```

Management group scope:

```
$ New-AzManagementGroupDeployment
    -ManagementGroupId <ManagementGroupId>
    -Location <Location>
    -TemplateFile <TemplateFile>
```

Tenant scope:

```
$ New-AzTenantDeployment
    -Location <Location>
    -TemplateFile <TemplateFile>
```

Managing and Updating Deployed Infrastructure

When you've added your initial infrastructure, you may need to make updates to keep it in line with evolving business requirements, security standards, or performance needs. Azure Bicep facilitates this process by providing deployment modes that determine how updates to the infrastructure are handled. The two primary deployment modes in Azure Bicep are *incremental* and *complete* modes.

Incremental Mode

Incremental mode is the default mode for Azure Bicep deployments. In this mode, only the resources defined in the Bicep file are updated or created. Existing resources not mentioned in the file remain unaffected. This mode is particularly useful when you need to add or modify resources without impacting the entire infrastructure setup. It allows for safer updates, minimizing the risk of accidental resource deletion or unintended changes. For example, if you deploy a new virtual machine or modify the configuration of an existing one, an incremental deployment ensures that other resources in the resource group, such as databases or storage accounts, are not altered unless explicitly specified.

Complete Mode

Complete mode, on the other hand, enforces a strict alignment between the resources defined in the Bicep file and the actual state of the resource group. In this mode, Azure ensures the deployed state exactly matches the template. Any resources not specified in the template are deleted. This mode is useful for situations where you need to ensure that only the intended resources are present, such as during a cleanup operation or when decommissioning unused services.

However, using complete mode requires careful planning and awareness of the existing resources that might be unintentionally removed. It is often employed in scenarios where the infrastructure must adhere strictly to a defined configuration, such as compliance-driven environments or during significant infrastructure reorganization. If you ever need to use complete mode, I recommend that you run the `what-if` command to see the changes that will be made before continuing with each deployment; for example:

```
$ az deployment group create
    --resource-group <resource-group>
    --template-file <template-file>
    --mode Complete
```

In this code snippet, the `--mode Complete` flag ensures the final state of the resource group matches exactly what is defined in the template bicep file.

Figure 4-2 provides a clear comparison between the incremental and complete deployment modes in Azure Bicep, showcasing how each mode manages infrastructure across two deployment phases.

In the incremental mode section on the left side of the illustration, two deployment phases are depicted. During the first deployment phase, the infrastructure consists of Virtual Machine 1, Key Vault 1, and Storage Account 1. When the second deployment occurs, the existing resources (Virtual Machine 1, Key Vault 1, and Storage Account 1) remain unchanged, while new resources, namely Storage Account 2 and Cosmos DB Account 1, are added. This highlights that incremental deployments only add or modify resources without altering any others that are not included in the deployment file.

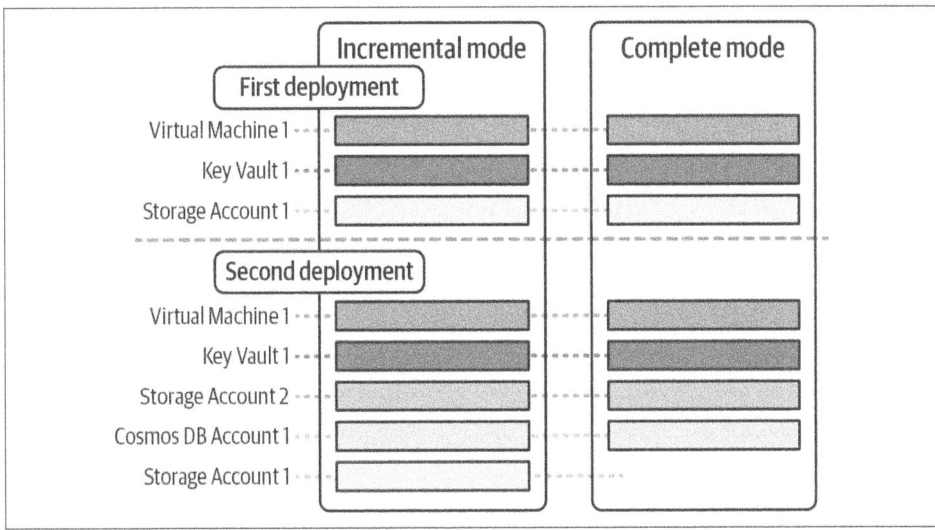

Figure 4-2. Incremental versus complete mode

On the right side, in the complete mode section, the illustration similarly shows two deployment phases. In the first deployment phase, Virtual Machine 1, Key Vault 1, and Storage Account 1 are initially deployed, just as in the incremental mode. However, in the second deployment phase, while Virtual Machine 1 and Key Vault 1 continue to exist, Storage Account 2 and Cosmos DB Account 1 are added. Notably, Storage Account 1 is removed. This representation emphasizes that complete mode ensures the actual infrastructure state strictly aligns with the current Bicep file definition, leading to the removal of any resources not specified in the latest deployment.

Let's see what the Bicep file definition looks like for both phases. First deployment:

```
targetScope = 'resourceGroup'

resource virtualMachine1 'Microsoft.Compute/virtualMachines@2021-07-01' = {
  name: 'virtualMachine1'
  location: 'eastus'
  // more code here
}

resource keyVault1 'Microsoft.KeyVault/vaults@2021-06-01' = {
  name: 'keyVault1'
  location: 'eastus'
  // more code here
}

resource storageAccount1 'Microsoft.Storage/storageAccounts@2021-04-01' = {
  name: 'storageAccount1'
  location: 'eastus'
  // more code here
}
```

Second deployment:

```
targetScope = 'resourceGroup'

resource virtualMachine1 'Microsoft.Compute/virtualMachines@2021-07-01' = {
  name: 'virtualMachine1'
  location: 'eastus'
  // more code here
}

resource keyVault1 'Microsoft.KeyVault/vaults@2021-06-01' = {
  name: 'keyVault1'
  location: 'eastus'
  // more code here
}

resource storageAccount2 'Microsoft.Storage/storageAccounts@2021-04-01' = {
  name: 'storageAccount2'
  location: 'eastus'
  // more code here
}

resource cosmosDBAccount1 'Microsoft.DocumentDB/databaseAccounts@2021-06-15' = {
  name: 'cosmosDBAccount1'
  location: 'eastus'
  // more code here
}
```

The first deployment template includes `virtualMachine1`, `keyVault1`, and `storageAccount1`. The second deployment template removes `storageAccount1` and adds `storageAccount2` and `cosmosDBAccount1` to the existing resources from the first deployment. As we've seen, the outcome in Azure depends on the mode we choose.

Best Practices for IaC in Azure

As you use IaC in Azure, I recommend following these practices because they can make your deployment processes more efficient and your infrastructure more resilient. Here, we discuss key best practices, including using modules, integrating with CI/CD pipelines, and using unique Bicep features.

Using Modules for Modularity and Maintainability

Modules help to promote modularity and maintainability. They allow you to encapsulate complex infrastructure configurations into reusable components, making your Bicep files more organized and easier to manage. This approach also aids consistency across projects and environments by centralizing common declarations.

For instance, you can create a module for standard application configurations and reuse it across multiple deployments, and we've seen how to do this already. This ensures any updates or changes need to be made in only one place, reducing the risk of configuration drift and simplifying management.

Using Modules to Enforce Naming Conventions

Modules can also be used to enforce naming conventions across multiple projects within a team, which helps maintain consistency and organization. By standardizing names, you simplify troubleshooting, ensure related resources are easily identifiable, and enhance overall operational efficiency.

This code snippet shows an example naming convention module:

```
param environment string
param baseName string
param instanceId string
param location string

output vnetResourceName string = '${baseName}-${environment}-vnet-${location}-${instanceId}'

output storageAccountResourceName string =
'st${environment}${baseName}${location}${instanceId}'

output keyvaultResourceName string =
'${baseName}-${environment}-kv-${location}-${instanceId}'

// additional outputs for other resource types
```

Using modules and enforcing a central naming convention like this has a few benefits:

Troubleshooting
: Consistent and meaningful names make it easier to identify and troubleshoot issues across different environments and resource types.

Organization
: Grouping related resources with similar names simplifies resource management and navigation.

Automation
: Scripts and tools can more easily target and manage resources based on predictable naming patterns.

Scalability
: As infrastructure grows, consistent naming prevents confusion and maintains clarity.

Cross-project consistency
: It ensures that resources across different projects adhere to a standard naming scheme, facilitating easier cross-team collaboration.

Operational efficiency
: It reduces the learning curve for new team members by providing a clear and standardized naming approach.

These naming convention practices through modules establish a foundation for consistent, manageable, and scalable infrastructure deployments across Azure environments.

Integrating Bicep with CI/CD Pipelines

Integrating Bicep with CI/CD pipelines helps with automating infrastructure deployments, tests, and code releases. CI/CD pipelines help streamline the deployment process, reduce the risk of human error, and ensure consistent and repeatable deployments. Let's consider the workflow:

Code changes
: When changes are made to the Bicep files, they are committed to a version control system.

Pipeline trigger
: The CI/CD pipeline is triggered by these changes, typically through a pull request, direct commit, or whatever trigger is in place.

Validation
: The pipeline validates the Bicep templates, checking for syntax errors and adherence to best practices.

Testing
: If applicable, the pipeline can deploy the infrastructure and application to a test environment and run automated tests to ensure everything works as expected.

Deployment
: Upon passing validation and tests, the pipeline deploys the infrastructure and application to the staging or production environment.

Monitoring
: Post-deployment, monitoring tools can be used to ensure the infrastructure is functioning correctly.

Using Bicep-Specific Features

Bicep has a few features that help you write optimal and secure IaC declarations. The first one is the `@secure` decorator. When you mark a parameter as secure, it ensures that sensitive information, like passwords or keys, is not written to deployment logs, thus enhancing security. This feature is crucial for maintaining the confidentiality of sensitive data during and after deployments.

Another significant feature is *parameterization*, which allows templates to be flexible and reusable across different environments. By defining parameters, you can easily adjust resource configurations without changing the core template, making it adaptable for various deployment scenarios. For example, you can set parameters for resource names, locations, or sizes, and provide default values that are safe and cost-effective for development environments.

Bicep also supports *string interpolation*, which is useful for constructing consistent and descriptive resource names. This feature helps enforce naming conventions that include key identifiers, such as project names, environments, or unique identifiers, facilitating easier management and troubleshooting of resources. Combining string interpolation with the `uniqueString()` function ensures unique names across different deployments. Note that it's important to prefix these with letters to avoid starting names with numbers, which some Azure services do not permit.

Last, Bicep has the `what-if` feature that previews the changes a deployment will make to the existing infrastructure. This feature helps identify what resources will be added, modified, or removed, allowing for a better understanding of the impact before applying changes. Using `what-if` can prevent unintentional deletions or modifications, providing a safer and more controlled deployment process.

Summary

This chapter covered IaC with Azure Bicep, highlighting the advantages of using IaC to automate and manage cloud infrastructure. Azure Bicep is a more readable and manageable alternative to ARM templates, making it easier to define and deploy resources. You learned the essential Bicep elements, including resource declarations, parameters, and modules, which help create modular and reusable infrastructure code. I also covered key features of Bicep, such as the `@secure` decorator for protecting sensitive information and the `what-if` analysis for previewing deployment impacts.

You should have a clearer understanding of best practices for using Bicep, such as enforcing naming conventions and integrating with CI/CD pipelines to automate and streamline deployments. It's important to maintain consistent and version-controlled infrastructure configurations, ensuring reliable and repeatable deployments. This chapter also addressed managing and updating infrastructure, focusing on deployment modes like incremental and complete, which control how changes are applied to the existing infrastructure. In the next chapter, you will learn about managing data on Azure.

CHAPTER 5

Managing Data in Azure

Data can be represented in different ways—it can be large and unstructured like media files or logs, semistructured like JSON documents, or structured like data in relational databases. Each type of data requires different storage solutions and management strategies. In this chapter, we will explore how to effectively manage data in Azure, focusing on both storage services and databases tailored for various data types.

We will also explore the different types of storage, including object, block, and file storage, and discuss which solution fits each scenario. Additionally, we'll cover how to manage data that gets stored in Azure databases, ensuring your data is secure, accessible, and efficiently managed. By the end of this chapter, you will have a comprehensive understanding of how to leverage Azure's storage services and database options to meet your specific data needs.

Introduction to Data Management in Azure

Data is everywhere around us, and it's how we make sense of the world. One very important thing is understanding that data comes in different forms, and the way we store and manage it can vary greatly depending on its type. Data can be categorized into three main types: unstructured, semistructured, and structured.

Unstructured data is data that doesn't have a predefined format or organization. Examples include documents, images, audio files, and videos. This type of data is often rich in information but challenging to analyze due to its lack of structure.

Semistructured data, on the other hand, has some organizational properties but doesn't fit neatly into a table or relational database. Examples include JSON files, XML documents, and emails. This data is more manageable than unstructured data because it has tags or markers to separate elements, but it still requires specialized tools for storage and analysis.

Structured data is the most organized form of data, typically stored in relational databases. It consists of clearly defined fields and records, such as numbers, dates, and strings, making it straightforward to query and analyze using SQL and similar tools.

Along with understanding data types, it's important to recognize the different storage formats that align with these types of data. *Block storage*, for example, is often used for structured data that needs to be frequently accessed and updated, such as databases. Block storage divides data into blocks and stores them separately, allowing for efficient access and modification. This type of storage is essential for applications requiring high performance, like transactional databases.

File storage is typically used for semistructured data, where files need to be stored in a hierarchical system. It's similar to how data is stored on a computer's hard drive, making it suitable for storing documents, media files, and shared content. File storage allows for easy access and sharing of data across multiple users or applications, making it ideal for collaborative environments.

Object storage, which is commonly used for unstructured data, stores data as objects, each with its own metadata. This type of storage is highly scalable and perfect for handling large volumes of data such as backups, archives, and multimedia files. Object storage is optimized for read-heavy operations and is often used in cloud environments where data needs to be accessed from various locations.

Choosing the right storage solution is crucial because it impacts not only how data is stored but also how it can be accessed, managed, and analyzed. The right choice can improve performance, reduce costs, and enhance the scalability of your applications. For example, using block storage for a high-performance database ensures that transactions are processed quickly and reliably. On the other hand, using object storage for large media files can significantly reduce storage costs while still providing easy access to the data.

Another reason why choosing the right storage solution is important is related to data management and governance. Different storage solutions offer different levels of control over data, which is critical for ensuring data integrity, security, and compliance with regulations. For instance, structured data stored in databases can be easily backed up, encrypted, and audited, providing a high level of security and compliance.

In contrast, unstructured data stored in object storage may require additional tools and processes to ensure it is protected and meets compliance requirements. Therefore, understanding the nature of your data and the specific requirements of your applications is essential in selecting the appropriate storage solution. By aligning the storage type with your data needs, you can optimize performance, scalability, and cost efficiency, while also ensuring that your data is secure and compliant with relevant regulations.

Understanding Azure Storage Services

Let's talk about some of the Azure storage services and how you can use them.

Object Storage with Azure Blob Storage

Azure Blob Storage is Microsoft's object storage solution, designed to handle massive amounts of unstructured data like documents, images, videos, and backups. Blob Storage is highly scalable, cost effective, and accessible from anywhere, making it an ideal choice for cloud-based applications and large-scale data storage needs.

Within Blob Storage, data is organized into containers, which act like directories, and blobs, which are the actual files stored within those containers. The hierarchy in Figure 5-1 depicts how this works.

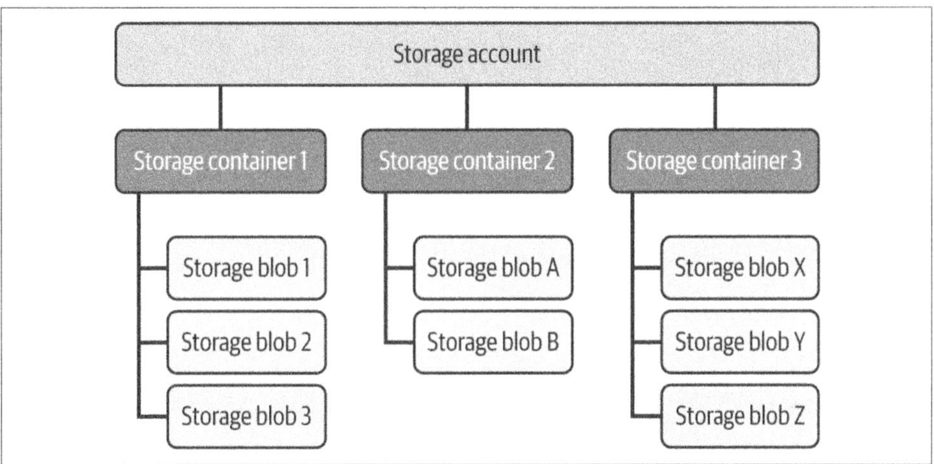

Figure 5-1. Storage account, container, and blob hierarchy

There are three types of blobs in Azure Blob Storage—block blobs, append blobs, and page blobs—each suited for different use cases:

Block blobs
: These are used to store text and binary data and are optimized for uploading large files.

Append blobs
: Append blobs are optimized for append operations, making them ideal for logging scenarios.

Page blobs
: These are used for scenarios that require random read/write access to data, such as virtual hard drives.

Managing storage accounts, containers, and blobs

To start using Azure Blob Storage, you first need to create a storage account, which is the top-level container that holds all your Azure storage data. Let's take a look at how to create a storage account, containers, and blobs using various methods.

Using Azure CLI. Create the storage account:

```
$ az storage account create
    --name <storage-account-name>
    --resource-group <storage-account-resource-group>
    --location <location>
    --sku <sku>
```

The SKU can be `Premium_LRS`, `Premium_ZRS`, `Standard_GRS`, `Standard_GZRS`, `Standard_LRS`, `Standard_RAGRS`, `Standard_RAGZRS`, or `Standard_ZRS`.

Each of these SKUs defines different levels of redundancy and performance for the storage account. Premium SKUs (e.g., `Premium_LRS` and `Premium_ZRS`) offer high-performance, low-latency storage, while Standard SKUs provide varying levels of redundancy, such as locally redundant storage (LRS), zone-redundant storage (ZRS), and geo-redundant storage (GRS), which replicate data across regions for higher availability and disaster recovery. For more information, you can visit the official Azure Storage redundancy documentation (*https://oreil.ly/5lbj6*) to explore the different SKUs and redundancy options in greater detail.

Create the storage container:

```
$ az storage container create
    --name <container-name>
    --account-name <storage-account-name>
```

Upload a blob to the storage container:

```
$ az storage blob upload
    --container-name <container-name>
    --name <blob-name>
    --file <path-to-file>
    --account-name <storage-account-name>
```

Using Azure PowerShell. Create the storage account:

```
$ New-AzStorageAccount
    -ResourceGroupName <resource-group-name>
    -Name <storage-account-name>
    -Location <location>
    -SkuName <sku>
```

Create the storage container:

```
$storageAccount = Get-AzStorageAccount
    -ResourceGroupName <resource-group-name>
    -Name <storage-account-name>
$ctx = $storageAccount.Context
New-AzStorageContainer
    -Name <container-name>
    -Context $ctx
```

Using Azure Bicep. Create the storage account and container:

```
param storageAccountName string
param containerName string
param location string
param skuName string
param storageKind string

resource storageAccount 'Microsoft.Storage/storageAccounts@2021-04-01' = {
  name: storageAccountName
  location: location
  sku: {
    name: skuName
  }
  kind: storageKind
}

resource container 'Microsoft.Storage/storageAccounts/blobServices/containers@2021-04-01' =
{
  name: containerName
  parent: storageAccount
  properties: {}
}
```

Beyond these three methods, you can also create and manage storage accounts, containers, and blobs directly from the Azure portal, which offers a user-friendly, intuitive graphical interface. This method allows you to configure, upload, and manage your storage resources without needing to write or execute command-line scripts.

To create a storage account, simply navigate to the Storage accounts section in the portal, click Create, and fill in the necessary details. Figure 5-2 shows the form for creating a storage account on Azure.

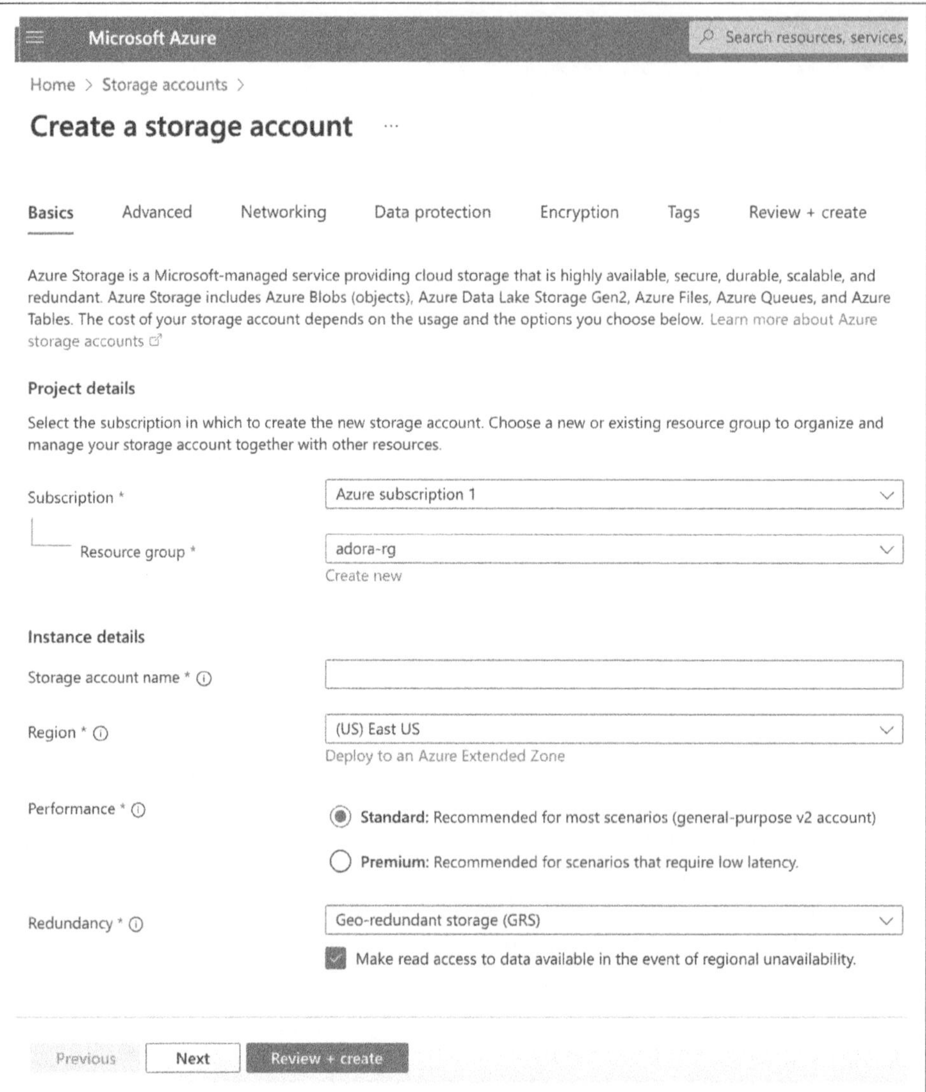

Figure 5-2. Creating a storage account

When creating a container, select your storage account, go to Containers, and add a new container with your desired settings (Figure 5-3).

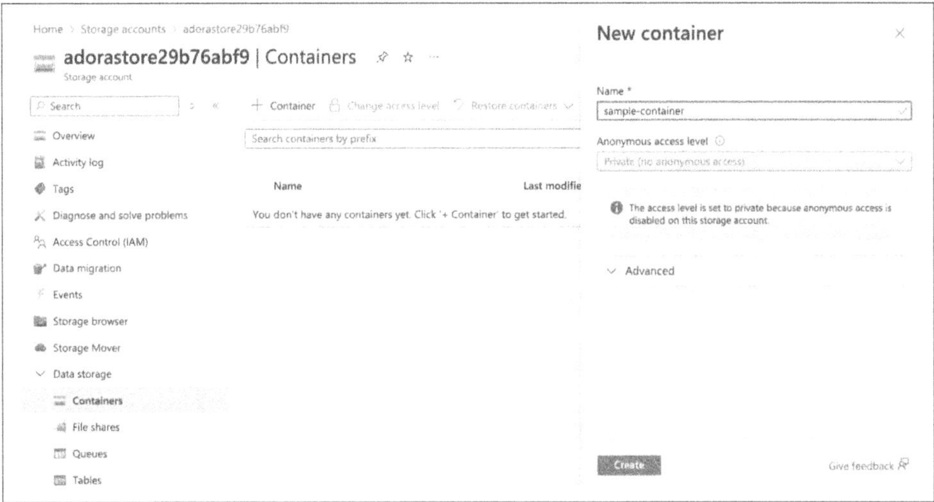

Figure 5-3. Creating a storage container

Uploading a blob in the Azure portal is just as straightforward. Once you have your container set up, you can easily upload blobs by selecting the container, clicking Upload, and choosing the file from your local system, as shown in Figure 5-4.

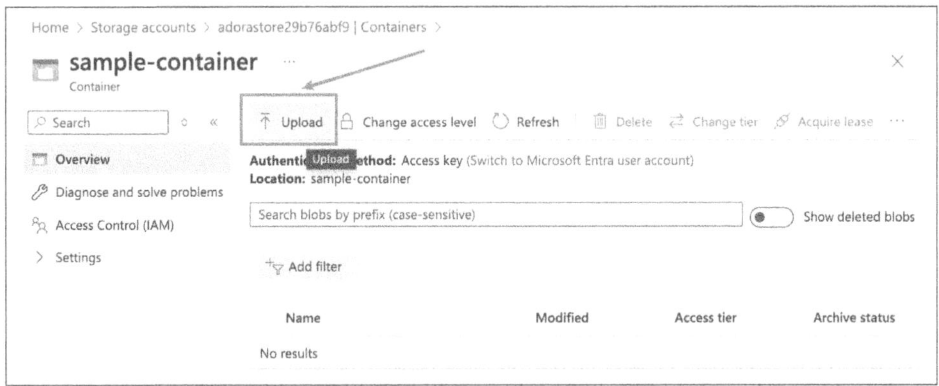

Figure 5-4. Uploading a blob to the storage container

Once you've uploaded your blobs to Azure Storage, you can access them in different ways.

If you prefer a visual approach, the Azure portal allows you to navigate directly to your storage account, select the container, and click on the blob you want to access. From there, you can view the blob, download it, or generate a shared access signature (SAS) URL, which provides controlled access without exposing your storage account credentials. This method is straightforward and ideal for manual management or quick access.

For those who prefer command-line tools, Azure CLI offers powerful commands to interact with your blobs. You can use the `az storage blob show` command to retrieve information about a blob or the `az storage blob download` command to download it directly to your local machine. The AZ CLI commands are shown here:

```
$ az storage blob show
    --name <blob-name>
    --container-name <container-name>
    --account-name <storage-account-name>

$ az storage blob download
    --name <blob-name>
    --container-name <container-name>
    --account-name <storage-account-name>
```

As a developer, you can also access blobs programmatically using Azure SDKs or the REST API. Azure provides SDKs for various programming languages, which allows you to integrate blob access directly into your applications.

If you need to share blobs securely, generating an SAS URL is the recommended approach. SAS tokens provide temporary, secure access to blobs without revealing your storage account credentials. You can share the SAS URL with others, granting them specific permissions (such as read or write) for a defined period. This method is particularly useful for sharing data with external collaborators or applications. To generate a SAS URL in Azure CLI, you can use the AZ CLI:

```
$ az storage container generate-sas
    --account-name <storage-account-name>
    --name <container-name>
    --permissions <permissions>  # e.g. rwdlac
    --expiry <expiry-date> # Datetime format (Y-m-d'T'H:M'Z')
    --https-only
    --output tsv
```

You can also do it programmatically through the Azure portal by clicking "Shared access tokens," as shown in Figure 5-5.

After creating the SAS token, you can now append it to the storage account URL:

```
https://<storage-account-name>.blob.core.windows.net/<container-name>?<sas-token>
```

You can also use storage account URLs even though you don't have SAS tokens. If you've configured your container with public access, you can directly access blobs using a URL in the following format:

> *https://<storage-account-name>.blob.core.windows.net/<container-name>/<blob-name>*

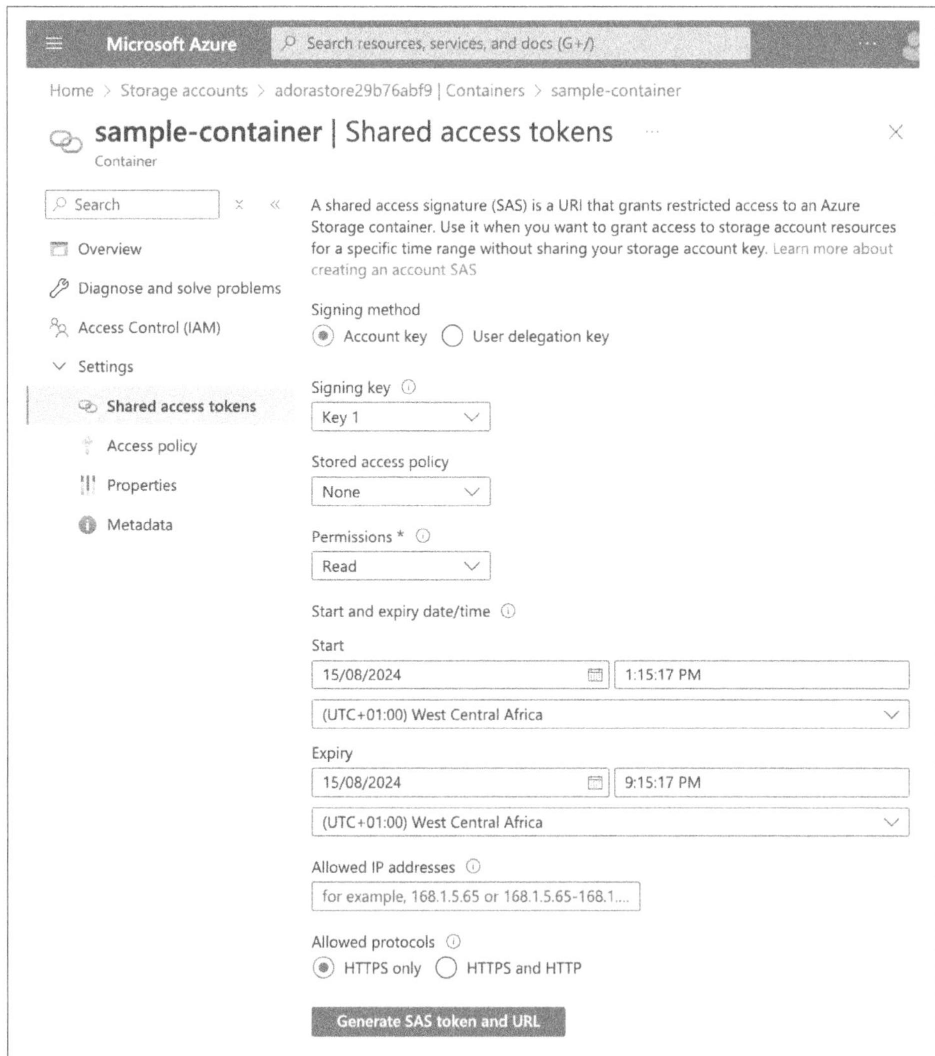

Figure 5-5. Creating an SAS token

This approach allows for straightforward access to blobs via a web browser or any application that can make HTTP requests. While convenient, public access should be used with caution, as it permits unrestricted access to the blobs within the container, which may not be appropriate for sensitive or private data.

Securing your data in Azure Storage

As you create complex distributed systems on the cloud and build innovative apps, it's important to understand that bad actors are also innovating on ways to hack you; security is everyone's responsibility. For that reason, securing your data in Azure Storage is critical to protecting your applications and data from unauthorized access and breaches. Let's explore a few ways that you can secure your data in Azure Storage.

Encryption. Azure automatically encrypts all data at rest using 256-bit Advanced Encryption Standard (AES) encryption, which is one of the strongest block ciphers available. This ensures that even if your data is compromised, it remains unreadable without the appropriate decryption keys. For additional control over encryption, you can implement customer-managed keys (CMK) stored in Azure Key Vault. This approach allows you to rotate, manage, and audit your encryption keys independently, giving you greater flexibility and security. When you use CMK, you can specify your encryption keys in the Azure Key Vault, and Azure will use these keys to encrypt and decrypt your data. This is useful for organizations that have strict regulatory requirements around encryption key management.

The following code snippet shows you how to use CMK in your storage accounts:

```
param storageAccountName string
param keyVaultUri string
param keyVersion string
param keyName string
param location string
param skuName string

resource storageAccount 'Microsoft.Storage/storageAccounts@2021-04-01' = {
  name: storageAccountName
  location: location
  sku: {
    name: skuName
  }
  kind: 'StorageV2'
  properties: {
    encryption: {
      services: {
        blob: {
          enabled: true
        }
        file: {
          enabled: true
        }
        table: {
          enabled: true
        }
        queue: {
          enabled: true
        }
      }
      keySource: 'Microsoft.Keyvault'
      keyVaultProperties: {
```

```
            keyname: keyName
            keyvaulturi: keyVaultUri
            keyversion: keyVersion
          }
        }
      }
    }
```

Access control. Access control is important because it allows you to make sure only the right people or applications can access your data in Azure Storage. Azure provides two main ways to control access: shared access signatures and role-based access control.

Shared access signatures (SAS) let you give temporary access to your storage resources. You can specify what actions the user can take (like read, write, or delete) and how long they can have access. This is useful when you need to share data with someone temporarily without exposing your main credentials. The following code snippet shows how to create SAS tokens in the Azure CLI:

```
$  az storage container generate-sas \
    --account-name <storage-account-name>
    --name <container-name>
    --permissions <permissions>  # e.g. rwdlac
    --expiry <expiry>   # e.g. 2022-12-31T23:59:59Z
    --https-only
    --output tsv
```

Role-based access control (RBAC) allows you to assign specific roles to users, groups, or applications. Each role comes with certain permissions, like the ability to read or modify data. For example, you can give someone the *Storage Blob Data Contributor* role, which allows them to upload, delete, and read blobs in your storage account. This ensures that each person or application only has the permissions they need. Let's look at the Azure CLI command:

```
$  az role assignment create
    --assignee <user-or-app-id>
    --role "Storage Blob Data Contributor"
    --scope /subscriptions/<subscription-id>/resourceGroups/<resource -group-name>/
            providers/Microsoft.Storage/storageAccounts/<storage-account-name>
```

In this example, you replace `<user-or-app-id>` with the ID of the user or application you're assigning the role to, and the role allows them to manage blobs within the specified storage account.

Using RBAC provides a more permanent and structured way to manage who has access to your storage, while SAS is great for temporary or specific access needs. Combining these methods gives you strong control over your data's security.

Network security. You can also use network security measures as a way to protect your data from unauthorized access. Azure offers several options to restrict access, including VNet service endpoints and IP whitelisting.

With VNet service endpoints, you can restrict access to your storage account so only resources within a specific virtual network can connect. This ensures your storage account is isolated from the public internet, adding a critical layer of security.

Here's how to configure a storage account to allow access only from a specific VNet:

```
param storageAccountName string
param vnetId string
param location string
param skuName string
Param storageKind string

resource storageAccount 'Microsoft.Storage/storageAccounts@2021-04-01' = {
  name: storageAccountName
  location: location
  sku: {
    name: skuName
  }
  kind: storageKind
  properties: {
    networkAcls: {
      bypass: 'AzureServices'
      defaultAction: 'Deny'
      virtualNetworkRules: [
        {
          id: vnetId
          action: 'Allow'
        }
      ]
    }
    supportsHttpsTrafficOnly: true
  }
}
```

You can also disable public access and whitelist certain IP addresses to further secure your storage account. By setting the `allowBlobPublicAccess` property to false, you prevent anyone from accessing your blobs publicly. Additionally, you can specify `ipRules` to allow only certain IP addresses to connect to your storage account, adding another layer of security.

Here's an example of how to whitelist IP addresses using Bicep:

```
param storageAccountName string
param allowedIPAddresses array = []
param location string
param skuName string

resource storageAccount 'Microsoft.Storage/storageAccounts@2021-04-01' = {
  name: storageAccountName
  location: location
  sku: {
    name: skuName
  }
  kind: 'StorageV2'
  properties: {
    networkAcls: {
      bypass: 'AzureServices'
```

```
        defaultAction: 'Deny'
        ipRules: [
          for ip in allowedIPAddresses: {
            action: 'Allow'
            value: ip
          }
        ]
      }
      supportsHttpsTrafficOnly: true
    }
  }
```

By combining VNet service endpoints with IP whitelisting, you can create a robust security perimeter around your Azure Storage account and ensure only trusted networks and devices have access to your data.

Block Storage with Azure Managed Disks

Azure Managed Disks are a flexible block storage solution designed for use with Azure VMs. These disks are fully managed by Azure, which means you don't need to worry about storage limits or managing the storage infrastructure. Azure Managed Disks simplify the process of creating, managing, and scaling disk storage for your VMs. They offer reliable performance and are designed to handle a variety of workloads, from small development environments to large-scale enterprise applications.

Benefits of Azure Managed Disks

Azure Managed Disks are engineered for exceptional availability and durability, with a design that ensures 99.999% availability. This high level of reliability is achieved by maintaining three replicas of your data within the Azure infrastructure. This ensures that even if one or two replicas experience issues, the remaining replica continues to function. This architecture not only protects your data from hardware failures but also contributes to Azure's industry-leading durability, boasting an impressive 0% annualized failure rate.

When it comes to performance, Azure Managed Disks offer several tiers to meet various workload requirements. The available disk types include ultra disks, premium solid-state drives (SSDs), standard SSDs, and standard hard disk drives (HDDs), each designed to deliver specific levels of IOPS (input/output operations per second) and throughput:

Ultra disks
: Provide the highest performance, ideal for mission-critical applications like large databases and high-performance computing

Premium SSDs
: Offer high IOPS and low latency, making them suitable for production workloads that require consistent performance

Standard SSDs
: Strike a balance between cost and performance, perfect for web servers and lightly used applications

Standard HDDs
: Most economical, suitable for archival and backup storage

These performance options ensure that Azure Managed Disks can meet the demands of a wide range of applications, from small-scale deployments to enterprise-grade solutions requiring robust performance and availability.

Managing Azure Managed Disks

Azure Managed Disks have a range of commands for creating, managing, and maintaining your disks, using Azure CLI, PowerShell, and Bicep. Here's how you can work with Azure Managed Disks across these tools.

Azure CLI commands. These commands will show you how to create a managed disk, attach the disk to a VM, detach the disk from a VM, and delete the managed disk.

Create a managed disk:

```
$ az disk create
    --resource-group <resource-group-name>
    --name <managed-disk-name>
    --size-gb <size>
    --location <location>
    --sku <sku>
    --zone <zone>
```

Attach a disk to a VM:

```
$ az vm disk attach
   --resource-group <resource-group-name>
   --vm-name <vm-name>
   --disk <managed-disk-name>
```

Detach a disk from a VM:

```
$ az vm disk detach
   --resource-group <resource-group-name>
   --vm-name <vm-name>
   --disk <managed-disk-name>
```

Delete a managed disk:

```
$ az disk delete
   --resource-group <resource-group-name>
   --name <managed-disk-name>
```

With these four commands, you can manage the complete lifecycle of managed disks in your Azure environment.

PowerShell commands. The following commands will show you how to create a managed disk, attach the disk to a VM, detach the disk from a VM, and delete the managed disk.

Create a managed disk:

```
$diskConfig = New-AzDiskConfig
    -SkuName <sku>
    -Location <location>
    -CreateOption Empty
    -DiskSizeGB <size>

New-AzDisk
    -ResourceGroupName <resource-group-name>
    -DiskName <managed-disk-name>
    -Disk $diskConfig
```

Attach a disk to a VM:

```
$vm = Get-AzVM
    -ResourceGroupName <resource-group-name>
    -Name <vm-name>

$disk = Get-AzDisk
    -ResourceGroupName <resource-group-name>
    -DiskName <managed-disk-name>

$vm = Add-AzVMDataDisk
    -VM $vm
    -Name <managed-disk-name>
    -CreateOption Attach
    -ManagedDiskId $disk.Id

Update-AzVM
    -VM $vm
    -ResourceGroupName <resource-group-name>
```

Detach a disk from a VM:

```
$vm = Get-AzVM
    -ResourceGroupName <resource-group-name>
    -Name <vm-name>

$vm = Remove-AzVMDataDisk
    -VM $vm
    -Name <managed-disk-name>

Update-AzVM
    -VM $vm
    -ResourceGroupName <resource-group-name>
```

Delete a managed disk:

```
Remove-AzDisk
    -ResourceGroupName <resource-group-name>
    -DiskName <managed-disk-name>
    -Force
```

Using these PowerShell cmdlets, you can programmatically manage all aspects of disk lifecycle for your Azure VMs.

Bicep code. This code snippet will show you how to create a managed disk, attach the disk to a VM, detach the disk from a VM, and delete the managed disk:

```
param location string
param vmName string
param diskSizeGB int
param diskSkuName string
param managedDiskName string

resource managedDisk 'Microsoft.Compute/disks@2021-04-01' = {
  name: managedDiskName
  location: location
  sku: {
    name: diskSkuName
  }
  properties: {
    creationData: {
      createOption: 'Empty'
    }
    diskSizeGB: diskSizeGB
  }
}

resource vm 'Microsoft.Compute/virtualMachines@2021-07-01' existing = {
  name: vmName
}

resource diskAttachment 'Microsoft.Compute/virtualMachines/dataDisks@2021-07-01' = {
  parent: vm
  name: managedDiskName
  properties: {
    lun: 0
    createOption: 'Attach'
    managedDisk: {
      id: managedDisk.id
    }
  }
}
```

`managedDisk` creates a new managed disk, `vm` references an existing virtual machine, and `diskAttachment` attaches the created managed disk to the specified virtual machine as a data disk.

File storage with Azure Files

Azure Files offers fully managed file shares in the cloud that can be accessed via the standard Server Message Block (SMB) protocol. Azure Files also has a feature called Azure File Sync that allows you to synchronize your on-premises file shares with Azure Files. This enables you to keep a local cache of your most frequently accessed files while storing the full set of files in Azure. Azure File Sync also includes multisite access, allowing you to sync the same file share across multiple locations.

You can create an Azure file share using the Azure CLI, PowerShell, or Bicep.

Using Azure CLI. The following Azure CLI commands demonstrate how to create a storage account and file share:

```
$ az storage account create
    --resource-group <resource-group-name>
    --name <storage-account-name>
    --location <location>
    --sku <sku>

$ az storage share-rm create
    --resource-group <resource-group-name>
    --storage-account <storage-account-name>
    --name <file-share-name>
    --quota <quota>
```

In the preceding code snippet, the `az storage account create` command creates a storage account, and the `az storage share-rm create` command creates a file share within that storage account.

Using PowerShell. The following PowerShell commands demonstrate how to create a storage account and file share:

```
New-AzStorageAccount
    -ResourceGroupName <resource-group-name>
    -Name <storage-account-name>
    -Location '<location>
    -SkuName <sku>

$ctx = (Get-AzStorageAccount -ResourceGroupName <resource-group
        -name> -Name <storage-account-name>).Context

New-AzStorageShare
    -Name <file-share-name>
    -Context $ctx
    -Quota <quota>
```

Using Bicep. The following Bicep template defines the resources needed to deploy a storage account with a file share:

```
param fileShareName string
param location string
param quota int
param skuName string
param storageAccountName string
param storageKind string

resource storageAccount 'Microsoft.Storage/storageAccounts@2021-04-01' = {
  name: storageAccountName
  location: location
  sku: {
    name: skuName
  }
  kind: storageKind
}
```

```
resource fileShare 'Microsoft.Storage/storageAccounts/fileServices/shares@2021-04-01' = {
  name: fileShareName
  parent: storageAccount
  properties: {
    quota: quota
  }
}
```

These three approaches give you flexibility to create Azure file shares using your preferred deployment method, whether through command-line tools or IaC templates.

Managing Data with Azure Databases

This section will cover databases on Azure and how to use them to manage structured and semistructured data effectively. These include services like Azure SQL Database, Azure Cosmos DB, and Azure Database for MySQL/PostgreSQL.

Using Azure SQL Database

Azure SQL Database runs the SQL Server database engine, which is a fully managed relational database service in the Azure cloud. It provides a high-performance, scalable, and secure environment for running SQL Server databases without the need to manage the underlying infrastructure. Azure SQL Database is designed for developers and businesses that need a powerful relational database service that can be easily scaled and managed, with built-in high availability, backup, and security features.

Understanding relational databases

Relational databases store data in tables with rows and columns, making it easy to manage and query structured data using SQL (Structured Query Language). They are ideal for applications that require ACID (atomicity, consistency, isolation, durability) transactions and complex queries. Azure SQL Database supports relational database features like indexing, stored procedures, triggers, and full-text search, making it suitable for a wide range of applications, from small web apps to large enterprise systems.

Database deployment options

Azure SQL Database provides several deployment options to meet diverse requirements, organized into three main categories: SQL databases, SQL managed instances, and SQL virtual machines. Each category serves different purposes and comes with specific configurations.

SQL databases. For this deployment, there are three options:

Single database
: This is a fully isolated database designed for modern cloud applications. It's highly scalable and offers serverless options, allowing you to pay only for what you use.

Elastic pool
: This is a collection of databases that share the same resources. It's ideal for managing multiple databases that experience varying workloads. This means the model has cost-effective scalability.

Database server
: This is a server hosting multiple databases and elastic pools, allowing you to manage several databases under a single server entity.

SQL managed instances. For this deployment, there are two options:

Single instance
: A fully managed SQL Server instance offering nearly 100% compatibility with on-premises SQL Server, making it an excellent choice for migrating existing SQL Server applications to Azure.

Single instance—Azure Arc
: Managed instances that can run on premises, at the edge, in multicloud environments, or in any other infrastructure you choose.

SQL virtual machines. For this deployment, there is only one option: *SQL Server on Virtual Machines* (Figure 5-6). SQL VMs provide full control over the database engine and the underlying VM. This is ideal for applications that require OS-level access or custom configurations not available in managed instances or databases.

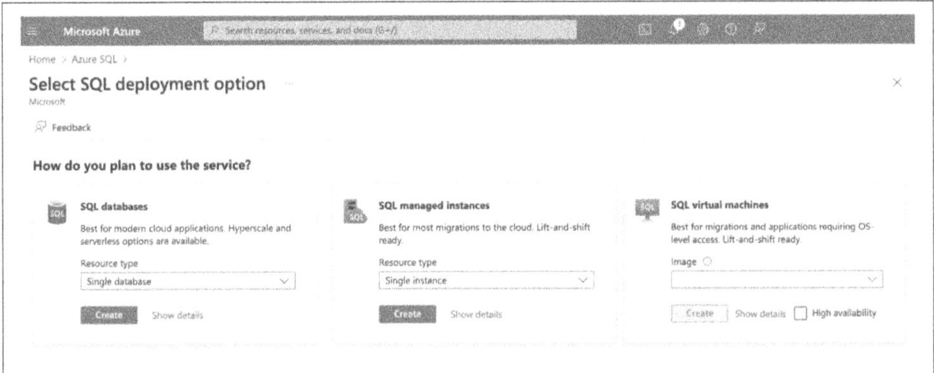

Figure 5-6. SQL deployment options

Managing Azure SQL databases

Like other Azure resources, you can manage Azure SQL Databases through the Azure portal, Azure CLI, PowerShell, or through IaC tools like Azure Bicep:

Azure CLI:

```
# Create a SQL server
$  az sql server create
    --name <server-name>
    --resource-group <resource-group-name>
    --location <location>
    --admin-user <username>
    --admin-password <password>

# Create a SQL database
$  az sql db create
    --resource-group <resource-group-name>
    --server <server-name>
    --name <database-name>
    --service-level-objective <slo>
```

PowerShell:

```
# Create a SQL server
$  New-AzSqlServer
    -ResourceGroupName <resource-group-name>
    -ServerName <server-name>
    -Location <location>
    -SqlAdministratorCredentials (Get-Credential)

# Create a SQL database
$  New-AzSqlDatabase
    -ResourceGroupName <resource-group-name>
    -ServerName <server-name>
    -DatabaseName <database-name>
    -RequestedServiceObjectiveName <slo>
```

Bicep:

```
param location string
resource sqlServer 'Microsoft.Sql/servers@2021-02-01' = {
  name: 'server-name'
  location: location
  properties: {
    administratorLogin: 'my-login'
    administratorLoginPassword: 'my-password123'
  }
}

resource sqlDatabase 'Microsoft.Sql/servers/databases@2021-02-01' = {
  name: 'database-name'
  parent: sqlServer
  properties: {
    requestedServiceObjectiveName: 'S0'
  }
}
```

These commands and templates provide the foundation for deploying and managing Azure SQL Database infrastructure across different tool sets.

Using Azure Database for PostgreSQL

Azure Database for PostgreSQL is a fully managed database service that offers built-in high availability, automated backups, and scaling capabilities, making it an ideal choice for running PostgreSQL in the cloud.

PostgreSQL is a powerful, open source relational database management system known for its robustness, extensibility, and compliance with SQL standards. Azure Database for PostgreSQL primarily provides the flexible server deployment option. This option gives you more control over your database configuration and maintenance, including the ability to define custom maintenance windows and achieve high availability across multiple availability zones. It also allows for dynamic scaling to meet varying workload demands.

You can create an Azure Database for PostgreSQL using the Azure CLI, PowerShell, or Bicep:

Azure CLI:

```
$ az postgres flexible-server create
    --resource-group <resource-group-name>
    --name <name>
    --location <location>
    --admin-user <admin-user>
    --admin-password <admin-password>
    --sku-name <sku>
```

PowerShell:

```
$ New-AzPostgreSqlFlexibleServer
    -ResourceGroupName <resource-group-name>
    -Name <name>
    -Location <location>
    -AdministratorLogin <admin-user>
    -AdministratorLoginPassword <admin-password>
    -SkuName <sku>
```

Bicep:

```
resource postgreSqlFlexibleServer 'Microsoft.DBforPostgreSQL/flexibleServers@2021-06-01' = {
  name: <pgserver-name>
  location: <location>
  properties: {
    administratorLogin: <admin-user>
    administratorLoginPassword: <admin-password>
    version: <version>
    storageProfile: {
      storageMB: <storage-mb>
      backupRetentionDays: <backup-retention-days>
    }
  }
  sku: {
```

```
        name: <name>
        tier: <tier>
        capacity: <capacity>
      }
    }
```

These deployment options provide flexible ways to provision Azure Database for PostgreSQL, allowing you to choose the method that best aligns with your infrastructure management approach.

Using Azure Cosmos DB

Azure Cosmos DB is a fully managed NoSQL database service designed to provide high availability, low latency, and global distribution for large-scale applications. Supporting multiple data models, including key-value, document, graph, and column-family, Cosmos DB is versatile and powerful, making it an excellent choice for modern applications that need to handle diverse data types and high volumes.

The Cosmos DB hierarchy

Cosmos DB's hierarchy is structured to optimize data management and access (Figure 5-7).

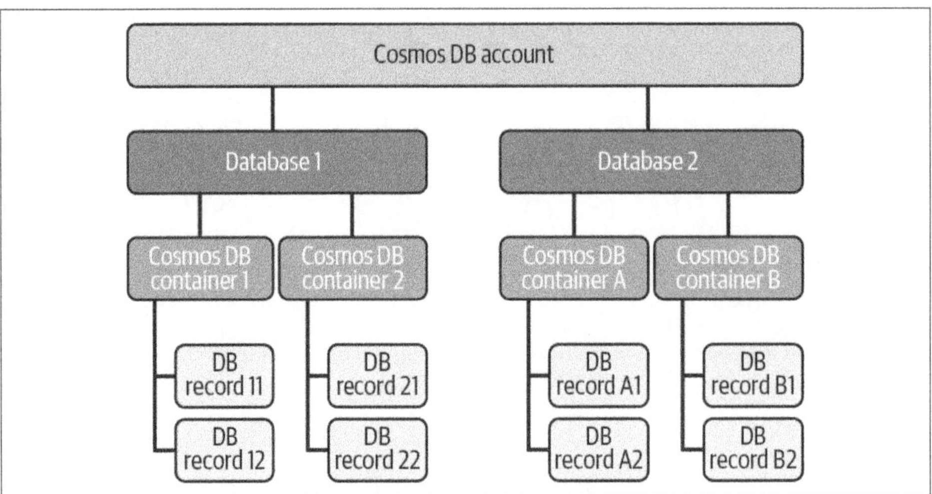

Figure 5-7. The Cosmos DB hierarchy

The hierarchy starts with:

Account
: The Cosmos DB account is the top-level container that holds all the databases and provides global distribution, consistency, and security settings.

Database
: Each database within a Cosmos DB account is a logical container that holds one or more containers, similar to how a database holds tables in a relational system.

Container
: Containers are schema-agnostic tables within the database, storing items. Containers are partitioned, and each item (document) is identified by a unique key.

Item (DB record)
: The actual records stored within containers. Items can be documents, key-value pairs, or graph nodes, depending on the data model.

Multimodel API support

One of the unique features of Cosmos DB is its *multimodel API support*, which allows you to use different data models depending on what your application needs:

SQL API
: For document-oriented applications using SQL syntax

MongoDB API
: For applications using the MongoDB driver and commands

Cassandra API
: For wide-column stores, compatible with Apache Cassandra

Gremlin API
: For graph databases, enabling traversal queries over graph structures

Table API
: For key-value stores, similar to Azure Table

When you create a Cosmos DB account, you must select one of these APIs as the storage model. This choice determines how data is stored and accessed, and it cannot be changed later. However, you can have different applications accessing the same database using the same API. Each application can leverage the strengths of its respective API, but the storage model remains consistent across the entire Cosmos DB account. For more details on Cosmos DB APIs, check the Azure Cosmos DB API documentation (*https://oreil.ly/dQdhJ*).

Global distribution and replication

Azure Cosmos DB excels at global distribution, allowing you to replicate your data across multiple Azure regions. This ensures your data is close to your users, providing low-latency access no matter where they are located. You can add or remove regions at any time and configure read/write regions based on your needs.

Cosmos DB supports automatic failover, ensuring high availability even in the event of a regional outage. The platform's multimaster replication allows for multiple regions to handle read and write operations simultaneously, improving both performance and resilience. Cosmos DB also has five consistency levels: Strong, Bounded Staleness, Session, Consistent Prefix, and Eventual. These options allow you to balance between consistency and performance based on your application's requirements.

The following code snippet is an example CLI command to create a Cosmos DB account with global distribution, a database, and a container:

```
# Create a Cosmos DB account
az cosmosdb create
  --name <cosmosdb-account-name>
  --resource-group <resource-group>
  --kind GlobalDocumentDB
  --enable-multiple-write-locations
  --default-consistency-level Session
  --locations regionName=EastUS failoverPriority=0 isZoneRedundant=False
  --locations regionName=WestUS failoverPriority=1 isZoneRedundant=False

# Create a database in the Cosmos DB account
az cosmosdb sql database create
  --account-name <cosmosdb-account-name>
  --name <db-name>
  --resource-group <resource-group>

# Create a container in the database
az cosmosdb sql container create
  --account-name <cosmosdb-account-name>
  --database-name <db-name>
  --name <container-name>
  --partition-key-path /<PartitionKey> # e.g. /Id or /User
  --throughput <throughput>
```

The following code snippet is an example PowerShell command to create a Cosmos DB account with global distribution, a database, and a container:

```
# Create a Cosmos DB account
New-AzCosmosDBAccount
    -ResourceGroupName <resource-group>
    -Name <cosmosdb-account-name>
    -Location <location>
    -DefaultConsistencyLevel "Session"
    -EnableAutomaticFailover $true
    -Locations @("EastUS", "WestUS")

# Create a database in the Cosmos DB account
New-AzCosmosDBSqlDatabase
    -ResourceGroupName <resource-group>
    -AccountName <cosmosdb-account-name>
    -Name <db-name>

# Create a container in the database
New-AzCosmosDBSqlContainer
    -ResourceGroupName <resource-group>
    -AccountName <cosmosdb-account-name>
    -DatabaseName <db-name>
```

```
    -Name <container-name>
    -PartitionKeyKind "Hash"
    -PartitionKeyPath /<PartitionKey> # e.g. /Id or /User
    -Throughput <throughput>
```

The following code snippet is an example Bicep script to create a Cosmos DB account with global distribution, a database, and a container:

```
resource cosmosAccount 'Microsoft.DocumentDB/databaseAccounts@2021-04-15' = {
  name: cosmosDBAccountName
  location: location
  kind: 'GlobalDocumentDB'
  properties: {
    consistencyPolicy: {
      defaultConsistencyLevel: 'Session'
    }
    locations: [
      {
        locationName: 'eastus'
        failoverPriority: 0
        isZoneRedundant: false
      }
      {
        locationName: 'westus'
        failoverPriority: 1
        isZoneRedundant: false
      }
    ]
    enableAutomaticFailover: true
  }
}

resource cosmosDatabase 'Microsoft.DocumentDB/databaseAccounts/sqlDatabases@2021-04-15' = {
  name: databaseName
  parent: cosmosAccount
  properties: {}
}

resource cosmosContainer 'Microsoft.DocumentDB/databaseAccounts/sqlDatabases/
containers@2021-04-15' = {
  name: containerName
  parent: cosmosDatabase
  properties: {
    partitionKey: {
      paths: ['/Id']
      kind: 'Hash'
    }
    throughput: throughput
  }
}
```

Each of these approaches allows you to provision a globally distributed Cosmos DB setup with automatic failover and multiregion replication, providing the foundation for resilient, low-latency applications worldwide.

Indexing and querying

Cosmos DB automatically indexes all the properties for all the items in the DB container, and this enforces fast and efficient querying without requiring manual index management. The indexing policy is flexible, allowing you to include or exclude specific fields and customize the indexing mode.

If your database is created to use the SQL API, you can query Cosmos DB using a SQL-like language, which is familiar to those with experience in relational databases. Additionally, Cosmos DB supports queries using MongoDB API, Cassandra API, Gremlin API (for graph databases), and Azure Table API, depending on the data model in use.

Let's look at an example SQL query:

```
SELECT * FROM TestContainer c WHERE c.Property = 'value'
```

This query retrieves all items from `TestContainer` where the specified property matches the given value.

Let's also look at customizing indexing policy with Bicep:

```
resource cosmosContainer 'Microsoft.DocumentDB/databaseAccounts/sqlDatabases/
containers@2021-04-15' = {
  name: containerName
  parent: cosmosDatabase
  properties: {
    partitionKey: {
      paths: ['/Id']
      kind: 'Hash'
    }
    indexingPolicy: {
      indexingMode: 'consistent'
      includedPaths: [
        {
          path: '/*'
        }
      ]
      excludedPaths: [
        {
          path: '/\"_etag\"/?'
        }
      ]
    }
  }
}
```

In the Bicep code provided, the `indexingPolicy` is customized to control how the data in the Cosmos DB container is indexed. The indexing mode is set to `consistent`, ensuring that all data is indexed as soon as it's written, allowing queries to return the most up-to-date results. The `includedPaths` specify that all properties in the documents should be indexed (`/*`), while the `excludedPaths` indicate that the `_etag` property should not be indexed.

Partitioning and scaling

Cosmos DB uses partitioning to manage large datasets efficiently. Each container in Cosmos DB is horizontally partitioned, meaning the data is distributed across multiple partitions. Each partition is identified by a partition key, which is a crucial aspect of scaling in Cosmos DB.

Selecting the right partition key is essential for achieving optimal performance and scalability. A good partition key ensures an even distribution of data and avoids hotspots, where one partition receives more requests than others.

In the Azure CLI, the `--partition-key-path` parameter is how you set this. For example:

```
az cosmosdb sql container create
    --account-name <cosmosdb-account-name>
    --database-name <db-name>
    --name <container-name>
    --partition-key-path /<PartitionKey> # e.g. /Id or /User
    --throughput <throughput>
```

Similarly, you can set the partition key with the `PartitionKeyPath` parameter in PowerShell:

```
New-AzCosmosDBSqlContainer
    -ResourceGroupName <resource-group>
    -AccountName <cosmosdb-account-name>
    -DatabaseName <db-name>
    -Name <container-name>
    -PartitionKeyKind "Hash"
    -PartitionKeyPath /<PartitionKey> # e.g. /Id or /User
    -Throughput <throughput>
```

Using Bicep, you can also set the partition key when creating the Cosmos DB container infrastructure:

```
resource cosmosContainer 'Microsoft.DocumentDB/databaseAccounts/sqlDatabases/
containers@2021-04-15' = {
  name: containerName
  ... // more code
  properties: {
    partitionKey: {
      paths: ['/Id']
      kind: 'Hash'
    }
    ... // more code
}
```

Security

Cosmos DB includes robust security features to protect your data. It supports encryption at rest and in transit, ensuring that your data is always secure. Additionally, integration with Microsoft Entra ID allows for fine-grained access control using RBAC.

You can also configure private endpoints to limit network access to your Cosmos DB account, ensuring traffic stays within the secure Microsoft backbone network.

The following code snippet shows an example of creating a private endpoint with the Azure CLI:

```
az network private-endpoint create
    --resource-group <resource-group-name>
    --name <private-endpoint-name>
    --vnet-name <vnet-name>
    --subnet <subnet-name>
    --private-connection-resource-id "/subscriptions/{subscriptionId}/resourceGroups/
        {resource-group-name}/providers/Microsoft.DocumentDB/
        databaseAccounts/{cosmosdb-account}"
    --group-id "Sql"
```

The following code snippet shows how you can use PowerShell to secure access:

```
New-AzPrivateEndpoint
    -ResourceGroupName <resource-group-name>
    -Name <private-endpoint-name>
    -Location <location>
    -SubnetId "/subscriptions/{subscriptionId}/resourceGroups/{resource-group-name}/
    providers/Microsoft.Network/virtualNetworks/{vnet-name}/subnets/{subnet-name}"
    -PrivateLinkServiceConnection @{"Name"="CosmosDBConnection"; "PrivateLinkServiceId"=
    "/subscriptions/{subscriptionId}/resourceGroups/{resource-group-name}/providers/
    Microsoft.DocumentDB/databaseAccounts/{cosmosdb-account}"; "GroupIds"=@("Sql")}
```

Collectively, these capabilities ensure that your Cosmos DB deployment is secure and aligns with best practices for data protection and access control in modern cloud environments.

Backup and restore

Azure Cosmos DB provides continuous backup with point-in-time restore, allowing you to recover data to any previous state within the retention period. This feature is crucial for data recovery in case of accidental deletion or corruption.

The backup and restore process is fully managed by Azure, so you don't have to worry about configuring or maintaining backup schedules. You can restore data at the database or container level, offering flexibility in data recovery.

The following code snippet shows a CLI command to trigger a restore:

```
$  az cosmosdb restore
    --resource-group <resource-group-name>
    --account-name <cosmosdb-account>
    --target-database-account-name <db-name>
    --restore-timestamp <timestamp>
    --location <location>
```

Integration with other Azure services

Cosmos DB integrates seamlessly with other Azure services, such as Azure Functions, Azure Logic Apps, and Azure Synapse Analytics. This allows you to build end-to-end solutions that can process, analyze, and visualize data stored in Cosmos DB. For example, you can use Azure Functions to trigger actions based on changes in your Cosmos DB data, or Azure Synapse Analytics to run complex analytical queries against large datasets.

The following code snippet shows example Bicep code for integration with Azure Functions by adding the database details as an app setting:

```
resource cosmosFunction 'Microsoft.Web/sites@2021-02-01' = {
  name: <function-name>
  location: <location>
  kind: 'functionapp'
  properties: {
    serverFarmId: appServicePlan.id
    siteConfig: {
      appSettings: [
        {
          name: 'AzureWebJobsStorage'
          value: 'DefaultEndpointsProtocol=https;AccountName=<cosmosdb-account-name>;
              AccountKey=<cosmosdb-account-key>;EndpointSuffix=core.windows.net'
        }
      ]
    }
  }
}
```

Summary

This chapter covered data and storage in a comprehensive way, explaining how to manage and store different types of data in Azure. We explored various data types like unstructured, semistructured, and structured and discussed suitable storage solutions like object, block, and file storage. It's important to select the right storage to ensure performance, scalability, and security.

We also looked into Azure storage services such as Blob Storage, Managed Disks, and Azure Files, providing practical steps for managing these resources. Prioritizing security is essential, and it's important to understand encryption, access control, and network security to protect your data. Last, we explored Azure's database offerings, including Azure SQL Database and Cosmos DB, covering their management and integration with other Azure services. This chapter has equipped you with the knowledge needed to effectively manage and secure data in Azure. In the next chapter, you will learn about building containerized solutions on Azure.

CHAPTER 6

Building Containerized Solutions on Azure

As we build more distributed and scalable applications, it's becoming increasingly important to use flexible and efficient ways to deploy and manage them across various environments. Containerization has changed the way we run applications by packaging them, along with their dependencies, into lightweight and portable units. These containers can run anywhere consistently, whether on a developer's laptop, in a data center, or in the cloud.

This chapter starts with an introduction to the basics of containerization, covering how it simplifies application deployment and management. Next, you'll learn how to deploy containers using Azure Kubernetes Service (AKS), a powerful platform that allows you to manage and scale your containerized applications. You will also explore the details of container orchestration and management, gaining insights into how to handle complex deployments with ease.

Then, we'll dive into the microservices architecture in Azure, where you'll see how containers play a vital role in building, deploying, and managing microservices-based applications. This chapter will also guide you through using Azure Container Registry (ACR), a service that helps you store, manage, and secure your container images effectively. By the end of this chapter, you'll have a strong understanding of how to build, deploy, and manage containerized solutions on Azure using modern tools and practices that enhance your application's flexibility and scalability.

Introduction to Containerization

To better understand how to build containerized applications on Azure, let's start with a basic illustration of how applications used to be deployed (Figure 6-1). Imagine a company that developed a software application to run on its internal servers. The application was built to work in a specific environment with a particular operating system, certain libraries, and specific configurations. Everything was tightly coupled, and deploying the application to a different environment often led to errors or failures because something in the new environment didn't match the original setup. This made scaling or moving the application to different servers or data centers a complex and risky task.

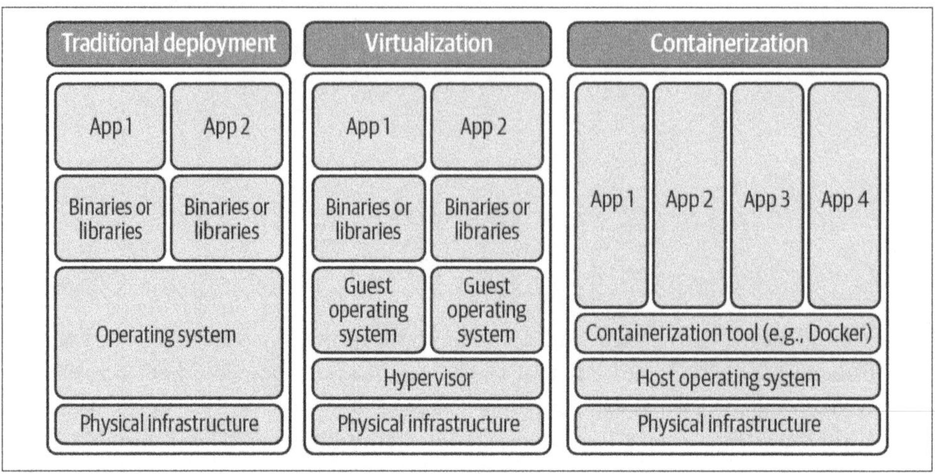

Figure 6-1. Traditional deployment versus virtualization versus containerization

While the scenario in Figure 6-1 is a simple example, it quickly became apparent that as businesses grew and their needs evolved, they required more flexible solutions. Enter virtualization. VMs allowed multiple operating systems to run on a single physical server, each isolated from the others. This was a significant improvement because it allowed better resource utilization and provided some level of flexibility. However, VMs were still heavy because each one included a full operating system, which consumed a lot of resources and took time to start up.

Then came containerization, which took flexibility to the next level. Containers are like lightweight VMs, but instead of virtualizing entire operating systems, they share the host OS kernel while keeping the application and its dependencies isolated. This means you can run multiple containers on a single OS without the overhead of running multiple operating systems. Containers start up quickly, use fewer resources, and can be easily moved between environments, making them ideal for modern, scalable applications.

To better understand the value of containerization, think of it as a way to package everything an application needs to run—code, runtime, libraries, and configurations—into a single, self-contained unit. This unit can run consistently on any environment that supports containers, whether it's your local development machine, a testing server, or a cloud platform. This consistency is one of the key benefits of containerization, as it eliminates the classic "it works on my machine" problem.

Containerization also brings with it the concept of microservices (Figure 6-2). In the past, applications were often built as monolithic entities, where all components were tightly integrated into a single unit. This made it difficult to update or scale individual parts of the application without affecting the whole system. With containers, you can break down your application into smaller, independent services, each running in its own container. These microservices can be developed, deployed, and scaled independently, allowing for greater agility and resilience.

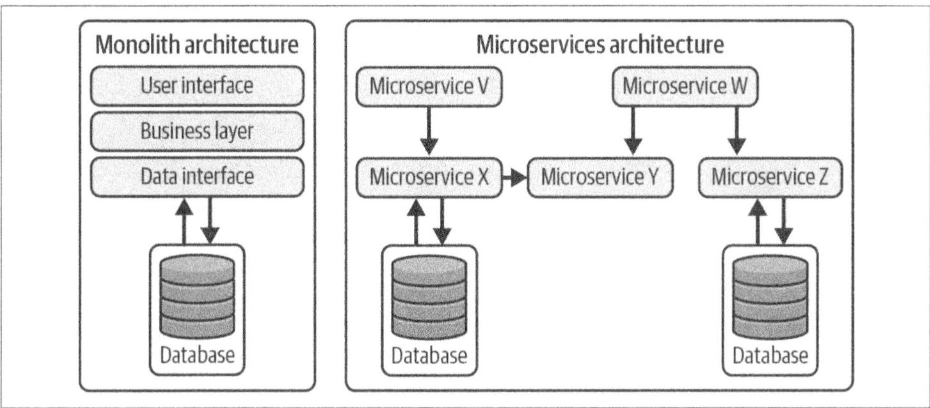

Figure 6-2. Monoliths versus microservices

Docker played a huge role in popularizing this technology. It made it easy for developers to create, deploy, and manage containers. It provided tools and a standard format for packaging applications into containers, which could then be easily shared and run across different environments.

But managing containers manually, especially in large numbers, can be a challenge. This is where container orchestration tools like Kubernetes come into play. Kubernetes, often referred to as K8s, is an open source platform that automates the deployment, scaling, and management of containerized applications. With Kubernetes, you can manage thousands of containers across multiple servers, ensuring your applications are resilient and can scale according to demand. For more details on how to get started with Kubernetes, consider reading *Kubernetes: Up & Running* by Brendan Burns, Joe Beda, Kelsey Hightower, and Lachlan Evenson.

As we continue to build more distributed and scalable applications, containerization has become a fundamental part of modern software development. It allows developers to focus on building features rather than worrying about the underlying infrastructure. Containers have made it possible to deploy applications faster, scale them more efficiently, and ensure they run consistently across different environments. Dealing with Kubernetes directly, though, can be challenging due to its complexity. To make this easier, cloud providers, including Azure, have managed Kubernetes services that handle much of the operational overhead.

Deploying Containers with AKS

Containerized apps follow the principle of encapsulating everything needed to run an application, including the code, runtime, libraries, and configurations, into a single package. When deploying containerized applications at scale, Kubernetes ensures they run consistently and can handle the complexities of production environments.

AKS is a fully managed container orchestration service provided by Microsoft Azure. AKS simplifies the deployment, management, and scaling of containerized applications using Kubernetes. Through this managed Kubernetes service, Azure takes care of many of the complexities associated with deploying and operating Kubernetes clusters, such as scaling, patching, and upgrading.

There are a few benefits you can get from using AKS, as described in the following sections.

Managed Kubernetes

AKS takes care of the complexities of managing Kubernetes clusters, such as performing upgrades, applying patches, and monitoring. This reduces the operational burden on you.

Integration with Azure Services

AKS integrates with a wide range of Azure services, including Microsoft Entra ID (for identity and access management), Azure Monitor (for observability and monitoring), and Azure DevOps (for CI/CD pipelines). This integration simplifies operations and enhances automation and engineering excellence because you're able to leverage tools that allow you to build great applications.

Scalability

AKS allows you to scale your applications effortlessly by adjusting the number of nodes in your cluster. You can do this manually, or you can set up autoscaling, which adjusts the number of nodes in your cluster based on CPU or memory usage.

You can manually scale your AKS cluster using the Azure CLI with the following command:

```
$  az aks scale
  --name <cluster-name>
  --node-count <node-count>
  --resource-group <resource-group>
```

This command increases the number of nodes in the AKS cluster to the value of `<node-count>`, allowing your application to handle more load. To automatically scale your AKS cluster, you can enable the cluster autoscaler. This feature allows AKS to automatically add or remove nodes based on the workload demand. For instance:

```
$ az aks update
    --resource-group <resource-group>
    --name <cluster-name>
    --enable-cluster-autoscaler
    --min-count 3
    --max-count 15
```

In this example, the cluster will automatically scale between 3 and 15 nodes, depending on the demand.

Security

Security is a top priority in any cloud environment. AKS integrates with Microsoft Entra ID (formerly known as Azure Active Directory) to manage access to your Kubernetes resources. Additionally, you can use Azure Key Vault to securely manage secrets, keys, and certificates used by your applications.

To enable Microsoft Entra ID integration for AKS, use this Azure CLI command:

```
$ az aks update
    --resource-group <resource-group>
    --name <cluster-name>
    --enable-aad
    --aad-admin-group-object-ids <your-aad-group-object-id>
```

This command integrates the AKS cluster with Microsoft Entra ID, which allows you to manage user access to the Kubernetes API using Microsoft Entra ID groups.

To securely manage your application secrets, you can integrate AKS with Azure Key Vault using the Secrets Store CSI (Container Storage Interface) driver. Azure Key Vault is a cloud service that safeguards cryptographic keys, secrets, and certificates, keeping them secure and accessible only to authorized applications. We'll dive into more details about Azure Key Vault in Chapter 7.

First, install the Secrets Store CSI driver:

```
$ az aks enable-addons
    --resource-group <resource-group>
    --name <cluster-name>
    --addons azure-keyvault-secrets-provider
```

Next, create an Azure Key Vault resource and set a secret:

```
$ az keyvault create
    --name <key-vault-name>
    --resource-group <resource-group>
    --location <location>

$ az keyvault secret set
    --vault-name <key-vault-name>
    --name <secret-name>
    --value <secret-value>
```

Next, create a `SecretProviderClass` to link the Key Vault to your AKS cluster:

```
apiVersion: secrets-store.csi.x-k8s.io/v1
kind: SecretProviderClass
metadata:
  name: azure-kvname
spec:
  provider: azure
  parameters:
    usePodIdentity: "false"
    keyvaultName: "<key-vault-name>"
    cloudName: ""
    objects: |
      array:
        - |
          objectName: "<secret-name>"
          objectType: secret
          objectVersion: ""
    tenantId: "<your-tenant-id>"
```

Next, deploy a Kubernetes Pod that references the secrets from Key Vault:

```
apiVersion: v1
kind: Pod
metadata:
  name: busybox-secrets-store-inline
spec:
  containers:
    - image: busybox
      name: busybox
      volumeMounts:
      - name: secrets-store-inline
        mountPath: "/mnt/secrets-store"
        readOnly: true
      command:
        - "/bin/sh"
        - "-c"
        - "sleep 10000"
  volumes:
    - name: secrets-store-inline
      csi:
        driver: secrets-store.csi.k8s.io
        readOnly: true
        volumeAttributes:
          secretProviderClass: "azure-kvname"
```

This setup allows the application running in the Pod to access secrets from Azure Key Vault securely.

Cost Management

AKS helps you optimize costs by allowing you to scale your cluster based on demand and by leveraging Azure Spot Virtual Machines for lower-cost, interruptible workloads. Azure Spot VMs allow you to run workloads on unused Azure capacity at a lower price, with the understanding the VMs can be evicted when Azure needs the capacity back. While the cluster autoscaler optimizes resource allocation, AKS also supports Azure Spot VMs to further reduce costs for noncritical workloads. To add a new node pool:

```
$ az aks nodepool add
    --resource-group <resource-group>
    --cluster-name <cluster-name>
    --name <pool-name>
    --priority Spot
    --eviction-policy Deallocate
    --spot-max-price -1
    --node-count <node-count>
    --min-count <min-count>
```

This command is used to add a new node pool to an AKS cluster using Azure Spot VMs, which are cost-effective because they run on unused Azure capacity. The `--priority Spot` flag designates these VMs as *spot* instances, which are cheaper but can be evicted when Azure needs the capacity. The `--eviction-policy Deallocate` ensures that the VMs' state is preserved upon eviction, and the `--spot-max-price -1` flag allows you to pay the current market price for these VMs. This setup helps reduce costs while maintaining flexibility for noncritical workloads.

Kubernetes Cluster Architecture in AKS

To understand how AKS works, it's important to grasp the basics of Kubernetes architecture, which AKS is built upon. In AKS, Azure manages the control plane, ensuring the API server, etcd, scheduler, and controller managers are highly available, secure, and up-to-date with the latest patches and features. Customers are responsible for managing the worker nodes, including configuring and maintaining the Kubelet, container runtime, and kube-proxy, as well as setting up node pools, handling scaling operations, and deploying and maintaining the applications running in the cluster. Figure 6-3 is an illustration of these components and how they interact.

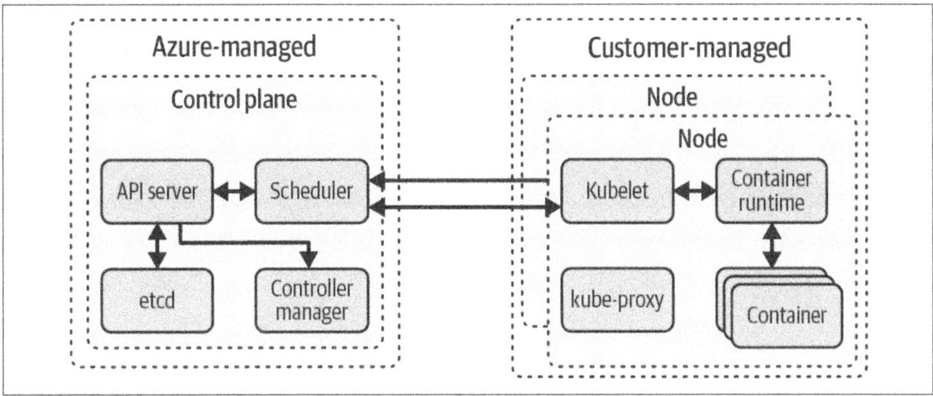

Figure 6-3. Kubernetes cluster components

Control plane components

The Kubernetes control plane consists of several key components that work together to manage and orchestrate the cluster:

API server
: The API server is the heart of the Kubernetes control plane, acting as the central management interface that processes and validates requests, exposing the Kubernetes API to users and other components.

etcd
: This is a distributed key-value store that holds all the data about the cluster's state, including configuration, secrets, and status of workloads. It's a critical component that ensures data persistence and high availability.

Scheduler
: The scheduler is responsible for assigning newly created Pods to nodes within the cluster based on their resource requirements and the current availability of resources on the nodes.

kube-controller-manager
: This component runs a set of controllers that are responsible for ensuring the desired state of the cluster matches the actual state. For example, the replication controller ensures that the specified number of Pod replicas are running.

cloud-controller-manager
: Unique to cloud environments, the cloud-controller-manager integrates the Kubernetes cluster with the underlying cloud provider's services. In AKS, it handles cloud-specific tasks such as managing load balancers, attaching storage volumes to nodes, and other Azure-specific operations.

Node components

The node components work together on each worker node to run your containerized applications and manage local networking:

Kubelet
: Kubelet is an agent that runs on each worker node. It is responsible for ensuring containers are running according to the configurations provided by the Kubernetes API server. It interacts with the container runtime to manage the lifecycle of containers.

Container runtime
: The container runtime, such as Docker or containerd, is the software responsible for running containers on the nodes. It handles tasks like pulling container images from registries, starting and stopping containers, and managing container execution.

Kube-proxy
: Kube-proxy runs on each node and manages the networking for the nodes. It handles the routing of network traffic between different Pods and ensures that requests reach the correct containers.

Beyond these essential components, AKS provides additional resources and abstractions to manage and operate containerized applications effectively:

Pods
: The smallest deployable unit in Kubernetes, typically representing a single instance of a running process. Pods usually contain one or more containers that share storage, networking, and a specification for how to run the containers.

Services
: Services define a logical set of Pods and a policy for accessing them, providing a stable endpoint for client requests, even as Pods are dynamically created or destroyed.

Deployments
: A higher-level Kubernetes object that manages the creation and scaling of Pods. Deployments ensure that the desired number of Pods are running and can automatically update or roll back Pods to previous versions.

StatefulSets
: This is similar to Deployments but specifically designed for stateful applications that require stable, persistent storage and ordered, predictable deployment and scaling.

DaemonSets
: DaemonSets are used to ensure a copy of a Pod is running on all or selected nodes in the cluster. This is often used for logging, monitoring, or other system services that need to run across the cluster.

Persistent volumes (PVs) and persistent volume claims (PVCs)
: These resources manage persistent storage for applications. A PV is a piece of storage in the cluster, while a PVC is a request for storage by a user. They allow applications to maintain data beyond the lifecycle of individual Pods.

ConfigMaps and secrets
: These resources allow you to decouple environment-specific configuration and sensitive information from your container images, making it easier to manage configurations and credentials securely.

Node pools
: Node pools are groups of worker nodes in an AKS cluster with similar configurations. Node pools can be independently scaled and tailored to different types of workloads, such as general-purpose nodes or Spot VMs for cost savings.

Ingress
: Ingress resources manage external access to services within the Kubernetes cluster, typically for HTTP/HTTPS traffic. They provide load balancing, SSL termination, and routing to services based on the host or path.

Simple Use Case: Deploying a Stateful Application

There's a lot to learn when it comes to Kubernetes that this book cannot cover. However, the previous sections have introduced the popular terms, what they mean, and what Kubernetes clusters are composed of. Now, it's time to get practical. Let's consider a use case where you need to deploy a MySQL database as a stateful application on AKS. Unlike stateless applications, stateful applications like databases require persistent storage, which must be carefully managed to ensure data persistence across Pod restarts and rescheduling. Deploying MySQL on AKS involves creating several Kubernetes components, such as PVs, PVCs, and a StatefulSet to manage the database Pods.

To follow through with this, you need to have `kubectl` installed and configured on your machine. `kubectl` is the Kubernetes command-line tool that allows you to run commands against Kubernetes clusters. You can find the installation instructions in the official Kubernetes documentation (*https://oreil.ly/69JEl*).

We'd do this in two ways: using the Azure CLI and PowerShell.

Using the Azure CLI

First, create an AKS cluster:

```
$ az aks create
    --resource-group <resource-group>
    --name <name>
    --node-count <node-count>
    --safeguards-level <safeguards-level>
    --enable-addons <addons>
    --generate-ssh-keys
```

Connect to your newly created AKS cluster:

```
$ az aks get-credentials
    --resource-group <resource-group>
    --name <name>
```

Define and create a PV to allocate storage. To do this, create a YAML file called *pv.yaml*:

```
apiVersion: v1
kind: PersistentVolume
metadata:
  name: mysql-pv
spec:
  capacity:
    storage: 10Gi
  accessModes:
    - ReadWriteOnce
  azureDisk:
    diskName: mysql-disk
    diskURI: <azure-disk-uri>
    kind: Managed
```

After creating the PV, create a PVC to request the storage:

```
apiVersion: v1
kind: PersistentVolumeClaim
metadata:
  name: mysql-pvc
spec:
  accessModes:
    - ReadWriteOnce
  resources:
    requests:
      storage: 10Gi
```

In the Azure CLI, apply these configurations using the `kubectl` command:

```
$ kubectl apply -f pv.yaml
$ kubectl apply -f pvc.yaml
```

Now, create the StatefulSet YAML file that will use the preexisting PVC:

```
apiVersion: apps/v1
kind: StatefulSet
metadata:
  name: mysql
spec:
  serviceName: "mysql"
  replicas: 1
  selector:
    matchLabels:
      app: mysql
  template:
    metadata:
      labels:
        app: mysql
    spec:
      containers:
      - name: mysql
        image: mysql:5.7
        ports:
        - containerPort: 3306
          name: mysql
        volumeMounts:
        - name: mysql-persistent-storage
```

```
          mountPath: /var/lib/mysql
        env:
        - name: MYSQL_ROOT_PASSWORD
          value: "my-secret-pw"
      volumes:
      - name: mysql-persistent-storage
        persistentVolumeClaim:
          claimName: mysql-pvc
```

Once this is done, apply the StatefulSet configurations using `kubectl` as well:

```
$ kubectl apply -f statefulset.yaml
```

Using Azure PowerShell

First, create an AKS cluster:

```
$ New-AzAksCluster
    -ResourceGroupName <resource-group-name>
    -Name <cluster-name>
```

Create the PV and PVC by first defining them in YAML files (*pv.yaml* and *pvc.yaml*) as shown in the Azure CLI example, and then apply them using PowerShell:

```
$ kubectl apply -f .\pv.yaml
$ kubectl apply -f .\pvc.yaml
```

Once this is done, define the StatefulSet in a YAML file (*statefulset.yaml*), and apply the StatefulSet configurations using `kubectl` as well:

```
$ kubectl apply -f statefulset.yaml
```

Beyond using the Azure CLI and PowerShell, you can also create your AKS cluster using Bicep. It could look similar to this:

```
resource myAksCluster 'Microsoft.ContainerService/managedClusters@2021-05-01' = {
  name: clusterName
  location: 'eastus'
  properties: {
    agentPoolProfiles: [
      {
        name: 'nodepool1'
        count: 3
        vmSize: 'Standard_DS2_v2'
        osType: 'Linux'
      }
    ]
    dnsPrefix: 'myaks'
    enableRBAC: true
    kubernetesVersion: '1.21.2'
    servicePrincipalProfile: {
      clientId: 'xxxxxxxx-xxxx-xxxx-xxxx-xxxxxxxxxxxx'
      secret: 'a-test-secret'
    }
  }
}
```

The preceding code snippet creates an AKS cluster using Azure's managed Kubernetes service. The cluster is set to deploy in the `eastus` region with three nodes in the `nodepool1` agent pool. Each node is a `Linux` VM of type `Standard_DS2_v2`, which provides a balanced CPU-to-memory ratio. The cluster also has RBAC enabled, which is important for managing user permissions within the cluster.

Advanced Use Case: Multinode Pool Deployment with AKS

Let's explore a more complex scenario where we deploy a microservices-based application on an AKS cluster with multiple node pools. This example will demonstrate how to manage different workloads by assigning them to specific node pools, optimizing resource usage, and scaling capabilities. We'll also integrate other advanced features like Microsoft Entra ID integration, ingress controllers, and autoscaling.

Imagine you are deploying a multitier web application consisting of the following components:

Frontend service
: A web frontend built with React.js served through Nginx

Backend API
: A set of RESTful APIs built with Node.js

Worker service
: A background worker that processes data using Python

Database
: A MySQL database managed by a StatefulSet with persistent storage

We'll create an AKS cluster with separate node pools to manage these services efficiently:

General-purpose node pool
: Handles the frontend and backend services

Compute-optimized node pool
: Handles the worker service, which requires high CPU resources

Stateful node pool
: Manages the database, ensuring high IOPS for persistent storage

Start by creating a resource group and then the AKS cluster with Microsoft Entra ID integration:

```
$ az group create
    --name <resource-group-name>
    --location <location>

$ az aks create
```

```
    --resource-group <resource-group-name>
    --name <cluster-name>
    --node-count <node-count>
    --enable-aad
    --aad-admin-group-object-ids <your-aad-group-object-id>
    --enable-addons monitoring
    --generate-ssh-keys
```

Once the AKS cluster is successfully created, create the node pools for specific workloads. For this example, there are three node pools—the general node pool, the compute-optimized node pool, and the stateful node pool.

```
#  General node pool
$  az aks nodepool add
    --resource-group <resource-group-name>
    --cluster-name <cluster-name>
    --name generalpool
    --node-count 2
    --node-vm-size Standard_DS2_v2

#   Compute-optimized node pool
$  az aks nodepool add
    --resource-group <resource-group-name>
    --cluster-name <cluster-name>
    --name computepool
    --node-count 2
    --node-vm-size Standard_F4s_v2
    --mode User
    --priority Spot
    --eviction-policy Deallocate

#   Stateful node pool
$  az aks nodepool add
  --resource-group <resource-group-name>
  --cluster-name <cluster-name>
  --name statefulpool
  --node-count 1
  --node-vm-size Standard_E4s_v3
  --node-taints storage=dedicated:NoSchedule
```

The `statefulpool` uses a node taint to ensure only Pods tolerant to this taint are scheduled, which is ideal for running stateful workloads like databases.

Once the node pools are created, you can deploy each component of your application to the appropriate node pools using `kubectl apply`. To make sure the application is using the appropriate node pool, your Kubernetes manifest should have the following:

```
template:
   ...
   spec:
      nodeSelector:
         kubernetes.io/hostname: <pool-name>
```

Here, `<pool-name>` should be `generalpool`, `computepool`, or `statefulpool`, depending on what is being deployed.

To route external traffic to the frontend and backend services, let's also add an Nginx Ingress Controller to our resources:

```
kubectl apply -f https://raw.githubusercontent.com/kubernetes/ingress-nginx/main/deploy/
                 static/provider/cloud/deploy.yaml
```

Once this is done, you should also use `kubectl apply` to create the ingress resource that ties everything together.

Finally, let's also imagine our application has varying workloads depending on the time of the year. We can accommodate this by adding autoscaling to the nodepool we created before:

```
$   az aks nodepool update
    --resource-group <resource-group-name>
    --cluster-name <cluster-name>
    --name generalpool
    --enable-cluster-autoscaler
    --min-count 2
    --max-count 5
```

There are more advanced things you can do in Kubernetes with AKS, and while this book cannot cover all of them, these examples give you an idea of what's possible.

Managing Container Images with Azure Container Registry

When dealing with containers, Azure has its own registry called Azure Container Registry (ACR). ACR is a managed Docker registry service that allows you to store, manage, and deploy container images in a secure and scalable way. Whether you're working with a single container or managing hundreds of microservices, ACR has the tools necessary to help with container lifecycle management. It also integrates seamlessly with other Azure services like AKS.

To get started with ACR, you first need to create a container registry. Here's how you can do it using Azure CLI, PowerShell, and Bicep.

Azure CLI

Use the following command to create a resource group and then set up a container registry with the Basic SKU:

```
$  az group create
    --name <resource-group-name>
    --location <location>

$  az acr create
    --resource-group <resource-group-name>
    --name <container-registry-name>
    --sku Basic
```

PowerShell

The PowerShell equivalent creates a resource group and a container registry with the same configurations as the Azure CLI example:

```
$ New-AzResourceGroup
    -Name <resource-group-name>
    -Location <location>

$ New-AzContainerRegistry
    -ResourceGroupName <resource-group-name>
    -RegistryName <container-registry-name>
    -Sku Basic
```

Bicep

The following Bicep template defines a container registry resource with the Basic SKU. The `adminUserEnabled` property allows for admin user access to the registry:

```
resource containerRegistry 'Microsoft.ContainerRegistry/registries@2021-06-01-preview' = {
  name: <container-registry-name>
  location: <location>
  sku: {
    name: 'Basic'
  }
  adminUserEnabled: true
}
```

Once your registry is set up, you can push Docker images to ACR and pull them when needed.

Pushing an Image with Azure CLI

This sequence of commands logs in to the ACR, builds a Docker image tagged as `myapp:v1`, and pushes it to the registry:

```
$ az acr login --name <container-registry-name>

$ docker build -t <container-registry-name>.azurecr.io/myapp:v1

$ docker push <container-registry-name>.azurecr.io/myapp:v1
```

Pulling an Image with Azure CLI

This command pulls the image from ACR to your local environment or any other environment where Docker is running:

```
$ docker pull <container-registry-name>.azurecr.io/myapp:v1
```

Managing ACR Repositories

In ACR, you can organize your container images using repositories. A repository is a collection of related images with different tags (e.g., `v1`, `v2`, `latest`). You can manage your ACR repositories using the `az acr repository` CLI command.

The following command lists all the repositories in your ACR instance:

```
$ az acr repository list
    --name <acr-name>
    --output table
```

The following command deletes the specified repository from your ACR instance:

```
$ az acr repository delete
    --name <acr-name>
    --repository <repository-name>
```

When managing ACR repositories, you can also do security and access control. One of the key features of ACR is its integration with Microsoft Entra ID and RBAC. You can define who has access to your container registry and what actions they can perform using the following:

```
$ az role assignment create
    --assignee <user-object-id>
    --role AcrPull
    --scope /subscriptions/<subscription-id>/resourceGroups/<resource-group>/providers/
    Microsoft.ContainerRegistry/registries/<container-registry>
```

The command assigns the `AcrPull` role to a specific Entra ID user, allowing them to pull images from the container registry.

Integrating ACR with AKS

AKS integrates seamlessly with ACR, and this enables Kubernetes clusters to pull container images directly from the registry. This integration simplifies deploying containerized applications on AKS by ensuring that images stored in ACR are easily accessible to the AKS cluster without requiring additional setup.

When deploying applications on AKS, it's important to have a reliable and secure source for your container images. Linking ACR to AKS enables the use of private container registries. Unlike public registries, where images are accessible to anyone, ACR provides a controlled environment where you can set permissions and manage who has access to your images. This is beneficial in enterprise environments where security and compliance are very important.

To link an ACR to an AKS cluster, you use the Azure CLI to attach the registry to the Kubernetes cluster. Here's the command:

```
$ az aks update
    --name <cluster-name>
    --resource-group <resource-group-name>
    --attach-acr <container-registry>
```

The `--attach-acr` flag configures the AKS cluster to have pull access to the container registry without needing extra login credentials. Azure handles the integration by creating a managed identity for the AKS cluster, granting it the necessary permissions to read from the ACR.

Running Containers with Azure Container Instances

Azure Container Instances (ACI) is a simple way to run your containers in the cloud. With ACI, you can run Docker containers in a managed, serverless environment so you don't have to worry about provisioning or managing any underlying infrastructure. This makes ACI a great choice when you need to deploy and scale containerized applications without the complexity of traditional setups. By contrast, AKS gives you a managed Kubernetes environment that's better suited for more complex, multicontainer deployments requiring orchestration, scaling, and detailed management.

With ACI, you can perform various actions, such as:

Deploying containers
: You can deploy single or multiple containers within a container group.

Scaling containers
: ACI allows you to scale out by deploying additional container instances or scale down by stopping or deleting instances.

Setting environment variables
: You can set environment variables for your containers to manage configurations and secrets.

Mounting volumes
: ACI supports mounting Azure file shares and managed disks as volumes to provide persistent storage to your containers.

Networking
: You can expose your containers to the internet using public IPs or keep them private within a VNet.

Logging and monitoring
: ACI integrates with Azure Monitor and Azure Log Analytics to provide robust monitoring and logging capabilities.

Scheduling
: You can schedule container workloads to run at specific times or intervals.

Let's take a closer look at each of these actions.

Deploying Containers

In this section, you will see how to deploy containers using Azure CLI, PowerShell, and Azure Bicep.

Here's an example of how to deploy a container instance using Azure CLI:

```
# Create a resource group
$  az group create
    --name <resource-group-name>
    --location <location>

# Deploy a container instance
az container create
    --resource-group <resource-group-name>
    --name <container-name>
    --image mcr.microsoft.com/azuredocs/aci-helloworld
    --cpu 1
    --memory 1
    --dns-name-label aci-demo
    --ports 80
```

The previous command creates a resource group and deploys a container instance running the `aci-helloworld` image. The container is allocated 1 CPU and 1 GB of memory, exposed on port 80, and made publicly accessible with a DNS name. Note that the image doesn't have to come from ACR; you can use any container image hosted on a public registry like Docker Hub or your own private registry.

Here's an example of how to deploy a container instance using Azure PowerShell:

```
# Create a resource group
New-AzResourceGroup
    -Name <resource-group-name>
    -Location <location>

# Deploy a container instance
New-AzContainerGroup
    -ResourceGroupName <resource-group-name>
    -Name <name>
    -Image mcr.microsoft.com/azuredocs/aci-helloworld
    -Cpu 1
    -MemoryInGB 1
    -DnsNameLabel aci-demo
    -Port 80
```

This PowerShell command creates a resource group and then deploys a container instance with the specified image, CPU, memory, DNS name, and port configuration.

Here's an example of how to deploy a container instance using Azure Bicep:

```
resource myContainerGroup 'Microsoft.ContainerInstance/containerGroups@2021-07-01' = {
  name: <container-group-name>
  location: <location>
  properties: {
    containers: [
      {
        name: <container-name>
        properties: {
          image: 'mcr.microsoft.com/azuredocs/aci-helloworld'
          resources: {
            requests: {
              cpu: 1
              memoryInGB: 1
            }
          }
          ports: [
            {
              port: 80
            }
          ]
        }
      }
    ]
    osType: 'Linux'
    ipAddress: {
      type: 'Public'
      dnsNameLabel: 'aci-demo'
      ports: [
        {
          port: 80
          protocol: 'TCP'
        }
      ]
    }
  }
}
```

This Bicep template defines a container group in ACI, specifying the image, CPU, memory, and DNS label. The container is exposed on port 80, making it accessible publicly.

Scaling and Managing Containers

ACI allows you to scale your container instances easily. If you need to increase the number of running containers, you can deploy additional container instances using the same configuration. Similarly, you can stop or delete containers when they are no longer needed to optimize resource usage.

For example, to scale out using Azure CLI, you can run:

```
$ az container create
    --resource-group <resource-group-name>
    --name <another-container-name>
    --image mcr.microsoft.com/azuredocs/aci-helloworld
```

```
--cpu 1
--memory 1
--dns-name-label aci-demo-2
--ports 80
```

This command deploys a second container instance using the same image and configuration, effectively scaling out the application.

Setting Environment Variables

Environment variables are crucial for managing configuration settings and secrets. You can set environment variables when deploying a container instance in ACI.

In the Azure CLI, you can add the following parameter to the `az container create` command:

```
--environment-variables ENV_VAR=<value>
```

In PowerShell, you can add the following parameter to the `New-AzContainerGroup` command:

```
-EnvironmentVariable @{ MY_ENV_VAR=<value> }
```

In Bicep, you can define environment variables within the `environmentVariables` property of the container resource. Here's an example:

```
resource myContainerGroup 'Microsoft.ContainerInstance/containerGroups@2023-05-01' = {
  properties: {
    containers: [
      {
        name: <container-name>
        properties: {
          image: 'mcr.microsoft.com/azuredocs/aci-helloworld:latest'
          environmentVariables: [
            {
              name: 'MY_ENV_VAR'
              value: <value>
            }
            {
              name: 'ANOTHER_ENV_VAR'
              value: <another-value>
            }
          ]
        }
      }
    ]
    // more code here
  }
}
```

Mounting Volumes for Persistent Storage

ACI supports mounting Azure file shares and managed disks as volumes to provide persistent storage for your containers. This may be useful when you need to persist data beyond the lifecycle of a container instance, share data between multiple containers, or handle workloads that require durable storage, such as saving logs, caching data, or storing files that need to be accessed by different container instances or applications.

The following code snippet shows how you can mount Azure file share with Azure CLI:

```
$  az container create
    --resource-group <resource-group-name>
    --name <name>
    --image mcr.microsoft.com/azuredocs/aci-helloworld
    --cpu 1
    --memory 1
    --dns-name-label aci-demo-vol
    --ports 80
    --azure-file-volume-account-name <storage-account-name>
    --azure-file-volume-account-key <storage-account-key>
    --azure-file-volume-share-name <file-share-name>
    --azure-file-volume-mount-path /mnt/azure
```

Here, an ACI is configured to mount an Azure file share as a persistent storage volume. The `--azure-file-volume-account-name` and `--azure-file-volume-account-key` parameters specify the storage account credentials, while `--azure-file-volume-share-name` identifies the specific file share within the storage account. The `--azure-file-volume-mount-path` parameter defines the directory path inside the container where the file share will be mounted, in this case, `/mnt/azure`. This setup allows the container to access and persist data on the Azure file share, ensuring the data remains available even if the container is stopped or restarted, making it ideal for stateful applications or shared storage scenarios.

You can also mount Azure file share with Bicep. This code snippet shows how you can do it with Bicep:

```
resource myContainerGroup 'Microsoft.ContainerInstance/containerGroups@2021-07-01' = {
  name: <resource-name>
  properties: {
    containers: [
      {
        name: <name>
        properties: {
          image: 'mcr.microsoft.com/azuredocs/aci-helloworld'
          volumeMounts: [
            {
              name: 'azurefile'
              mountPath: '/mnt/azure'
            }
          ]
        }
      }
    ]
    volumes: [
      {
        name: 'azurefile'
        azureFile: {
```

```
            shareName: '<file-share-name>'
            storageAccountName: '<storage-account-name>'
            storageAccountKey: '<storage-account-key>'
          }
        }
      ]
    }
  }
```

Networking and Security

The Azure ecosystem has networking capabilities that allow you to manage how your containers are accessed and how ACI supports networking. You can expose containers to the internet using public IPs or keep them private within a VNet for secure internal communication. This flexibility ensures your containers can interact with other Azure resources securely and efficiently.

Additionally, ACI allows you to configure network security groups (NSGs) to control inbound and outbound traffic. You can set rules that restrict access to your containers, ensuring only authorized users or services can communicate with them. This is useful in scenarios where containers handle sensitive data or provide critical services.

Here's how you can create a container instance and place it within a VNet using Azure CLI:

```
// Create the vnet
$  az network vnet create
    --resource-group <resource-group-name>
    --name <vnet-name>
    --subnet-name <subnet-name>

// Create the container and place it in the vnet
$  az container create
    --resource-group <resource-group-name>
    --name <name>
    --image mcr.microsoft.com/azuredocs/aci-helloworld
    --vnet <vnet-name>
    --subnet <subnet-name>
    --cpu 1
    --memory 1
    --dns-name-label aci-secure
    --ports 80
```

To achieve the same with PowerShell, you can use commands similar to these:

```
$  New-AzVirtualNetwork
    -ResourceGroupName <rg-name>
    -Location <location>
    -Name <vnet-name>
    -AddressPrefix 10.0.0.0/16

$Vnet = Get-AzVirtualNetwork
    -Name <vnet-name>
    -ResourceGroupName <rg-name>

$  Add-AzVirtualNetworkSubnetConfig
```

```
    -Name <subnet-name>
    -AddressPrefix 10.0.0.0/24
    -VirtualNetwork $Vnet

$  New-AzContainerGroup
    -ResourceGroupName <rg-name>
    -Name <name>
    -Image mcr.microsoft.com/azuredocs/aci-helloworld
    -Cpu 1
    -MemoryInGB 1
    -VirtualNetwork <vnet-name>
    -Subnet <subnet-name>
    -DnsNameLabel aci-secure
    -Port 80
```

Logging and Monitoring

ACI integrates with Azure Monitor and Azure Log Analytics to provide monitoring and logging capabilities. You can track metrics like CPU and memory usage, network activity, and container restarts. These metrics help you understand how your containers are performing and identify potential issues before they impact your application.

ACI also allows you to collect logs directly from your containers, making it easier to debug issues and monitor application behavior. Logs can be sent to Azure Log Analytics, where they can be analyzed using queries, or to Azure Storage for long-term retention. For more on monitoring and observability, you'll find extra details in Chapter 10.

Here's how you can create a workspace that uses log analytics:

```
$  az monitor log-analytics workspace create
    --name <log-analytics-workspace-name>
    --resource-group <resource-group>

$  az container create
    --resource-group <resource-group>
    --name <name>
    --log-analytics-workspace <log-analytics-workspace-name>
```

Scheduling

While ACI does not have built-in support for scheduled workloads, you can still automate the running of ACI tasks using other Azure services. For instance, you can create timer-triggered functions with Azure Functions, set up schedules with Azure Logic Apps, or use cron jobs to trigger the ACI workload at specified times. Let's assume you want to run ACI workloads for 30 minutes every day starting from 6 A.M. Here's how you can set that up using a cron job.

First, create a shell script (`manage-aci.sh`) that starts the container at 6 A.M. and stops it after 30 minutes. While the following script uses `sleep 1800` to pause for 30 minutes before stopping the container, note that for a more robust solution you might consider using an Azure Function with a timer trigger instead. Here's the setup using a cron job:

```
#!/bin/bash

# Start the ACI container
az container start
    --resource-group <resource-group-name>
    --name <container-group-name>

# Check if the container started successfully
if [ $? -ne 0 ]; then
echo "Error: Failed to start the container."
exit 1
fi

# Wait for 30 minutes (1800 seconds)
sleep 1800

# Stop the ACI container
az container stop
    --resource-group <resource-group-name>
    --name <container-group-name>
```

Make sure the script is executable:

```
chmod +x /path/to/manage-aci.sh
```

To run this script every day at 6 A.M., open the cron table by running:

```
crontab -e
```

Add the following line:

```
0 6 * * * /path/to/manage-aci.sh
```

This cron job will start the ACI container at 6 A.M., let it run for 30 minutes, and then stop it.

Building Distributed Systems with Azure Service Fabric

Beyond AKS and ACI, Azure offers other options for building and managing distributed systems, such as Azure Service Fabric. For example, consider a financial services company that handles millions of transactions daily and requires high availability, low latency, and real-time processing. Azure Service Fabric is ideal for this scenario because it can manage stateful microservices with built-in failover and replication. This ensures that even if part of the infrastructure fails, the system remains operational, processing transactions without losing data or experiencing downtime.

Here is how you can define an Azure Service Fabric cluster using Bicep:

```
resource sfCluster 'Microsoft.ServiceFabric/clusters@2021-06-01' = {
  name: 'myServiceFabricCluster'
  location: 'eastus'
  properties: {
    reliabilityLevel: 'Silver'
```

```
        upgradeMode: 'Automatic'
        clusterCodeVersion: '7.2.432.9590'
      }
    }
```

Using the Azure CLI, you can create an Azure Service Fabric cluster with a few commands:

```
$  az group create
     --name <resource-group-name>
     --location <location>

$  az sf cluster create
     --resource-group <resource-group-name>
     --location <location>
     --cluster-name <cluster-name>
     --cluster-size <cluster-size>
     --vm-password <password>
     --vm-user-name <username>
```

Here's how to create an Azure Service Fabric cluster using PowerShell:

```
$  New-AzResourceGroup
     -Name <resource-group-name>
     -Location <location>

$  New-AzServiceFabricCluster
     -ResourceGroupName <resource-group-name>
     -Name <cluster-name>
     -Location <location>
     -ClusterSize <cluster-size>
     -VmUserName <username>
     -VmPassword <password>
```

Once your Azure Service Fabric cluster is set up, you can deploy applications to it. Here's how you will do it using the Azure CLI:

```
$  az sf application create
            --application-name <application-name>
            --application-type-name <application-type-name>
            --application-type-version <application-type-version>
            --cluster-name <cluster-name>
            --resource-group <resource-group>
            --application-parameters <application-parameters>
            --max-nodes <max-nodes>
            --min-nodes <min-nodes>
            --package-url <package-url>
```

An Azure Service Fabric cluster node type is a specific configuration within an Azure Service Fabric cluster that defines a group of VMs with similar settings, such as size, capabilities, and roles. Each node type serves as a blueprint for scaling out VMs that will run your microservices or containerized applications.

Node types are important because they allow you to customize the resources allocated to different parts of your application. For example, you can have a node type optimized for frontend services with lower memory requirements and another for backend services that need more processing power and memory.

Figure 6-4 shows a sample microservices architecture that demonstrates how Azure Service Fabric can manage distributed applications with different components working together seamlessly. In this example, you will see how node types can be used.

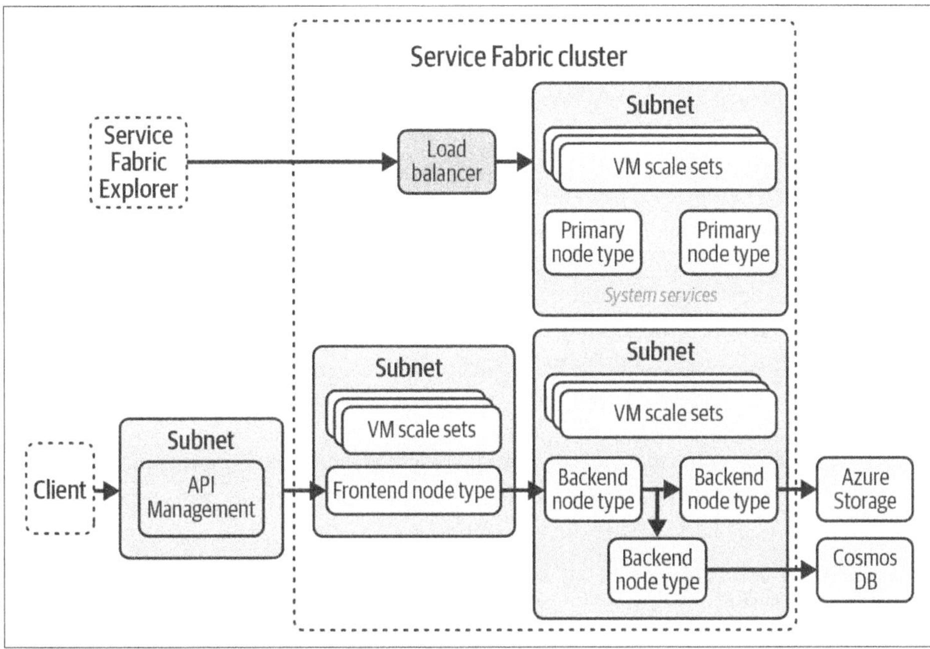

Figure 6-4. Microservices architecture with Azure Service Fabric

In this setup, the Azure Service Fabric cluster is at the center, consisting of VMs grouped into different types, known as node types, each located in separate sections called subnets. The *primary node type* is responsible for essential system services that keep the cluster running, like managing workloads, maintaining cluster state, and handling updates.

The *frontend node type* manages incoming user requests using an API Management gateway that routes these requests to the appropriate microservices within the cluster. This helps ensure requests are processed correctly and efficiently.

The *backend node type* handles the core business logic and processing tasks. These nodes run microservices that perform specific functions such as processing data, managing transactions, or connecting to external systems. They interact with external data stores like Azure Storage and Azure Cosmos DB, which provide solutions for structured and unstructured data.

A *load balancer* distributes network traffic evenly across the node types, ensuring that no single node type becomes overwhelmed. This improves the reliability and stability of the entire application.

Now, let's see how we can use the Azure CLI to create an Azure Service Fabric node type:

```
$ az sf cluster node-type add
    --cluster-name <cluster-name>
    --resource-group <resource-group-name>
    --node-type frontEndNodeType
    --capacity 2
    --vm-sku <vm-sku>
```

Building Apps with Azure Container Apps

Azure also has serverless containers. It has Azure Container Apps, a service where you can run microservices and apps in containers without worrying about managing servers or Kubernetes clusters. This makes it great for event-driven and microservices-based applications that need to scale automatically based on demand, like handling HTTP requests, events, or custom metrics.

Let's go through the steps to set up Azure Container Apps using the Azure CLI.

First, create a Container Apps environment. A Container Apps environment is like a sandbox where your container apps run. It provides the necessary resources and configurations for your apps to operate smoothly:

```
$ az containerapp env create
    --name <name>
    --resource-group <resource-group-name>
    --location <location>
```

Now that you have the environment ready, you can deploy your container app. For this example, we'll use a sample container image that runs a simple web application:

```
$ az containerapp create
    --name <name>
    --resource-group <resource-group-name>
    --environment <environment-name>
    --image <image>
    --target-port <target-port>
    --ingress 'external'
```

Azure Container Apps can automatically scale based on traffic or other metrics. Let's set up autoscaling based on the number of HTTP requests:

```
$ az containerapp update
    --name <name>
    --resource-group <resource-group-name>
    --min-replicas 1
    --max-replicas 5
    --scale-rule-name http-rule
    --scale-rule-type http
    --scale-rule-metadata concurrentRequests=50
```

Azure Container Apps is built on top of Kubernetes and uses some of the same technologies as AKS. However, it simplifies the experience by hiding the complexities of managing Kubernetes clusters. This makes it a good choice if you need some Kubernetes features but don't want the operational overhead.

If you're already using AKS, you can integrate Container Apps to offload certain workloads, such as handling bursty or event-driven tasks that benefit from serverless scaling. Both services can coexist, with AKS handling more complex or stateful microservices, while Container Apps manage lighter, stateless, or temporary workloads.

Extending the Cloud with Azure Arc

Azure Arc is a set of technologies that extends Azure management and governance capabilities to resources outside of Azure, including on-premises, multicloud, and edge environments. With Azure Arc, you can bring Azure services and management to any infrastructure, allowing you to manage and secure these resources consistently using familiar Azure tools.

Azure Arc can be used to manage Kubernetes clusters, including AKS clusters, as well as clusters running in other environments like AWS, Google Cloud, or on premises. This integration allows you to apply consistent configurations and security policies and deploy applications across all your Kubernetes clusters using GitOps, regardless of where they are running.

To connect an existing Kubernetes cluster to Azure Arc using the Azure CLI, you'd need to install the Azure Arc extension:

```
$ az extension add --name connectedk8s
```

Once the Azure Arc extension is added, you can onboard a connected Kubernetes cluster with Azure Arc:

```
$ az connectedk8s connect
    --name <name>
    --resource-group <resource-group-name>
    --location <location>
```

Summary

This chapter covered the different ways you can build containerized solutions on Azure. I introduced you to the basics of containerization, helping you learn how it simplifies application deployment by packaging applications and their dependencies into containers. You explored deploying containers using AKS, which manages and scales containerized apps, and ACI, which offers a simpler, serverless way to run containers without managing the infrastructure.

The chapter also discussed ACR, which securely stores and manages container images, and Azure Container Apps, which runs microservices and event-driven applications without the complexity of Kubernetes. Integration between ACR and AKS was highlighted, demonstrating how to pull images directly into Kubernetes clusters.

Additionally, the chapter introduced Azure Service Fabric, focusing on building and managing complex distributed systems with stateful and stateless services. Finally, it concluded with Azure Arc, which extends Azure's management capabilities to resources outside of Azure, allowing you to manage Kubernetes clusters and other resources consistently across on-premises, multicloud, and edge environments using Azure tools. In the next chapter, you will learn about Azure security.

CHAPTER 7
Implementing Azure Security

Security is a very important part of building and maintaining applications. It's everyone's job—the business, the engineers, and even the customers—to keep systems safe. As companies build innovative products, bad actors are also innovating on ways to hack you. Security is about staying one step ahead and protecting your data, applications, and systems from these threats.

In this chapter, we will explore different aspects of security in Azure. We'll start with identity and access management, which includes tools like Microsoft Entra ID (formerly Azure AD) and RBAC to ensure that only the right people have access to your resources. We'll also dive into data protection, covering encryption methods and secure ways to manage keys and secrets with Azure Key Vault.

Next, we'll look at network security, where you'll learn how to use firewalls, network security groups, and secure connections to protect your data as it travels across the network. We've touched on some of these concepts in previous chapters, but we'll cover them in depth here. Threat protection will help you understand how to detect and respond to threats in real time using Microsoft Defender for Cloud.

We'll also discuss compliance and governance, ensuring your systems meet regulatory requirements and best practices. Finally, we'll go over security best practices, and you'll see tips and recommendations for keeping your systems secure. By the end of this chapter, you'll have a comprehensive understanding of how to secure your Azure environment against today's evolving threats.

Identity and Access Management

Identity and access management (IAM) in Azure is all about ensuring that the right people have the right access to the right resources. It's a framework that helps control who can do what within your Azure environment, which is very important when protecting sensitive data and maintaining compliance. IAM encompasses tools like Microsoft Entra ID and RBAC, which manage identities and control permissions. It also includes features like multifactor authentication (MFA) and conditional access to enhance security further.

Role-Based Access Control

With RBAC, you'll be assigning specific roles to identities, such as users, groups, or service principals, to manage access to resources in Azure. It's a way to ensure each identity only has the permissions they need to perform their job, which helps to minimize security risks. RBAC operates on the principle of least privilege, meaning permissions are granted based on the specific tasks a user needs to perform rather than giving blanket access. In Azure, roles define a set of permissions, and these roles are assigned to identities within a defined scope, such as a subscription, resource group, or individual resource.

Azure RBAC provides several built-in roles that cover common scenarios:

Owner
: Full access to all resources, including the ability to delegate access to others

Contributor
: Can create and manage resources but cannot grant access to others

Reader
: Can view resources but cannot make changes

User access administrator
: Can manage access to Azure resources

Role-based access control administrator
: Can manage role assignments across all scopes

Beyond these general roles, there are built-in roles across the different segments of Azure resources (e.g., compute, storage, network, databases, containers, and more). Additionally, Azure allows for the creation of custom roles when the built-in roles do not meet specific requirements. Custom roles can be tailored to include only the permissions necessary for a particular task or role within the organization.

Scope determines where the permissions apply, and it can be set at the management group, subscription, resource group, or resource level. Assigning roles at a broader scope, such as the subscription, means the permissions will inherit down to all contained resources. This hierarchical approach helps in organizing and managing access across large Azure environments.

Creating custom roles with Azure CLI

Creating custom roles allows you to define a set of permissions tailored to specific needs. Here's how to create a custom role with the Azure CLI:

```
# Define the properties of the custom role
customRole='{
  "Name": "AssetReadOnlyRole",
  "Description": "Read-only access to storage and network resources.",
  "Actions": [
    "Microsoft.Storage/*/read",
    "Microsoft.Network/*/read"
  ],
  "AssignableScopes": ["/subscriptions/<subscription-id>"]
}'

# Create the custom role
az role definition create --role-definition "$customRole"
```

The custom role named `AssetReadOnlyRole` grants read-only access to storage and network resources within the specified subscription.

Creating custom roles with PowerShell

In PowerShell, there are two ways to create a custom role. You either do it using the `PSRoleDefinitionObject` or using a JSON file.

Creating a custom role using the `PSRoleDefinitionObject` looks similar to the following code snippet:

```
# Create the PSRoleDefinitionObject
$role = New-Object -TypeName Microsoft.Azure.Commands.Resources.Models.Authorization.
        PSRoleDefinition

# Set the properties for the custom role
$role.Name = 'AssetReadOnlyRole'
$role.Description = 'Read-only access to storage and network resources.'
$role.IsCustom = $true
$role.AssignableScopes = @("/subscriptions/<subscription-id>")
$role.Actions = @(
    "Microsoft.Storage/*/read"
    "Microsoft.Network/*/read"
)

# Create the role definition
New-AzRoleDefinition -Role $role
```

When using a JSON file that defines the role, here's how you'd do it:

```
New-AzRoleDefinition -InputFile <path-to-json-role>
```

Creating custom roles with Bicep

For infrastructure as code, you can use Bicep to define custom roles within your Azure environment:

```
resource customRole 'Microsoft.Authorization/roleDefinitions@2021-04-01-preview' = {
  name: guid(subscription().id, 'CustomReadOnlyRole')
  properties: {
    roleName: 'AssetReadOnlyRole'
    description: 'Read-only access to storage and network resources.'
    permissions: [
      {
        actions: [
          'Microsoft.Storage/*/read'
          'Microsoft.Network/*/read'
        ]
        notActions: []
      }
    ]
    assignableScopes: [
      subscription().id
    ]
  }
}
```

Whether using command-line tools or IaC templates, these approaches allow you to define granular permissions that enforce the principle of least privilege across your Azure environment.

Assigning roles with Azure CLI

To assign a role using the Azure CLI, you can use the `az role assignment create` command. Here is an example of how to assign the Contributor role to a user at the resource group level:

```
$  az role assignment create
     --assignee sampleuser@email.com
     --role Contributor
     --scope /subscriptions/<subscription>/resourceGroups/<rg-name>
```

This command assigns the Contributor role to `sampleuser@email.com` for the resource group named `<rg-name>`. The user will have permission to create and manage resources within this group. The scope can also be another kind of Azure resource. In this case, the value of the `--scope` parameter will be the full resource ID, which looks similar to this format:

```
/subscriptions/<subscriptionId>/resourcegroups/<resourceGroupName>/providers/
<providerName>/<resourceType>/<resourceSubType>/<resourceName>
```

Beyond the built-in roles, you can also assign custom roles like the `AssetReadOnly Role` we created in the previous sections as well. It will look like this:

```
$  az role assignment create
    --assignee sampleuser@email.com
    --role AssetReadOnlyRole
    --scope /subscriptions/<subscription>/resourceGroups/<rg-name>
```

Assigning roles with PowerShell

Using PowerShell, you can assign roles with the `New-AzRoleAssignment` cmdlet:

```
$objectId = (Get-AzADUser -DisplayName <userName>).id

New-AzRoleAssignment
-ObjectId $objectId
    -RoleDefinitionName "Contributor"
    -Scope /subscriptions/<subscription>/resourceGroups/<rg-name>
```

Assigning roles with Bicep

To assign a role using Bicep, you can use the following:

```
resource role 'Microsoft.Authorization/roleAssignments@2020-04-01' = {
  name: guid(subscription().id, customRole.id, 'sampleuser@email.com')
  properties: {
    roleDefinitionId: customRole.id
    principalId: 'user-object-id'
    scope: subscription().id
  }
}
```

Microsoft Entra ID

Microsoft Entra ID, previously known as Azure AD, is Microsoft's IAM service in the cloud. It provides identity services for managing users, groups, and devices and secures access to various Azure resources, applications, and SaaS offerings. Entra ID simplifies security with single sign-on (SSO), MFA, conditional access, and privileged identity management (PIM). We'll explore these capabilities with practical code examples using Azure CLI and PowerShell in the following sections.

Microsoft Entra ID has the following key features:

Single sign-on
: SSO allows users to access multiple applications with a single set of credentials, simplifying the user experience and reducing the number of passwords they need to manage.

Multifactor authentication
: MFA adds an extra layer of security by requiring users to provide additional verification, such as a code sent to their mobile device, in addition to their password.

Conditional access
: Conditional access policies help control how and when users access resources. For instance, you can require MFA when accessing sensitive data or block access from certain geographic locations.

Identity protection
: This feature uses machine learning to detect suspicious behavior and automatically respond to potential identity risks, such as compromised credentials or sign-ins from unfamiliar locations.

Privileged identity management
: PIM helps manage, monitor, and control access within Entra ID, allowing you to reduce the risks associated with excessive, unnecessary, or misused access permissions.

Managing Microsoft Entra ID with Azure CLI

To manage users in Microsoft Entra ID, you can use the `az ad user` command. The following command creates a new user in Microsoft Entra ID:

```
$ az ad user create
    --display-name <display-name>
    --user-principal-name <user-principal-name>
    --password <password>
```

The following command lists all users in Microsoft Entra ID:

```
$ az ad user list --output table
```

The following command creates a group in Microsoft Entra ID:

```
$ az ad group create
    --display-name "Developers"
    --mail-nickname "developers"
```

The following command adds a user to a group in Microsoft Entra ID:

```
$ az ad group member add
    --group "Developers"
    --member-id <user-object-id>
```

Managing Microsoft Entra ID with PowerShell

To manage users in Microsoft Entra ID, you can use the `New-AzureADUser` cmdlet. The following command creates a new user in Microsoft Entra ID:

```
# Create Password Profile
$passwordProfile = New-Object
    -TypeName Microsoft.Open.AzureAD.Model.PasswordProfile
    -ArgumentList ("password-value-here")

# Create a new user in Microsoft Entra ID
New-AzureADUser
    -DisplayName "Adora Nwodo"
```

```
    -UserPrincipalName "adoranwodo@website.com" `
    -AccountEnabled $true
    -PasswordProfile $passwordProfile
```

The following command creates a group in Microsoft Entra ID:

```
New-AzureADGroup
    -DisplayName "Developers"
    -MailNickname "developers"
    -SecurityEnabled $true
    -MailEnabled $false
```

The following command adds a user to a group in Microsoft Entra ID:

```
$groupid=(Get-AzADGroup -DisplayName "Developers").Id
$members=@()
$members+=(Get-AzADUser -DisplayName "Adora").Id
$members+=(Get-AzADServicePrincipal -ApplicationId $appid).Id

Add-AzADGroupMember
    -TargetGroupObjectId $groupid
    -MemberObjectId $members
```

Creating a service principal using Azure CLI

Creating a service principal in Microsoft Entra ID allows applications or automation tools to access specific Azure resources securely. A service principal is essentially an identity used by applications, services, or automation tools to access Azure resources. It's a critical part of automating and managing Azure environments because it enables secure, programmatic access to Azure without needing a user's credentials. To create a service principal using Azure CLI, you can use the `az ad sp create-for-rbac` command. Here's an example:

```
$  az ad sp create-for-rbac
    --name <name>
    --role Contributor
    --scopes /subscriptions/<subscription>/resourceGroups/<rg-name>
```

Creating a service principal using PowerShell

With PowerShell, you can use the `New-AzADServicePrincipal` cmdlet:

```
$sp = New-AzADServicePrincipal
    -DisplayName <service-principal-name>

New-AzRoleAssignment
    -RoleDefinitionName "Reader"
    -ApplicationId $sp.ApplicationId
```

In the preceding code snippet, the first command creates the service principal with the specified display name, while the second command assigns the Reader role to the newly created service principal.

Data Protection

When improving the security posture of the apps you build, protecting your data is very important. Data protection in Azure involves securing your data at rest and in transit, managing sensitive information, and ensuring only authorized individuals have access. Azure provides several tools and services to help safeguard data, including encryption, key management, and data classification. These tools ensure your data is protected from unauthorized access, whether it's stored in databases, moving across the network, or managed in applications. In this section, we'll explore key services like Azure Key Vault and Azure Storage encryption to understand how they contribute to data protection in Azure.

Azure Key Vault

In Azure Key Vault, you can store and manage keys, secrets, and certificates securely. It's a service that helps keep your sensitive information safe, like passwords, API keys, or encryption keys. By using Azure Key Vault, you can control access to your secrets and ensure only authorized applications or users can access them.

> **What Are Keys, Certificates, and Secrets?**
>
> *Keys*
> : Cryptographic keys used for data encryption and decryption. They can be symmetric keys (for encryption and decryption) or asymmetric keys (public and private key pairs).
>
> *Secrets*
> : These are pieces of sensitive information, such as passwords, connection strings, or API keys. Secrets are stored securely and should only be accessed by applications or services that need them.
>
> *Certificates*
> : Digital certificates that are used for securing communication channels, such as SSL/TLS certificates for websites.

Managing a key vault using Azure CLI

To create a key vault using Azure CLI, you can use the following command:

```
$ az keyvault create
    --name <key-vault-name>
    --resource-group <resource-group-name>
    --location <location>
```

You can use the `az keyvault key` command to manage keys in your key vault. To create a key in Azure Key Vault with Azure CLI, you can use the following command:

```
$ az keyvault key create
    --vault-name <key-vault-name>
    --name <key-name>
    --protection software
```

You can use the `az keyvault secret` command to manage secrets in your key vault. To create a secret in Azure Key Vault with Azure CLI, you can use the following command:

```
$ az keyvault secret set
    --vault-name <key-vault-name>
    --name <secret-name>
    --value <secret-value>
```

You can use the `az keyvault certificate` command to manage certificates in your key vault. To add a certificate in Azure Key Vault with Azure CLI, you can use the following command:

```
$ az keyvault certificate create
    --vault-name <key-vault-name>
    --name <cert-name>
    --policy "$(az keyvault certificate get-default-policy)"
```

Managing a key vault using Azure PowerShell

To create a key vault using PowerShell, you can use the following command:

```
$ New-AzKeyVault
    -VaultName <key-vault-name>
    -ResourceGroupName <resource-group-name>
    -Location <location>
```

You can use the `Add-AzKeyVaultKey` cmdlet to manage keys in your key vault. To create a key in Azure Key Vault with PowerShell, you can use the following command:

```
$ Add-AzKeyVaultKey
    -VaultName <key-vault-name>
    -Name <key-name>
    -Destination "Software"
```

You can use the `Set-AzKeyVaultSecret` command to manage secrets in your key vault. To create a secret in Azure Key Vault with PowerShell, you can use the following command:

```
$ Set-AzKeyVaultSecret
    -VaultName <key-vault-name>
    -Name <secret-name>
    -SecretValue <secret-value>
```

You can use the Add-AzKeyVaultCertificate command to manage certificates in your key vault. To add a certificate in Azure Key Vault with PowerShell, you can use the following command:

```
# Create certificate policy
$Policy = New-AzKeyVaultCertificatePolicy
    -SecretContentType "application/x-pkcs12"
    -SubjectName <cert-subject-name>
    -IssuerName "Self"
    -ValidityInMonths 6
    -ReuseKeyOnRenewal

# Create certificate
Add-AzKeyVaultCertificate
    -VaultName <key-vault-name>
    -Name <cert-name>
    -CertificatePolicy $Policy
```

Managing a key vault using Azure Bicep

You can define key vault resources in a Bicep template to automate the creation and management of keys and secrets. To create a key vault using Bicep, you can use the following code snippet:

```
resource keyVault 'Microsoft.KeyVault/vaults@2021-06-01-preview' = {
  name: <key-vault-name>
  location: <location>
  properties: {
    sku: {
      family: 'A'
      name: 'standard'
    }
    tenantId: subscription().tenantId
    accessPolicies: []
  }
}
```

To create a key in Azure Key Vault with Bicep, you can use the following command:

```
resource key 'Microsoft.KeyVault/vaults/keys@2021-06-01-preview' = {
  parent: <key-vault-name>
  name: <key-name>
  properties: {
    keySize: 2048
    keyOps: ['encrypt', 'decrypt', 'sign', 'verify', 'wrapKey']
    kty: 'RSA'
  }
}
```

To create a secret in Azure Key Vault with Bicep, you can use the following command:

```
resource secret 'Microsoft.KeyVault/vaults/secrets@2021-06-01-preview' = {
  parent: <key-vault-name>
  name: <secret-name>
  properties: {
    value: <secret-value>
  }
}
```

Rotating certificates in Azure Key Vault

Rotating certificates is important because it helps maintain the security and trustworthiness of your applications. Regular rotation prevents certificates from expiring unexpectedly, which can lead to service disruptions. It also minimizes the risk of old or compromised certificates being used by bad actors, ensuring that your encryption remains strong and up to date.

To create a certificate with auto-renewal enabled, you first need to define the certificate policy that includes the validity period and auto-renewal settings. Your certificate policy may look similar to this:

```
echo '{
  "issuerParameters": {
    "name": "Self"
  },
  "keyProperties": {
    "exportable": true,
    "keySize": 2048,
    "keyType": "RSA",
    "reuseKey": false
  },
  "secretProperties": {
    "contentType": "application/x-pkcs12"
  },
  "x509CertificateProperties": {
    "subject": <cert-subject-name>,
    "keyUsage": ["digitalSignature", "keyEncipherment"],
    "validityInMonths": 12
  },
  "lifetimeActions": [{
    "trigger": {
      "daysBeforeExpiry": 30
    },
    "action": {
      "actionType": "AutoRenew"
    }
  }]
}' > policy.json
```

In this code snippet, the policy defines the certificate settings, including its validity period of 12 months, and sets a trigger to auto-renew the certificate 30 days before it expires. After this, create a certificate with the defined policy:

```
$  az keyvault certificate create
     --vault-name <key-vault-name>
     --name <certificate-name>
     --policy @"policy.json"
```

In this code snippet, the `--policy` parameter in the `az keyvault certificate create` command points to the policy file, which configures the auto-renewal behavior.

You can also use PowerShell to create a certificate with auto-renewal enabled:

```
# Create a certificate policy with auto-renew settings
$policy = New-AzKeyVaultCertificatePolicy
    -IssuerName 'Self'
    -KeyType RSA
    -RenewAtNumberOfDaysBeforeExpiry 30
    -SecretContentType application/x-pkcs12
    -SubjectName <cert-subject-name>
    -ValidityInMonths 12

# Create the certificate with the specified policy
Add-AzKeyVaultCertificate
    -VaultName <key-vault-name>
    -Name <certificate-name>
    -CertificatePolicy $policy
```

Managing key vault permissions with access policies

You can manage key vault permissions with RBAC, but we covered RBAC in a previous section, so here we'll talk about an alternative way to manage this access. In Azure Key Vault, access to keys, secrets, and certificates is controlled through access policies (Figure 7-1). These policies define who can access what in the key vault and what actions they can perform. Setting the right access policies is crucial for ensuring that only authorized users or applications have access to sensitive information.

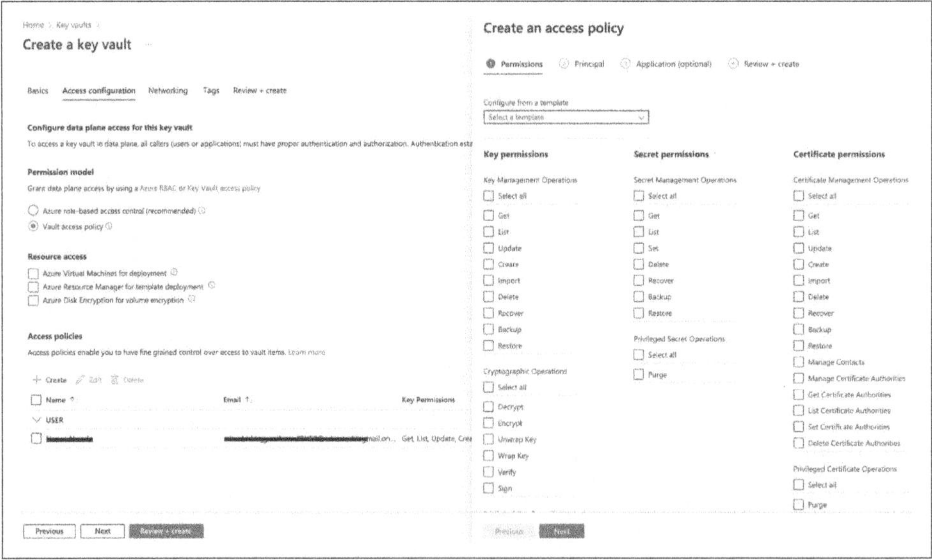

Figure 7-1. Access policies in the Azure portal

Access policies in Azure Key Vault can grant permissions for various actions, including:

Keys
: `get`, `list`, `update`, `create`, `import`, `delete`, `backup`, `restore`, `recover`, `purge`, `encrypt`, `decrypt`, `sign`, `verify`, and more

Secrets
: `get`, `list`, `set`, `delete`, `backup`, `restore`, `recover`, `purge`

Certificates
: `get`, `list`, `update`, `create`, `import`, `delete`, `managecontacts`, `recover`, `purge`, and more

You can set access policies using the Azure CLI with the `az keyvault set-policy` command. Here's an example:

```
$ az keyvault set-policy
    --name <key-vault-name>
    --object-id <user-object-id>
    --key-permissions get list create update delete
    --secret-permissions get list set delete
```

This command sets an access policy for a user identified by `object-id` to manage keys and secrets in the specified key vault.

To set access policies with PowerShell, you can use the `Set-AzKeyVaultAccessPolicy` cmdlet:

```
Set-AzKeyVaultAccessPolicy
    -VaultName <key-vault-name>
    -ObjectId <user-object-id>
    -PermissionsToKeys get, list, create, update, delete
    -PermissionsToSecrets get, list, set, delete
```

You can also do this in Bicep. Bicep allows you to define access policies declaratively as part of your infrastructure code. Here's how you can set an access policy with Bicep:

```
resource keyVault 'Microsoft.KeyVault/vaults@2021-06-01-preview' = {
  name: <key-vault-name>
  properties: {
    // … more code
    accessPolicies: [
      {
        tenantId: subscription().tenantId
        objectId: <user-object-id>
        permissions: {
          keys: [
            'get'
            'list'
          ]
          secrets: [
            'get'
```

```
                'list'
              ]
              certificates: []
            }
          }
        ]
      }
    }
```

Connecting certificates to Azure services

Certificates stored in Azure Key Vault can be used with other Azure services, like App Service, to secure communication. Here's how you can connect an Azure Key Vault certificate to an app service using Azure CLI:

```
$  az webapp config ssl import
     --resource-group <resource-group-name>
     --name <web-app-name>
     --key-vault <key-vault-name>
     --key-vault-certificate-name <key-vault-certificate-name>
```

Purge protection

Purge protection ensures that even if items are deleted, they can't immediately be permanently removed, adding extra security against accidental or malicious deletions.

Here's how to enable purge protection with Azure CLI:

```
$  az keyvault update
     --name <key-vault-name>
     --enable-purge-protection true
```

Azure Storage Encryption

Azure Storage encryption automatically encrypts data stored in Azure Blob Storage, Azure Files, Azure Queue Storage, and Azure Table Storage to protect data at rest. You can use CMK stored in Azure Key Vault to control encryption of your data at rest. You can enable encryption with CMK using Azure CLI, PowerShell, and Bicep.

Here's how to do it using Azure CLI:

```
# Create a Key Vault
az keyvault create
     --name <key-vault-name>
     --resource-group <resource-group-name>
     --location <location>

# Create a Key in Key Vault
az keyvault key create
     --vault-name <key-vault-name>
     --name <storage-key-name>
     --protection software

# Create a storage account with encryption enabled using customer-managed keys
az storage account create
```

```
    --name <storage-account-name>
    --resource-group <resource-group-name>
    --location <location>
    --sku <sku>
    --encryption-key-source Microsoft.Keyvault
    --encryption-key-vault https://<key-vault-name>.vault.azure.net
    --encryption-key-name <storage-key-name>
```

Here's how to do it using PowerShell:

```
# Create a Key Vault
$keyVault = New-AzKeyVault
    -ResourceGroupName <resource-group-name>
    -VaultName <key-vault-name>
    -Location <location>

# Create a Key in Key Vault
Add-AzKeyVaultKey
    -VaultName <key-vault-name>
    -Name <storage-key-name>
    -Destination "Software"

# Create a storage account with encryption enabled using customer-managed keys
New-AzStorageAccount
    -ResourceGroupName <resource-group-name>
    -Name <storage-account-name>
    -Location <location>
    -SkuName <sku>
    -Kind <storage-account-kind>
    -KeyVaultUri $keyVault.VaultUri
    -KeyName <storage-key-name>
```

Here's how to do it using Bicep:

```
// Create a Key Vault
resource keyVault 'Microsoft.KeyVault/vaults@2021-06-01-preview' = {
  name: <key-vault-name>
  location: <location>
  // ... more code here
}

// Create a Key in Key Vault
resource key 'Microsoft.KeyVault/vaults/keys@2021-06-01-preview' = {
  parent: <key-vault-name>
  name: <storage-key-name>
  // ... more code here
}

// Create a storage account with encryption enabled using customer-managed keys
resource storageAccount 'Microsoft.Storage/storageAccounts@2021-02-01' = {
  name: <storage-account-name>
   // ... more code here
  properties: {
    encryption: {
      services: {
        blob: {
          enabled: true
        }
        file: {
          enabled: true
```

```
        }
        table: {
          enabled: true
        }
        queue: {
          enabled: true
        }
      }
      keySource: 'Microsoft.Keyvault'
      keyVaultProperties: {
        keyname: <storage-key-name>
        keyvaulturi: <key-vault-uri>
        keyversion: <key-version>
      }
    }
  }
}
```

Network Security

Network security in Azure involves protecting resources from unauthorized access and threats by controlling traffic to and from Azure resources. It includes a range of tools and services to ensure data and applications are secure as they move through the network. Azure provides various features like Azure Firewall for centralized security management, Azure DDoS Protection to defend against distributed denial-of-service attacks, and NSGs for filtering traffic. Additionally, Azure Bastion offers secure Remote Desktop Protocol (RDP) and Secure Shell (SSH) connectivity to VMs without exposing them directly to the internet. In this section, we will explore some of these network security components in Azure and how they help secure your cloud environment. In Chapter 12, we'll go deeper into networking and cover this topic in a lot more detail.

Azure Firewall

Azure Firewall helps protect your applications and data by blocking unauthorized access and only allowing traffic that meets your security rules. For example, imagine a company that hosts several web applications in Azure. They want to ensure only trusted IP addresses can access their applications and block any traffic from suspicious or unknown sources. By using Azure Firewall, they can set up rules to allow access only from these trusted IP ranges and block all other incoming traffic. This setup helps keep their applications secure while giving them a central point to manage and monitor their security rules.

Azure Firewall offers three tiers—Basic, Standard, and Premium—each designed to meet different levels of security and performance needs.

The Basic tier is designed for small- to medium-sized businesses or environments that need essential firewall capabilities at a lower cost. It provides basic security features, such as L3/L4 filtering, to allow or deny traffic based on IP addresses, ports, and protocols.

The Standard tier is suitable for most organizations and has more advanced features, including stateful firewall capabilities, built-in high availability, and scalability. It supports application rules that filter traffic based on fully qualified domain names (FQDNs) and integrates with Azure Monitor for logging and analytics.

The Premium tier is designed for highly sensitive or regulated environments that require enhanced security. It includes all features of the Standard tier, plus advanced protection, including intrusion detection and prevention systems (IDPS), URL filtering, and Transport Layer Security (TLS) inspection. The Premium tier is ideal for enterprises that need to meet strict compliance and security requirements.

Here's a simple example of how to set up Azure Firewall using Azure CLI. To do this, we'll create a VNet and a dedicated subnet for the Azure Firewall. The firewall will be deployed within the VNet, and we'll add a rule to allow HTTP traffic out from a specific subnet. First, create a VNet:

```
az network vnet create
    --name <vnet-name>
    --resource-group <resource-group-name>
    --address-prefixes 10.0.0.0/16
```

Next, create a subnet named for Azure Firewall (it must be named `AzureFirewallSubnet`):

```
az network vnet subnet create
     --name AzureFirewallSubnet
     --resource-group <resource-group-name>
     --vnet-name <vnet-name>
     --address-prefixes 10.0.1.0/24
```

Once you have the subnet and VNet, deploy Azure Firewall:

```
az network firewall create
    --name <firewall-name>
    --resource-group <resource-group-name>
    --tier Standard
    --vnet-name <vnet-name>
```

Finally, add a firewall rule to allow outbound HTTP traffic:

```
az network firewall application-rule create
    --resource-group <resource-group-name>
    --firewall-name <firewall-name>
    --collection-name "AllowWebTraffic"
    --name "AllowHTTP"
    --protocols "Http=80"
    --target-fqdns "*.*"
    --source-addresses "10.0.1.0/24"
    --action "Allow"
    --priority 100
```

Azure DDoS Protection

Distributed denial-of-service (or DDoS) attacks are attempts to make an online service, website, or network unavailable by overwhelming it with a flood of internet traffic. Imagine thousands of people all trying to enter a small door at the same time, causing a jam. In DDoS attacks, attackers use many compromised computers or devices to send plenty of requests to the target, causing it to slow down, crash, or become unavailable to legitimate users.

When you combine the Azure DDoS Protection service with a good architecture for your services, you can effectively defend against DDoS attacks. Azure DDoS Protection helps by automatically monitoring and mitigating large amounts of unwanted traffic, similar to managing a crowd where hundreds of people are trying to enter a small door at the same time. It identifies these traffic surges as malicious and works to keep your services available to legitimate users.

Azure DDoS Protection provides automatic protection for your Azure resources by analyzing traffic patterns in real time and applying mitigation techniques when it detects an attack (Figure 7-2). It helps ensure your services remain available, even under a heavy DDoS attack, by scaling to absorb the attack traffic and by blocking malicious requests. It operates at the network layer, specifically layers 3 (network) and 4 (transport) of the OSI (Open Systems Interconnection) model because its focus is on defending against large-scale volumetric attacks that target the network and transport layers, such as SYN/ACK (synchronize/acknowledge) floods, UDP (User Datagram Protocol) reflection attacks, and other types of malicious traffic meant to overwhelm your service.

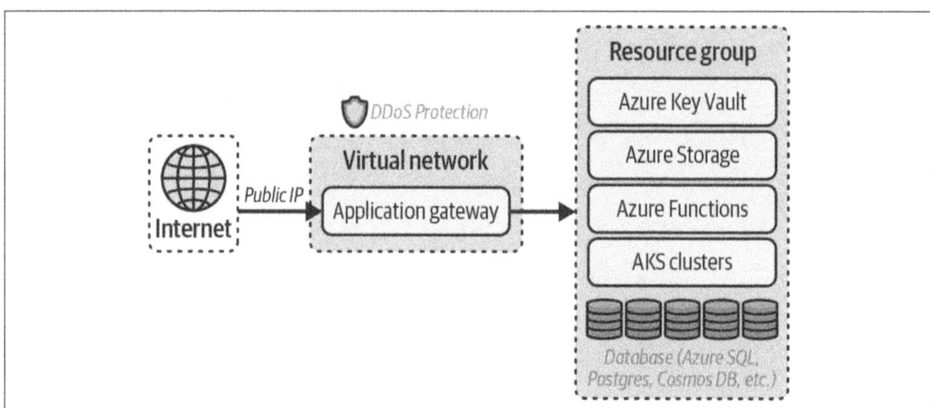

Figure 7-2. Azure DDoS Protection

To enable Azure DDoS Protection on a VNet, you first need to create a DDoS protection plan and then associate it with your VNet. Here's how to do it in the Azure CLI:

```
# Create a DDoS protection plan
az network ddos-protection create
    --resource-group <resource-group-name>
    --name <ddos-protection-plan>

# Associate the DDoS protection plan with a virtual network
az network vnet update
    --name <vnet-name>
    --resource-group <resource-group-name>
    --ddos-protection-plan <ddos-protection-plan-resource-id>
    --ddos-protection true
```

Beyond using Azure DDoS Protection in your VNets, there are other best practices you can implement to mitigate DDoS attacks in Azure:

- Use services like Azure Front Door or Azure Application Gateway, as these services provide additional layers of protection by distributing traffic across multiple locations and using web application firewall (WAF) rules to block malicious requests. We'll discuss Azure Front Door and Azure Application Gateway in more depth in Chapter 12.
- Use Azure's autoscaling features to automatically adjust the number of resources to handle unexpected surges in traffic. This helps absorb the impact of traffic spikes caused by DDoS attacks.
- Use NSGs to limit traffic to only what is necessary, reducing the attack surface. We'll cover NSGs in the next section.
- Implement rate limiting and throttling in your application to control the number of requests allowed from a single source.
- Use Azure Monitor or other monitoring and observability tools to set up alerts and monitor your resources. This allows you to respond quickly if an attack is detected.

Network Security Groups

You can also use NSGs to achieve data protection in Azure by controlling the flow of network traffic to and from your Azure resources. NSGs act like virtual firewalls, allowing you to create rules that specify which types of traffic are permitted or denied to your VMs, subnets, or other networked resources. These rules can be based on factors such as source and destination IP addresses, ports, and protocols.

NSGs allow you to create inbound and outbound security rules to filter traffic at the network level. This helps protect your Azure resources from unauthorized access and potential threats by only allowing legitimate traffic that meets your specified criteria.

NSGs are applied at both the subnet and network interface level, providing a flexible approach to securing your Azure environment.

Imagine you have a web application running on a VM in Azure, and you want to ensure that only HTTP (port 80) and HTTPS (port 443) traffic is allowed from the internet, while blocking all other traffic. By creating an NSG with rules that allow traffic on these ports and deny all others, you effectively secure your application from unwanted access, similar to locking specific doors and leaving others closed.

Here's how you can set up an NSG using Azure CLI. First, create a network security group:

```
$ az network nsg create
    --resource-group <resource-group-name>
    --name <nsg-name>
```

Once you've created your network security group, you can now add security rule:

```
$ az network nsg rule create
    --resource-group <resource-group-name>
    --nsg-name <nsg-name>
    --name AllowHTTP
    --priority 100
    --protocol Tcp
    --direction Inbound
    --source-address-prefixes Internet
    --source-port-ranges '*'
    --destination-address-prefixes '*'
    --destination-port-ranges 80 443
    --access Allow
```

You can also decide to add another rule in your NSG. To deny outbound traffic to a specific destination, you can create an NSG rule that blocks the desired traffic. Here is a sample command that sets up an NSG rule to deny outbound traffic to a specific destination IP address:

```
$ az network nsg rule create
    --resource-group <resource-group-name>
    --nsg-name <nsg-name>
    --name DenyOutboundToDestination
    --priority 200
    --direction Outbound
    --access Deny
    --protocol '*'
    --source-address-prefixes '*'
    --source-port-ranges '*'
    --destination-address-prefixes '192.168.1.100'
    --destination-port-ranges '*'
```

After setting all your rules, you can now associate the NSG with a subnet:

```
$ az network vnet subnet update
    --vnet-name <vnet-name>
    --name <subnet-name>
    --resource-group <resource-group-name>
    --network-security-group <nsg-name>
```

Azure Bastion

Azure Bastion acts as a gateway for managing VMs securely. By connecting through the Azure portal, you can access your VMs using RDP or SSH directly in your web browser without opening any ports like 3389 or 22 on your VMs. This helps prevent external attacks such as port scanning, which is often the first step in a malicious attack.

To set up Azure Bastion, you need to create an Azure Bastion host within your VNet and configure it to provide access to your VMs. First, create a subnet within your VNet and name it `AzureBastionSubnet`. This name is mandatory for Azure Bastion:

```
$ az network vnet subnet create
    --name AzureBastionSubnet
    --vnet-name <vnet-name>
    --resource-group <resource-group-name>
    --address-prefixes 10.0.1.0/27
```

Next, create a public IP address for the Bastion host:

```
$ az network public-ip create
    --resource-group <resource-group-name>
    --name <public-ip-name>
    --sku <sku>
    --location <location>
```

Finally, create the bastion host using the VNet and public IP:

```
$ az network bastion create
    --name <bastion-host-name>
    --public-ip-address <public-ip-name>
    --resource-group <resource-group-name>
    --vnet-name <vnet-name>
    --location <location>
```

Threat Protection

Threat protection in Azure involves identifying, assessing, and defending against security threats to your cloud environment. It includes tools and services designed to detect vulnerabilities, monitor for suspicious activities, and provide actionable insights to protect your resources.

Microsoft Defender for Cloud enhances the security of your Azure resources by providing real-time insights and recommendations. It detects threats like suspicious login attempts, malware, and unauthorized changes to resources. Defender for Cloud also assesses your environment for vulnerabilities, such as weak configurations or missing patches, and guides you on how to remediate these issues.

Consider a scenario where an organization uses Azure Virtual Machines, Azure SQL Databases, and Azure Storage accounts for their operations. Defender for Cloud monitors these resources and detects an unusual spike in failed login attempts on a

VM, suggesting a potential brute-force attack. The service generates an alert and provides recommendations to block the IP address, enable multifactor authentication, and review access logs. This enables the security team to act quickly, protecting their resources from a potential breach.

You can enable Microsoft Defender for Cloud on your subscription using the `az security pricing` command in the Azure CLI. Here's how to enable the Microsoft Defender for Cloud plan for your subscription:

```
$ az security pricing create
    --name default
    --tier standard
```

Compliance and Governance

Compliance and governance in Azure involve managing your cloud environment to ensure that it meets regulatory requirements, organizational standards, and best practices.

Azure Policy is a service in Azure that allows you to create, assign, and manage policies to enforce rules and standards across your Azure resources. These policies help ensure your environment stays compliant with corporate standards, security requirements, or industry regulations. For example, you can enforce policies that restrict the types of resources that can be deployed, ensure resources are tagged correctly, or require certain security configurations like encryption on storage accounts.

Azure Policy works by evaluating your resources and comparing them against policy definitions you have set up. If a resource is found to be noncompliant, Azure Policy can take action to enforce the rule, such as automatically remediating the resource or notifying you of the violation. These policies can be created through *policy as code*. Policy as code is a practice where policies are defined and managed using code, similar to infrastructure as code. By using JSON or other scripting formats, you can define policies, deploy them using automation tools, and maintain them in source control for versioning and collaboration. This approach enables you to manage your policies consistently across environments, integrate them into CI/CD pipelines, and apply changes programmatically. Let's see how to create policies using the Azure CLI and Bicep.

Creating and Assigning a Policy Using Azure CLI

To create and assign a policy in Azure, you can use the Azure CLI. Here's an example of how to create a policy requiring all storage accounts to have secure transfer enabled. First, create a policy definition that requires secure transfer on storage accounts:

```
az policy definition create --name "enforce-secure-transfer-policy"
    --display-name "Enforce Secure Transfer for Storage Accounts"
    --description "Ensures that secure transfer is enabled for all storage accounts."
    --rules '{
         "if": {
                    "field": "Microsoft.Storage/storageAccounts/enableHttpsTrafficOnly",
                    "equals": "false"
         },
         "then": {
                    "effect": "deny"
         }
     }'
    --mode "Indexed"
```

Once the policy is created, you can assign it to a particular scope:

```
$  az policy assignment create
    --name "enforce-secure-transfer-policy-assignment"
    --display-name "Enforce Secure Transfer for Storage Accounts"
    --policy "enforce-secure-transfer-policy"
    --scope "/subscriptions/<subscription>/resourceGroups/<rg-name>"
```

Using Bicep for Policy as Code

Here's how you can define and assign a policy using Bicep:

```
// Create the policy definition
resource policyDefinition 'Microsoft.Authorization/policyDefinitions@2021-06-01' = {
  name: 'enforceSecureTransferPolicy'
  properties: {
    displayName: 'Enforce Secure Transfer for Storage Accounts'
    description: 'Ensures that secure transfer is enabled for all storage accounts.'
    policyRule: {
      if: {
        field: 'Microsoft.Storage/storageAccounts/enableHttpsTrafficOnly'
        equals: 'false'
      }
      then: {
        effect: 'deny'
      }
    }
    mode: 'Indexed'
  }
}

// Assign the policy to a scope (in this case, a resource group)
resource policyAssignment 'Microsoft.Authorization/policyAssignments@2021-06-01' = {
  name: 'enforceSecureTransferPolicyAssignment'
  scope: resourceGroup().id
  properties: {
    displayName: 'Enforce Secure Transfer for Storage Accounts'
    policyDefinitionId: policyDefinition.id
  }
}
```

Security Best Practices

Securing your applications and infrastructure is very important as we build and deploy on the cloud because of the negative impact an insecure application can have on customer trust and business operations. Cyberattacks, data breaches, and other security incidents can damage your reputation and lead to significant financial losses. To mitigate these risks, it's very important to follow security best practices when building on Azure.

One fundamental approach is implementing *zero trust principles*, which assume that threats could come from anywhere, both outside and inside the network. Zero trust involves verifying the identity of users, devices, and services before granting access and continuously monitoring for unusual activity. This includes using MFA, restricting access to only the resources needed for a specific job, and regularly reviewing access permissions.

Secure DevOps practices are also important. Security should be a part of the process, and not an afterthought. Integrating security into the DevOps pipeline, often referred to as DevSecOps, ensures that security checks are part of every phase of development and deployment.

Conducting regular security assessments and audits helps identify weaknesses in your infrastructure and applications. Azure has services that can continuously monitor your resources for security misconfigurations and vulnerabilities and also provide recommendations for improvements. Regular audits help ensure compliance with security policies and industry regulations, reducing the risk of potential threats.

Using *Azure Key Vault* to manage sensitive information, such as API keys, passwords, and certificates, is another best practice. Storing secrets securely in Azure Key Vault keeps them out of your code and minimizes the risk of accidental exposure. Implementing policies that enforce the use of Azure Key Vault can further ensure secrets are managed safely.

Network security is also critical. Utilize NSGs to filter traffic to and from Azure resources, only allowing the necessary traffic. Additionally, Azure Firewall and Azure DDoS Protection provide further layers of security, helping to block unwanted traffic and protect against attacks that aim to overwhelm your services.

Another key practice is ensuring *data encryption*, both at rest and in transit. Azure provides built-in encryption options for services. Encrypting your data helps protect it from unauthorized access, even if the data is intercepted or stored inappropriately.

Implementing strong IAM practices is vital. Use Microsoft Entra ID to manage user identities and enforce access policies. PIM can help control and monitor access to critical resources, ensuring high-level permissions are only granted when necessary and for a limited time.

For applications exposed to the internet, using *web application firewalls* (WAFs) can protect against common web threats such as SQL injection and cross-site scripting (XSS). Azure provides WAF capabilities through services like Azure Application Gateway and Azure Front Door, helping to filter out malicious traffic before it reaches your applications. Chapter 12 covers how these two services work in depth.

Regularly updating and patching your software and systems is another essential practice. Outdated software can contain vulnerabilities attackers can exploit. Use Azure Update Management to automate the patching process for your VMs and ensure all systems are kept up-to-date with the latest security patches.

Additionally, *just-in-time (JIT) access* is a critical security feature that reduces exposure to attacks by allowing access to VMs only when needed and for a limited time. This helps reduce the risk of unauthorized access by minimizing the window of opportunity for attacks.

Last, fostering a culture of security awareness within your organization is essential. Educating your team about security best practices, potential threats, and the importance of adhering to security guidelines can greatly enhance your overall security posture.

There are a lot more recommendations. However, by following these best practices, you can significantly reduce the risk of security incidents as you build your cloud applications on Azure.

Summary

This chapter covered Azure security. It emphasized the importance of security in building and maintaining applications, highlighting it is a shared responsibility among businesses, engineers, and even customers. You explored various aspects of security in Azure, starting with identity and access management using tools like Microsoft Entra ID and RBAC to manage permissions and access. Data protection strategies, such as encryption and key management with Azure Key Vault are an important way to keep data safe along with network security measures including firewalls, secure connections, and NSGs.

The chapter further examined threat protection, illustrating how to detect and respond to security threats using Microsoft Defender for Cloud. It covered compliance and governance to ensure systems meet regulatory standards, and concluded with security best practices, offering tips and recommendations for securing Azure environments against evolving threats. In the next chapter, you will learn about API management in Azure.

CHAPTER 8

API Management in Azure

APIs make it easier for apps to work together, and they allow data and services to be reused and shared widely. As APIs become more common and essential, organizations must treat them as important resources and manage them carefully. Proper API management ensures that APIs are secure, reliable, and perform well, enabling businesses to connect systems, automate processes, and enhance digital experiences for users.

In this chapter, we will cover the fundamentals of Azure API Management (APIM), exploring how to create, secure, and monitor APIs effectively. You'll learn about the core components, how to set up and publish APIs, and best practices for managing them throughout their lifecycle. We'll also dive into securing APIs with authentication, adding policies for transforming and enhancing APIs, and how to integrate APIM with other Azure services. By the end of this chapter, you'll have a solid understanding of how to leverage APIM to streamline your API strategy, ensuring your APIs are scalable, secure, and ready for modern application demands.

Introduction to Azure API Management

Azure API Management (APIM) acts as a cloud-based service that sits on top of your backend APIs, functioning like a proxy. It allows you to create, manage, secure, and monitor your APIs efficiently. For instance, if you have APIs like a temperature API and a music API, every call to these backend services passes through the APIM service. This setup helps centralize control, applying security measures, usage policies, and monitoring, all while making sure your APIs are protected and perform consistently (Figure 8-1).

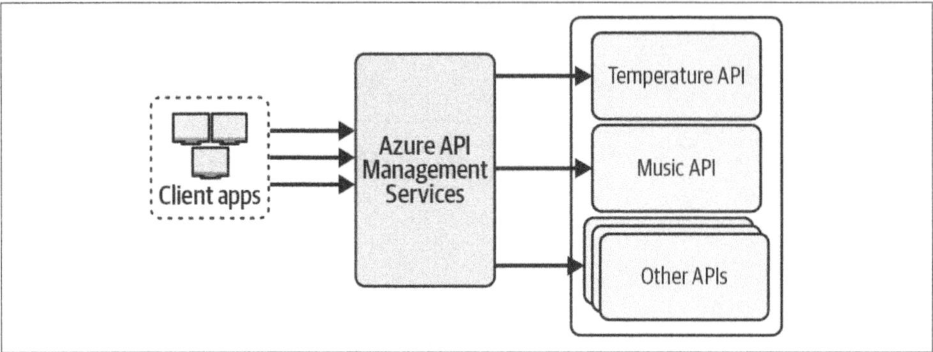

Figure 8-1. APIM overview

The primary components of APIM include the API gateway, developer portal, and management plane:

API gateway
: This acts as the core component that handles all API requests. It provides features like rate limiting, authentication, request/response transformation, caching, and traffic management. These features help control access, protect backend services from threats, and maintain efficient traffic flow.

Developer portal
: This is an automatically generated, customizable website enabling developers to explore APIs, read documentation, and subscribe to APIs. It serves as a self-service platform where developers can register, obtain API keys, and test APIs, fostering easier adoption and integration.

Management plane
: This provides the tools and interfaces for API publishers to define API policies, monitor API usage, and manage the API lifecycle. Through the Azure portal or other management interfaces, administrators can configure APIs, apply policies for caching, security, and logging, and monitor performance metrics to ensure the APIs meet their desired standards.

APIs have become the backbone of modern applications because they enable different systems to communicate and share data seamlessly. They allow companies to break down complex systems into manageable, reusable services that can be developed, maintained, and scaled independently.

In technology today, APIs are not just used internally but are also exposed to partners, third-party developers, and even the public. This exposure can drive new business opportunities, enable integration with other services, and expand the reach of an organization's products. APIs are critical for mobile applications, cloud computing, Internet of Things (IoT) devices, and virtually any scenario where systems need to interact with each other. They provide the means for different applications and platforms to work together, extending the functionality of services and enabling new, connected experiences.

In cloud native architecture, where applications are built using microservices, serverless functions, and other distributed components, managing APIs effectively becomes very important. APIM fits into this architecture by acting as a central hub for managing all APIs, regardless of where they are hosted—whether on Azure, on premises, or in other cloud environments. It provides the tools needed to ensure that APIs are consistent, secure, and perform well across all parts of an application.

Who Uses Azure API Management

Azure API Management caters to three main types of users: API providers, API consumers, and API administrators, each with distinct roles and needs.

For API providers, APIM allows them to publish APIs securely and efficiently. Providers can define the APIs they want to expose, set rules for how data is handled, and protect their APIs with security features like authentication and rate limiting. This helps in ensuring APIs are used properly and backend services are protected from misuse or overload.

API consumers, often developers, use the API Management developer portal to discover, test, and integrate APIs into their applications. The portal provides an easy way to explore available APIs, access documentation, and obtain the necessary keys or tokens to use the APIs. This simplifies the process of using APIs and speeds up the integration into various applications or services.

For API administrators, APIM offers tools to monitor and manage the APIs. Administrators can set policies to control how APIs behave, such as caching responses to improve performance or transforming requests and responses to fit specific needs. They also have access to analytics that provide insights into how APIs are used, helping them make informed decisions about scaling, improving, or deprecating APIs as needed.

This structure ensures that API providers can easily share their services, consumers can efficiently access and utilize APIs, and administrators can maintain oversight and control over the API environment.

Creating and Publishing APIs

APIM allows you to easily create and publish APIs by importing from existing specifications or defining them from scratch. This process involves setting up API endpoints, defining operations, configuring versions, and finally publishing the API. The platform supports multiple ways to manage these tasks, including the Azure portal and Azure CLI, giving you flexibility depending on your preferred method.

Creating an Azure API Management Instance

Before you can create and publish APIs, you need an APIM instance. This instance acts as a centralized hub where you can manage, secure, and monitor your APIs.

```
// Create a resource group
$  az group create
    --name <resource-group-name>
    --location <location>

// Create the API Management instance
$  az apim create
    --resource-group <resource-group-name>
    --name <api-management>
    --publisher-email <publisher-email>
    --publisher-name <publisher-name>
    --sku-name Consumption
```

Available SKUs include Consumption, Developer, Basic, Standard, and Premium, so you can select the one that best fits your needs. You can also create your APIM instance in Bicep or through the Azure portal. From the Azure portal, search for "API Management services" and follow the prompts. You should see something that looks like the screenshot shown in Figure 8-2.

Here's how you can create the API Management instance in Bicep:

```
resource apiManagement 'Microsoft.ApiManagement/service@2021-08-01' = {
  name: 'myApiManagement'
  location: 'eastus'
  sku: {
    name: 'Consumption'
  }
  properties: {
    publisherEmail: 'admin@contoso.com'
    publisherName: 'Contoso'
  }
}
```

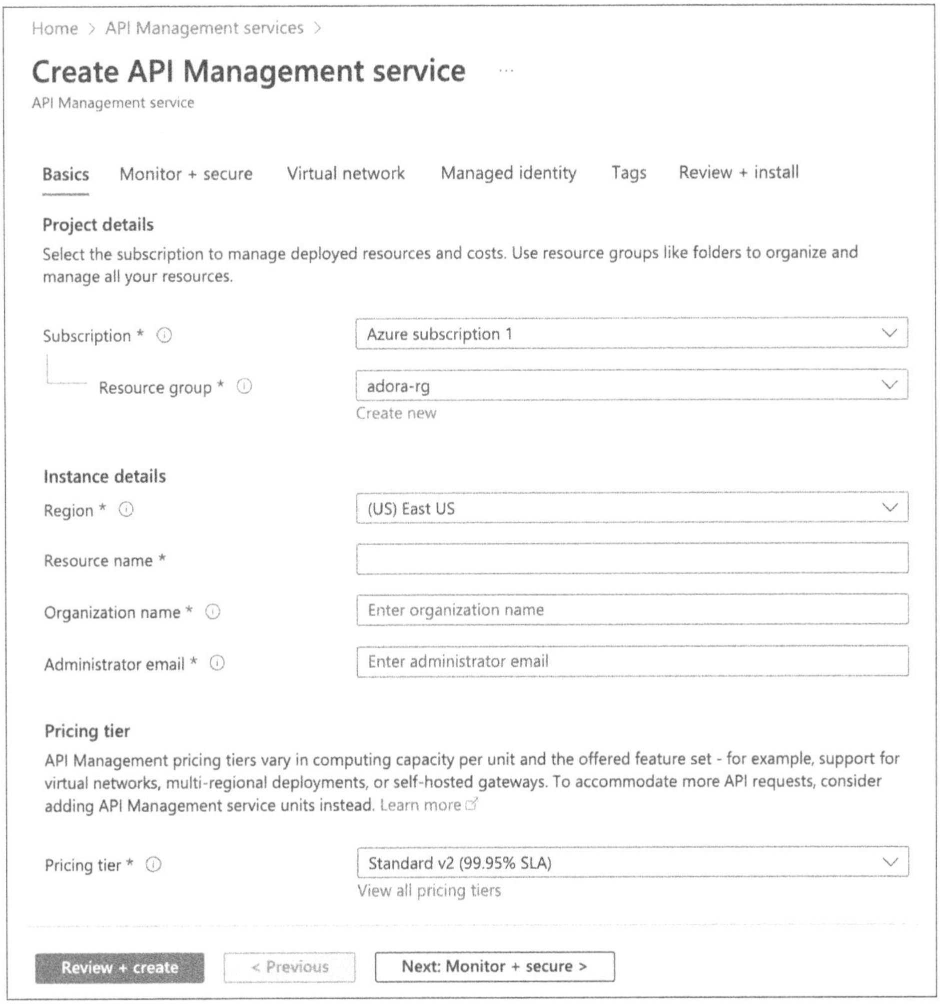

Home > API Management services >

Create API Management service ...

API Management service

Basics | Monitor + secure | Virtual network | Managed identity | Tags | Review + install

Project details

Select the subscription to manage deployed resources and costs. Use resource groups like folders to organize and manage all your resources.

Subscription * | Azure subscription 1

Resource group * | adora-rg

Create new

Instance details

Region * | (US) East US

Resource name *

Organization name * | Enter organization name

Administrator email * | Enter administrator email

Pricing tier

API Management pricing tiers vary in computing capacity per unit and the offered feature set - for example, support for virtual networks, multi-regional deployments, or self-hosted gateways. To accommodate more API requests, consider adding API Management service units instead. Learn more

Pricing tier * | Standard v2 (99.95% SLA)

View all pricing tiers

Review + create | < Previous | Next: Monitor + secure >

Figure 8-2. Creating an Azure API Management instance

Importing APIs from OpenAPI, WSDL, and Other Formats

One of the key features of APIM is the ability to import APIs from existing specifications like OpenAPI (formerly known as Swagger), WSDL (Web Services Description Language) for SOAP (Simple Object Access Protocol) services, or even from Postman collections. This makes it straightforward to bring existing APIs into Azure without needing to redefine endpoints manually.

For example, to import an API from an OpenAPI specification using the Azure CLI, you can use the following command:

```
$  az apim api import
    --resource-group <resource-group-name>
    --service-name <service-name>
    --path <path>
    --api-id <api-id>
    --specification-url "https://path-to-your-openapi-specification"
```

This command creates an API in the APIM instance by pulling the specification from a URL, allowing you to quickly set up endpoints and operations based on the existing documentation.

You can also do this in Bicep using the following code snippet:

```
resource api 'Microsoft.ApiManagement/service/apis@2021-08-01' = {
  name: <api-id>
  parent: <reference-to-api-management-instance>
  properties: {
    path: <path>
    displayName: <display-name>
    protocols: [
      'https'
    ]
    serviceUrl: 'https://path-to-your-openapi-specification'
    format: 'swagger-link-json'
  }
}
```

After successfully importing the API from OpenAPI, you should be able to view the API in the Azure portal, as shown in Figure 8-3.

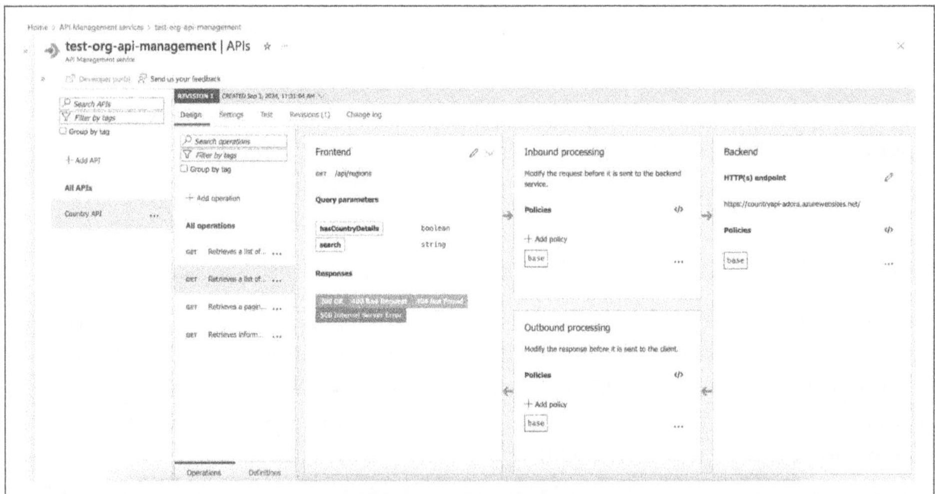

Figure 8-3. An imported API in Azure API Management

For SOAP services, APIM supports importing WSDL files, which describe the service and its operations. Here's how to import a SOAP API using Azure CLI:

```
$  az apim api import
    --resource-group <resource-group-name>
    --service-name <service-name>
    --path <path>
    --api-id <api-id>
    --specification-format Wsdl
    --specification-url "https://path-to-your-wsdl-file"
    --soap-api-type <soap-api-type>
    --wsdl-endpoint-name <wsdl-endpoint-name>
    --wsdl-service-name <wsdl-service-name>
```

You can also do this using Bicep:

```
resource soapApi 'Microsoft.ApiManagement/service/apis@2021-08-01' = {
  name: <api-name>
  parent: <reference-to-api-management-instance>
  properties: {
    path: <path>
    displayName: <display-name>
    protocols: [
      'https'
    ]
    serviceUrl: 'https://path-to-your-wsdl-file'
    format: Wsdl
    wsdlSelector: {
      wsdlEndpointName: '<endpoint-name>'
      wsdlServiceName: '<service-name>'
    }
  }
}
```

Defining API Endpoints, Operations, and Versions

Defining API endpoints involves specifying the paths that the API will expose, such as */products* or */orders*, and the operations like `GET`, `POST`, `PUT`, and `DELETE` that will be available on those endpoints. Each operation can be configured with different settings, such as request parameters, response formats, and error handling.

When creating APIs manually, you can define endpoints and operations directly using Azure CLI commands. For instance, you can create a basic API with a simple endpoint like this:

```
# Create a new API with a basic endpoint
$  az apim api create
    --resource-group <resource-group-name>
    --service-name <service-name>
    --api-id <api-id>
    --display-name <display-name>
    --path <path>
    --protocols <protocols>

# Add an operation to the API
$  az apim api operation create
```

```
    --resource-group <resource-group-name>
    --service-name <service-name>
    --api-id <api-id>
    --operation-id <operation-id>
    --display-name <display-name>
    --method <method>
    --url-template <url-template>
    --template-parameters <template-parameters>
```

Packaging APIs into Products

Azure API Management enables you to group multiple APIs into products, simplifying management and providing a structured way to control access and usage. A product can consist of one or more APIs, each governed by shared policies, quotas, and access rules. This setup allows you to present APIs in a way that aligns with your business needs, making it easier to offer tiered access levels, such as basic and premium versions of your API offerings.

To manage products using Azure CLI, you can create products, add APIs to products, and configure other settings to control how your APIs are consumed. Following are some examples demonstrating how to perform these tasks using Azure CLI.

To create a new product in APIM, use the following command:

```
$  az apim product create
    --resource-group $RESOURCE_GROUP
    --service-name $SERVICE_NAME
    --product-name $PRODUCT_NAME
    --description "$PRODUCT_DESCRIPTION"
    --approval-required false
    --subscriptions-limit 5
```

Once the product is created, you can add APIs to it with the following command:

```
$  az apim product api add
    --api-id $API_ID
    --product-id $PRODUCT_ID
    --resource-group $RESOURCE_GROUP
    --service-name $SERVICE_NAME
```

Securing APIs

To secure your APIs using OAuth 2.0 and Microsoft Entra ID, you first need to create an Entra ID application that serves as the identity provider for your API. This application will handle authentication, allowing users to obtain tokens that authorize them to access your API securely.

First, create a Microsoft Entra ID application:

```
$  az ad app create
    --display-name "My Entra App"
```

After creating the application, note down the Application (client) ID and the Directory (tenant) ID. These will be needed to configure OAuth 2.0 in API Management:

```
$ az ad app credential reset
    --id <application-id>
    --append
    --create-cert
    --years 1
```

To ensure your application can request tokens for the API, configure the necessary API permissions in the Entra ID application:

```
$ az ad app permission add
    --id <app-id>
    --api <api-id>
    --api-permissions <permissions>

$ az ad app permission grant
    --id <app-id>
    --api <api-id>
    --scope Directory.Read.All
```

Once your Entra ID application is ready, configure it as an OAuth 2.0 authorization server in APIM. This setup allows APIM to validate incoming requests using tokens issued by Microsoft Entra ID.

To do this, go to your API Management instance in the Azure portal, as shown in Figure 8-4. From there, select "Developer portal" and then OAuth 2.0 + OpenID Connect, or you can directly search for OAuth 2.0 + OpenID Connect.

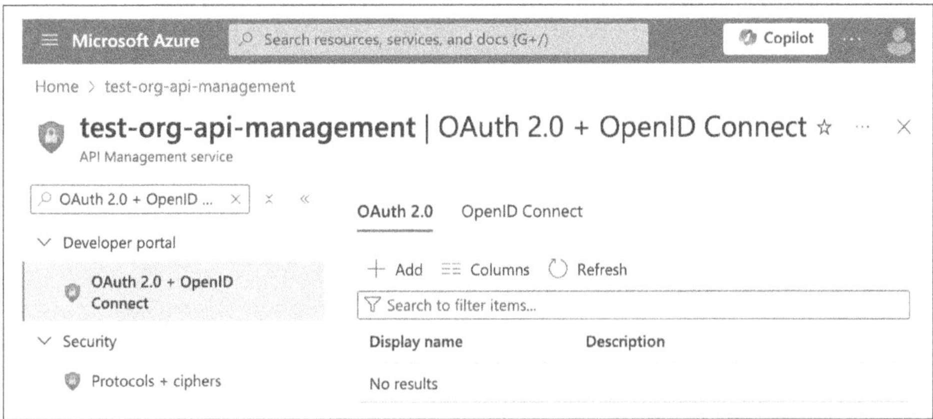

Figure 8-4. OAuth 2.0 + OpenID Connect in the Developer portal

Click + Add to create a new OAuth 2.0 server. In the form that appears, fill in all the necessary information. First, you can start by setting the Authorization endpoint URL to *https://login.microsoftonline.com/{tenant-id}/oauth2/authorize* and the Token endpoint URL to *https://login.microsoftonline.com/{tenant-id}/oauth2/token*. Next, provide your Entra ID Application ID as the client ID, and enter the client secret that you created earlier. You should have something similar to the screenshot shown in Figure 8-5.

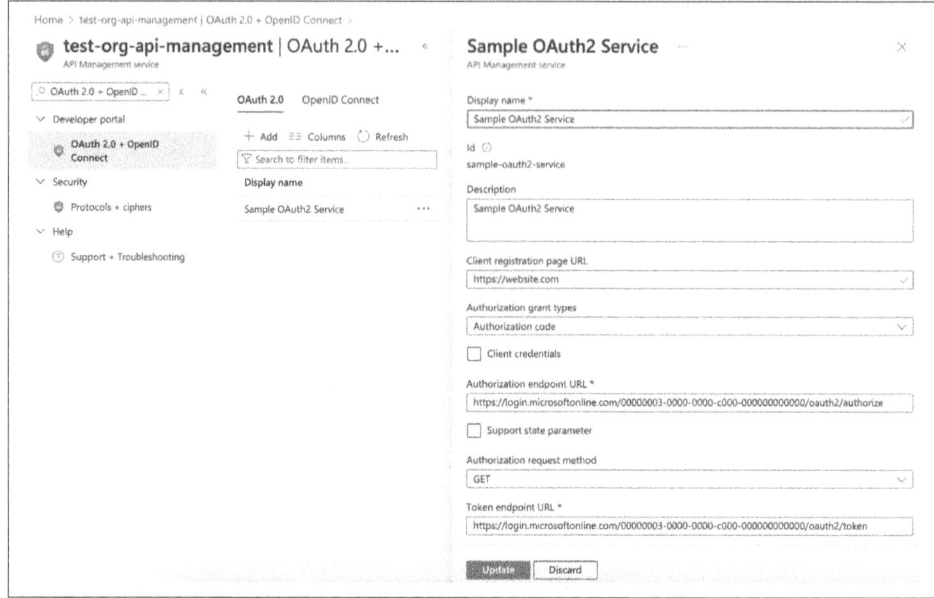

Figure 8-5. Creating an OAuth 2.0 Service

After configuring the OAuth 2.0 server, add a `validate-jwt` policy to your API to check the JSON web tokens:

```
resource symbolicname
'Microsoft.ApiManagement/service/apis/operations/policies@2023-09-01-preview' = {
  name: 'policy'
  parent: api
  properties: {
    format: 'xml'
    value: ```<inbound>
<validate-jwt header-name="Authorization" failed-validation-httpcode="401"
failed-validation-error-message="Unauthorized. Access token is missing or invalid.">
    <openid-config url="https://login.microsoftonline.com/{aad-tenant}/v2.0/.well-known/
        openid-configuration" />
    <audiences>
        <audience>{audience-value - (ex:api://guid)}</audience>
    </audiences>
    <issuers>
        <issuer>{issuer-value - (ex: https://sts.windows.net/{tenant id}/)}</issuer>
    </issuers>
    <required-claims>
        <claim name="aud">
            <value>{backend-app-client-id}</value>
        </claim>
    </required-claims>
</validate-jwt>
</inbound>
```

```
    ...
    }
}
```

The previous example policy should be in the `<inbound>` section of your APIM policy (as depicted). It checks if the *audience* claim in the access token from Microsoft Entra ID (provided in the Authorization header) matches the expected value. If the token is invalid, an error is returned. The `aad-tenant` in the `openid-config` URL should be the value of your Microsoft Entra tenant ID, which you can find in the Azure portal.

Once your setup is complete, you can ensure it works by requesting a token from Microsoft Entra ID and calling your API with the token. The `validate-jwt` policy will verify the token and grant access if valid.

Versioning APIs

API versioning is the practice of managing changes to your APIs while ensuring backward compatibility. Imagine building a library: you want to add new book editions without removing the old ones so readers can choose which editions to use. APIM provides three strategies for versioning—path-based, query string, and header-based—and each is suited to different scenarios. Let's explore how to implement them using Bicep.

Path-Based Versioning

Path-based versioning embeds the version directly into the API's URL path, such as */v1/products* or */v2/products*. This approach is intuitive because the version is visible to developers in the endpoint itself. For example, a weather API might use */v1/forecast* for its initial release and */v2/forecast* when adding humidity data.

In Bicep, you configure path-based versioning by including the version segment in the API's `path` property and setting the `versioningScheme` to `Segment`. Here's how to deploy a v2 API for a product catalog:

```
resource productsApiV2 'Microsoft.ApiManagement/service/apis@2021-08-01' = {
  name: 'products-api-v2'
  parent: apimService // Reference to api management instance
  properties: {
    displayName: 'Products API v2'
    path: 'v2/products'  // The version is part of the URL path
    protocols: [ 'https' ]
    serviceUrl: 'https://backend-v2.website.com'
    apiVersion: 'v2'
    apiVersionSet: {
      versioningScheme: "Segment"  // Enables path-based versioning
      displayName: 'Products Version Set'
    }
    isCurrent: true
  }
}
```

The path property explicitly includes the version (*v2/products*), and the versioningScheme is set to Segment to signal path-based routing. This method requires no additional parameters, making it simple to set up. One advantage is its transparency. Developers can see the version in the URL, which reduces confusion. However, it does clutter the URL structure, and changing versions requires updating all client code to reference the new path.

Query String Versioning

Query string versioning passes the version as a URL parameter, such as *products?api-version=2.0*. This keeps the base URL clean while allowing version selection through a key-value pair. For instance, an inventory API might use *inventory?version=2023* to differentiate between yearly updates.

To configure query string versioning in Bicep, set the versioningScheme to Query and define the parameter name using versionQueryName. Here is an example for a v2 orders API:

```
resource ordersApiV2 'Microsoft.ApiManagement/service/apis@2021-08-01' = {
  name: 'orders-api-2.0'
  parent: apimService // Reference to api management instance
  properties: {
    displayName: 'Orders API 2.0'
    path: 'orders'  // No version in the path
    protocols: [ 'https' ]
    serviceUrl: 'https://orders-latest.contoso.com'
    apiVersion: '2.0'
    apiVersionSet: {
      versioningScheme: "Query"       // Query parameter versioning
      versionQueryName: "api-version"  // Custom parameter name
      displayName: 'Orders Version Set'
    }
    isCurrent: true
  }
}
```

Here, the versionQueryName defines the query parameter (api-version), which clients append to requests (e.g., GET /orders?api-version=2.0). This method is flexible because clients can switch versions without altering the base URL. Although, query parameters can be overlooked in documentation, and caching systems sometimes ignore them, leading to inconsistent behavior.

Header-Based Versioning

Header-based versioning uses a custom HTTP header, such as X-API-Version: 2023-07, to specify the version. This approach is ideal for APIs requiring strict control, such as financial services, where URLs must remain static for compliance.

In Bicep, configure header-based versioning by setting `versioningScheme` to `Header` and specifying the header name with `versionHeaderName`. For example, a billing API might use headers to manage versions:

```
resource billingApi2023 'Microsoft.ApiManagement/service/apis@2021-08-01' = {
  name: 'billing-api-2023'
  parent: apimService // Reference to api management instance
  properties: {
    displayName: 'Billing API (2023)'
    path: 'billing'  // No version in the URL
    protocols: [ 'https' ]
    serviceUrl: 'https://billing-2023.contoso.com'
    apiVersion: '2023'
    apiVersionSet: {
      versioningScheme: "Header"        // Header-based versioning
      versionHeaderName: "X-API-Version"  // Custom header name
      displayName: 'Billing Version Set'
    }
    isCurrent: true
  }
}
```

Clients must include the `X-API-Version` header in their requests, which makes this method less visible but highly secure. While it keeps URLs clean, it requires clients to modify their HTTP headers, which can be challenging for tools like browsers or simple scripts. Table 8-1 shows the different available methods.

Table 8-1. Comparison table for API versioning strategies

Method	Parameter/header name	Version location	Client-friendly?
Path	N/A	URL path (e.g., */v2/*)	✅Easy
Query String	versionQueryName	URL parameter	✅Easy
Header	versionHeaderName	Custom HTTP header	❌Advanced

Version Sets: Organizing Your APIs

All versioning methods rely on version sets, containers that group related API versions. A version set defines the scheme (path, query, or header) and stores metadata like display names. For example, you might create a version set for a Weather API that includes v1 and v2.

To create a standalone version set in Bicep, use the `apiVersionSets` resource:

```
resource weatherVersionSet 'Microsoft.ApiManagement/service/apiVersionSets@2021-08-01' = {
  name: 'weather-version-set'
  parent: apimService
  properties: {
    displayName: 'Weather API Versions'
    versioningScheme: "Header"   // Applies to all APIs in this set
    versionHeaderName: "X-Weather-Version"
    description: 'Manages versions for the Weather API'
  }
}
```

Once created, reference the version set in your API definitions using its `id` property. This ensures consistency across versions and simplifies management. Here's the code demonstrating how to do this:

```
// Step 1: Create the version set separately
resource ordersVersionSet 'Microsoft.ApiManagement/service/apiVersionSets@2021-08-01' = {
  name: 'orders-version-set'
  parent: apimService
  properties: {
    displayName: 'Orders Version Set'
    versioningScheme: 'Header'
    versionHeaderName: 'X-API-Version'
    description: 'Centralized version configuration for Orders APIs'
  }
}

// Step 2: Reference the version set in your API
resource ordersApi2023 'Microsoft.ApiManagement/service/apis@2021-08-01' = {
  name: 'orders-api-2023'
  parent: apimService
  properties: {
    displayName: 'Orders API (2023)'
    path: 'orders'
    protocols: [ 'https' ]
    serviceUrl: 'https://orders-2023.contoso.com'
    apiVersion: '2023'  // Identifier for this specific version
    apiVersionSet: {
      id: ordersVersionSet.id  // Link to the pre-created version set
      // No need to repeat versioningScheme/versionHeaderName here
    }
    isCurrent: true
  }
}
```

The `id: ordersVersionSet.id` property establishes a critical link between the API and its centralized version set. When an API references a version set through this identifier, it adopts the versioning rules defined in that set. For instance, if the version set specifies header-based versioning with `X-API-Version`, every API linked to it will require that header. This linkage ensures uniformity—all APIs in the group follow the same versioning scheme, whether path, query, or header. Centralizing these rules in a version set eliminates repetitive configurations and reduces maintenance overhead. Updates to the versioning strategy, such as changing a header name or switching from query to path-based versioning, need only be applied once in the version set, propagating automatically to all connected APIs. This pattern works particularly well for large-scale APIs or teams managing multiple versions, where consistency and simplicity are critical.

Advanced Use Cases

APIM allows mixing versioning strategies. For example, you might use path-based versioning for public APIs and header-based for internal services. The `serviceUrl` property can route different versions to separate backends, `v1` might point to a legacy system, while `v2` connects to a modern microservice.

Deprecating old versions is straightforward. Set `isCurrent: false` to hide them from developer portals, and use Azure's policies to notify users. For instance, you could add a response header like `Deprecation: true` or return warnings in API responses.

Integrating with Other Azure Services

You can also integrate APIM with Azure services like Functions, Logic Apps, and App Service, among others, to create powerful and scalable API solutions. APIM works seamlessly with many Azure services to enhance API management, security, monitoring, and performance. Here's an overview of how APIM integrates with various Azure services to build robust enterprise solutions.

Azure API Center

Azure API Center helps you keep a complete inventory of all APIs in your organization, whether they are internal, external, or in different stages of their lifecycle. It allows for easy API discovery, reuse, and governance, making it simpler for teams to find and use APIs effectively. By integrating APIM with Azure API Center, you can manage your APIs more efficiently and ensure they meet your organization's standards.

Copilot in Azure

Copilot in Azure is an AI-powered assistant that helps you author APIM policies or understand existing ones. This integration is particularly useful for configuring policies such as rate limiting, authentication, and data transformation, as it provides intelligent suggestions and explanations. Copilot makes it easier to set up and manage complex API policies, reducing the time and expertise needed to configure your APIs correctly.

Azure Key Vault

Azure Key Vault is a service that stores and manages secrets, such as API keys, certificates, and passwords, securely. By integrating APIM with Azure Key Vault, you can securely manage sensitive information without exposing it in your code or API configurations. This integration ensures secrets are stored in a secure environment and can be accessed safely by your APIs at runtime.

Azure Monitor and Application Insights

Azure Monitor and Application Insights are essential for tracking the performance and health of your APIs. Azure Monitor provides logging, reporting, and alerting on management operations and API requests, while Application Insights offers live metrics, end-to-end tracing, and troubleshooting capabilities. By integrating APIM with these services, you can gain deep visibility into your API performance, quickly identify issues, and ensure your APIs are running smoothly.

Virtual Networks, Private Endpoints, Application Gateway, and Azure Front Door

For network-level security, APIM integrates with Azure Virtual Networks, Private Endpoints, Application Gateway, and Azure Front Door. These services help protect your APIs from unauthorized access, provide load balancing, and ensure high availability and performance. By using these integrations, you can secure your APIs within your private network or expose them securely to the internet while maintaining control over traffic flows.

Azure Defender for APIs and Azure DDoS Protection

Security is a top priority for any API solution. Azure Defender for APIs and Azure DDoS Protection provide runtime protection against malicious attacks. These integrations help detect and mitigate threats in real time, ensuring your APIs are protected against vulnerabilities and denial-of-service attacks. This level of security integration gives you peace of mind that your APIs are safeguarded against potential threats.

Microsoft Entra ID

Microsoft Entra ID is used for managing user identities and access. By integrating APIM with Microsoft Entra ID, you can secure your APIs with robust authentication and authorization mechanisms. This integration ensures only authorized users or applications can access your APIs, enhancing security and compliance with organizational policies.

Event Hubs

Azure Event Hubs is a big data streaming platform and event ingestion service. Integrating APIM with Azure Event Hubs allows you to stream events from your APIs, enabling real-time data processing and analytics. This is particularly useful for scenarios that require high-throughput data ingestion and real-time monitoring of API usage patterns.

Azure Compute Services

APIM also integrates with various Azure compute services commonly used for building and hosting APIs, such as Azure Functions, Logic Apps, Web Apps, and Service Fabric. These integrations enable you to expose your serverless functions, workflows, and web applications as managed APIs, complete with security, rate limiting, and monitoring features provided by APIM. Additionally, integrating with the Azure OpenAI service can bring advanced AI capabilities to your APIs, allowing for innovative solutions that leverage natural language processing, image recognition, and more.

Summary

This chapter covered API management in Azure. I presented the fundamentals of APIM, including how to create, secure, and monitor APIs effectively. Key components discussed were the API gateway, developer portal, and management plane, which help centralize control, enforce security measures, and streamline the API lifecycle. This chapter also detailed the process of setting up and publishing APIs, including creating instances, importing APIs from various formats, and defining endpoints and operations.

We explored securing APIs using OAuth 2.0 with Microsoft Entra ID, versioning APIs to manage changes, and packaging APIs into products for better access control. Additionally, the chapter highlighted the integration of APIM with other Azure services like Azure Functions, Azure Logic Apps, Azure Key Vault, and Azure Monitor, enhancing the overall API strategy.

In the next chapter, you will learn about event-driven architecture with Azure.

CHAPTER 9

Event-Driven Architecture with Azure

As we build out distributed systems, these different systems or nodes need ways to interact or send messages to one another. Some of these messages can be classified as events. Event-driven architectures are becoming increasingly popular because they allow systems to respond to events in real time, making them more efficient and reactive.

In this chapter, you will learn about event-driven architectures on Azure and how they can help you build modern, responsive applications. We'll explore the key components of event-driven systems, such as event producers, event consumers, and event brokers, and how Azure services like Event Grid, Event Hubs, and Service Bus can be used to implement these components. You'll see how these services allow you to handle various scenarios, from simple event notification systems to complex, high-throughput data streaming applications.

We'll also look at the benefits of using event-driven architectures on Azure, such as improved scalability, better resource utilization, and the ability to handle varying loads gracefully. By the end of this chapter, you'll have a solid understanding of how to design and implement event-driven systems using Azure's powerful tools and services, enabling you to build solutions that are both robust and responsive to changes in your environment.

Understanding Event-Driven Architecture

Placing an order, joining a group chat, or initiating a transaction are different types of *events* in distributed systems. Computers consistently communicating with one another creates a network of interactions where events play a crucial role. In distributed systems, an event is essentially a signal that something notable has occurred, triggering a response or a sequence of actions. Events are the lifeblood of these systems, enabling different components, often spread across multiple servers or even geographic locations, to interact and work together seamlessly without being tightly connected.

Events in distributed systems typically carry information about what happened, where it happened, and any relevant data that needs to be processed. They allow systems to be reactive, meaning they respond to changes and actions in real time. This event-driven approach helps keep the system components loosely coupled. Each part knows only enough to do its job based on the events it receives, without needing a full understanding of other parts of the system. This design leads to more flexible, scalable, and maintainable systems that can adapt quickly to new requirements or changes.

For example, in a distributed ecommerce platform, an event like `OrderPlaced` could trigger several actions across different services. When a customer places an order, this event is generated and sent to an event broker that routes it to various subscribers. The payment service picks up this event to handle the transaction, the inventory service updates stock levels, the shipping service begins processing the delivery, and a notification service sends a confirmation email to the customer. Each service acts independently but is coordinated through the events they consume, allowing the platform to function as a cohesive unit, as shown in Figure 9-1.

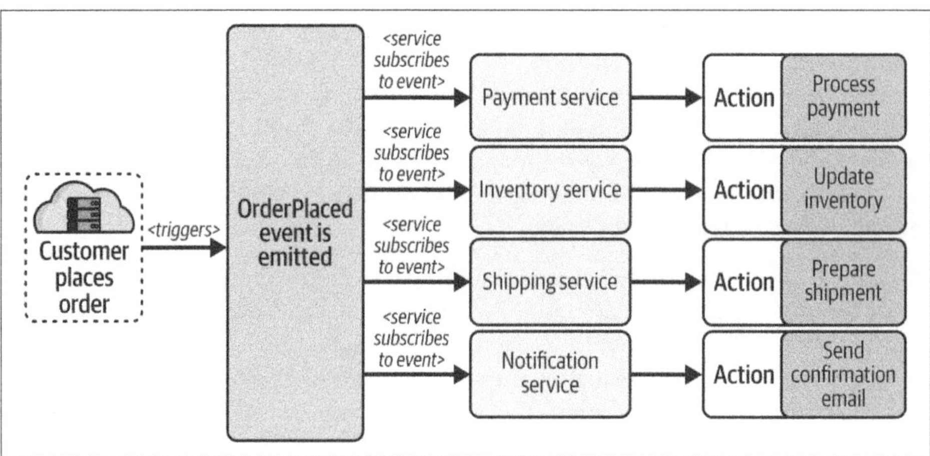

Figure 9-1. How events are triggered

This event-driven approach is powerful because it allows for adding new features or modifying existing ones without disrupting the whole system. For instance, if the ecommerce platform decides to add a new recommendation engine that suggests related products after a purchase, a new service can simply subscribe to the `OrderPlaced` event. This new service can start functioning immediately without any changes required in the existing payment, inventory, or notification services. This kind of flexibility and adaptability makes event-driven architectures particularly well suited for distributed systems.

Key Components of Event-Driven Systems

In event-driven architectures, different parts of a system react to events as they happen, allowing everything to work together in real time. To make this kind of system work, there are three main components: event producers, event consumers, and event brokers. Each of these plays an important role in how the system handles events and processes them smoothly.

Event producers

Event producers are the sources that generate events within an event-driven system. These producers can be various components, applications, or services that detect changes or perform actions significant enough to be broadcast as events. Producers don't need to know who will handle the events; they simply emit them when something notable occurs, such as a user action, a system state change, or data being updated. This decoupling allows event producers to function independently of the consumers that respond to these events, making the system more modular and scalable.

For example, in an online retail platform, an event producer could be the order management system. When a customer places an order, the order management system generates an `OrderPlaced` event. This event includes details like the order ID, customer information, and items purchased. The system simply emits the event without needing to be aware of which other parts of the application will use it. This way, the producer remains focused on its core functionality of processing orders, while other components like inventory, shipping, or notifications can subscribe to the event and perform their respective tasks.

Event consumers

Event consumers are the components that listen for and act on events emitted by producers. They subscribe to certain types of events that are relevant to their operations and perform actions in response, such as updating data, executing business logic, or triggering further processes. Consumers are designed to handle specific tasks based on the information contained in the events, allowing for specialized and distributed processing. This setup enables different parts of a system to react independently to the same event, thus enhancing flexibility and responsiveness.

In the same online retail platform example, event consumers could include services such as inventory management, payment processing, and the email notification system. When the `OrderPlaced` event is generated, each of these consumers reacts accordingly. The inventory management service updates stock levels, the payment processing service handles the transaction, and the notification system sends a confirmation email to the customer. Each consumer operates independently, reacting to the event in a way that aligns with its specific role within the broader system.

Event brokers

Event brokers act as intermediaries that manage the flow of events between producers and consumers. They are responsible for receiving events from producers and delivering them to the appropriate consumers based on subscriptions. Brokers decouple the producers and consumers further, allowing for scalability, reliability, and easier management of event distribution. They often include features like filtering, routing, buffering, and retry mechanisms to ensure that events are delivered correctly and efficiently.

A common example of an event broker in action is Azure Event Grid. In the online retail platform scenario, Azure Event Grid would receive the `OrderPlaced` event from the order management system and route it to the subscribed services, such as inventory, payment, and notification services.

Common Patterns in Event-Driven Architecture

In event-driven architecture, there are common patterns that help systems handle events effectively. These patterns describe how events are generated, processed, and managed across different parts of a system. Let's look at some patterns in event-driven architecture: publish/subscribe, event sourcing, and Command Query Responsibility Segregation (CQRS).

Publish/Subscribe

The publish/subscribe pattern, often called pub/sub, is one of the most common ways to handle events (Figure 9-2). In this pattern, event producers publish events to a central place, often called a message broker. Event consumers then subscribe to the types of events they are interested in. When an event is published, the broker sends it to all the subscribers that want that event. This allows multiple consumers to react to the same event independently, without knowing about each other.

For example, in an online store, when a customer places an order, an `OrderPlaced` event is published. Different services, like payment processing, inventory management, and shipping, can all subscribe to this event. When the event is published, each service does its part: the payment service processes the payment, the inventory service updates stock, and the shipping service prepares the package for delivery. This way, each service only does its job and doesn't need to worry about the other services. There are different services you can use to incorporate pub/sub into your architecture. In Azure, consider using Service Bus, Event Hubs or Event Grid. Other technologies that can be used for pub/sub messaging include Redis, RabbitMQ, and Apache Kafka.

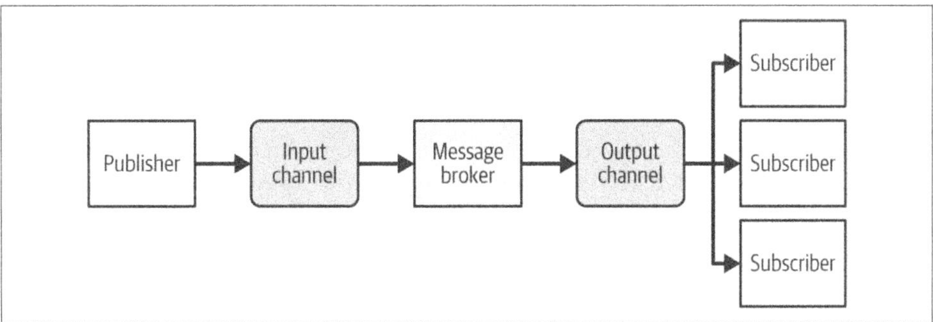

Figure 9-2. The pub/sub pattern

Event sourcing

Event sourcing is another pattern, where every change in the system is stored as a series of events (Figure 9-3). Instead of just storing the current state, like the final balance in a bank account, event sourcing keeps track of every deposit, withdrawal, and transfer as separate events. This means you can always see what happened in the past and even rebuild the state of the system by replaying these events from the beginning.

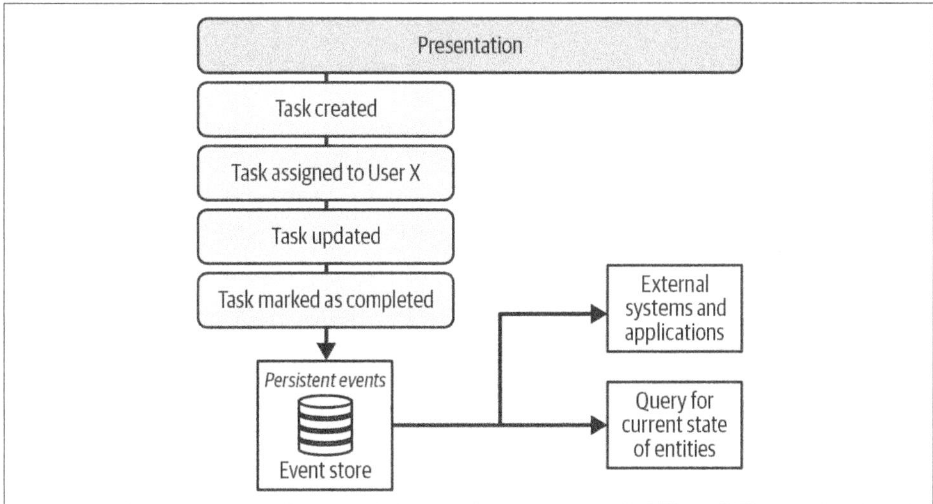

Figure 9-3. The event sourcing pattern

For example, imagine a project management application where tasks can be created, assigned, updated, or completed. Instead of just keeping the current state of each task, the system records each change as an event: *Task Created*, *Task Assigned to User X*, *Task Updated*, *Task Marked as Completed*. If there's ever a need to track what happened to a task, you can simply replay these events to see the full history of actions taken. This way, if a user needs to know why a task ended up with a certain status, they can trace back through all the recorded events to understand the journey of that task, making the system much more transparent and easy to troubleshoot.

Command Query Responsibility Segregation

CQRS separates the way a system handles commands (which change data) from how it handles queries (which read data). By splitting these two responsibilities, CQRS helps systems handle events more efficiently and allows them to scale better.

For instance, in an ecommerce site, commands like Place Order or Update Product would change the data and are handled differently from queries like Get Order Details or Search Products, which just read the data. With CQRS, commands can be processed by one part of the system, while queries are handled by another, allowing each to be optimized for its specific job. This separation makes the system more efficient, especially when dealing with lots of data or complex processing needs.

Azure Services for Event-Driven Architecture

Azure has several services that help you build event-driven systems, where parts of your application can respond to events as they happen. The key services that support this approach are Azure Event Grid, Azure Event Hubs, and Azure Service Bus.

Azure Event Grid

Azure Event Grid is a service that helps you route events from one place to another. It allows different parts of your system to communicate by sending and receiving events. Event Grid works like a traffic controller for events, making sure they get from event producers (where events start) to event consumers (where events are handled) efficiently.

Event Grid can be used to automate tasks based on events. For example, you can set it up so that when a new file is uploaded to Azure Blob Storage, an event triggers an Azure Function to process the file. It's also great for sending real-time notifications. For instance, when a new resource is created in Azure, Event Grid can send a notification to alert administrators or trigger other workflows.

Event Grid uses a publish/subscribe model. Event producers publish events to a topic, and event consumers subscribe to the events they care about. Event Grid then makes sure the events are delivered to the right consumers, like Azure Functions or Logic Apps. Here's how you can set it up in Bicep:

```
resource eventGridTopic 'Microsoft.EventGrid/topics@2025-02-15' = {
  name: <event-grid-topic-name>
  location: <location>
}
```

```
resource function 'Microsoft.Web/sites@2024-04-01' = {
  name: <function-name>
  location: <location>
  kind: 'functionapp'
  properties: {
    serverFarmId: <app-service-plan-id>
  }
}

resource eventSubscription 'Microsoft.EventGrid/eventSubscriptions@2025-02-15' = {
  name: <event-subscription-name>
  scope: <resource-scope>
  properties: {
    destination: {
      endpointType: 'AzureFunction'
      properties: {
        resourceId: function.id
      }
    }
    filter: {
      subjectBeginsWith: 'order/'
    }
  }
}
```

You can also do this in the Azure CLI and PowerShell. Here's how to do it in the Azure CLI:

```
# Create an Event Grid topic
$  az eventgrid topic create
    --resource-group <resource-group>
    --name <name>
    --location <location>

# Create a subscription to an Azure Function
$  az eventgrid event-subscription create
    --resource-group <resource-group>
    --name <event-subscription-name>
    --source-resource-id <event-grid-topic-id>
    --endpoint-type azurefunction
    --endpoint <azure-function-endpoint>
    --subject-begins-with "order/"
```

Here's how to do it in PowerShell:

```
# Create an Event Grid topic
New-AzEventGridTopic
    -ResourceGroupName <resource-group>
    -Name <name>
    -Location <location>

# Create a subscription to an Azure Function
New-AzEventGridSubscription
    -ResourceGroupName <resource-group>
    -Scope <event-grid-topic-id>
    -Destination <endpoint>
```

Azure Event Hubs

Azure Event Hubs is a big data streaming service that helps you collect and process large amounts of data in real time. It's designed for high-speed data streaming, making it great for scenarios where you need to handle a lot of events quickly, like telemetry data from devices or logs from applications. Event Hubs is perfect for collecting data from sensors, devices, or applications. For example, you can use it to gather telemetry data from IoT devices in real time. It also works well with analytics tools, allowing you to process data in real time. For example, it can feed data into Azure Stream Analytics or Apache Spark to create live dashboards. Here's how you can set it up with Bicep:

```
resource eventHubNamespace 'Microsoft.EventHub/namespaces@2021-11-01' = {
  name: <event-hub-namespace-name>
  location: <location>
  sku: {
    name: <sku-name>
    tier: <sku-tier>
  }
}

resource eventHub 'Microsoft.EventHub/namespaces/eventhubs@2021-11-01' = {
  parent: <event-hub-namespace-reference>
  name: <event-hub-name>
  properties: {
    partitionCount: <partition-count>
    messageRetentionInDays: <message-retention-in-days>
  }
}
```

In the preceding code snippet, we are creating an Event Hub namespace and then creating an event hub that references that namespace. An Event Hub namespace is like a container or a big folder that holds one or more event hubs, along with all the settings needed to manage them. Think of it as a way to organize and manage your event hubs in Azure.

The following command also shows how to create the event hub in the Azure CLI using the `az eventhubs` command:

```
# Create an Event Hub namespace
$  az eventhubs namespace create
    --resource-group <resource-group-name>
    --name <namespace-name>
    --location <location>
    --sku <sku>
    --enable-auto-inflate
    --maximum-throughput-units <max-units>

# Create an Event Hub
$  az eventhubs eventhub create
    --resource-group <resource-group-name>
    --name <eventhub-name>
    --namespace-name <namespace-name>
```

```
    --cleanup-policy <cleanup-policy>
    --partition-count <partition-count>
```

The following command also shows how to create the event hub in the PowerShell:

```
# Create an Event Hub namespace
New-AzEventHubNamespace
    -ResourceGroupName <resource-group-name>
    -Name <namespace-name>
    -SkuName <sku>
    -Location <location>
    -IdentityType <identity-type>

# Create an Event Hub
New-AzEventHub
    -Name <eventhub-name>
    -ResourceGroupName <resource-group-name>
    -NamespaceName <namespace-name>
    -RetentionTimeInHour <retention-time>
    -PartitionCount <partition-count>
    -CleanupPolicy <cleanup-policy>
```

Azure Event Hubs can be used for simple event streaming, and it's also powerful enough to handle complex scenarios that require high-throughput data processing. A feature of Event Hubs is its support for Apache Kafka, a popular open source platform for building real-time data pipelines and streaming applications. With Event Hubs, you can use Kafka without needing to set up or manage Kafka clusters yourself. This makes it much easier to get started with Kafka on Azure. You can enable Kafka support by setting the `kafkaEnabled` property to `true` when creating your Event Hub namespace. This feature allows you to use Kafka clients and applications directly with Azure Event Hubs, leveraging all the benefits of a managed service without the need to configure or maintain Kafka infrastructure.

Here's how you can enable Kafka support in Event Hubs using Bicep:

```
resource eventHubNamespace 'Microsoft.EventHub/namespaces@2021-11-01' = {
  name: '<namespace-name>'
  location: '<location>'
  sku: {
    name: '<sku>'
    tier: '<tier>'
  }
  properties: {
    kafkaEnabled: true
  }
}
```

Here's how you can enable Kafka support in Event Hubs using Azure CLI:

```
# Create an Event Hub namespace with Kafka support enabled
$  az eventhubs namespace create
    --resource-group <resource-group-name>
    --name <namespace-name>
    --location <location>
    --sku <sku>
    --enable-kafka true
```

Azure Service Bus

Azure Service Bus is a messaging service that helps different parts of an application communicate with each other reliably. It's great for sending messages between services, especially when those services don't need to respond instantly or are running on different schedules. Service Bus uses uses two main messaging patterns—queues and topics—to handle these messages, making it easier to build systems where components are loosely connected but can still work together smoothly.

Queues are like mailboxes where messages are stored until the receiving service is ready to pick them up. A queue ensures each message is processed by only one consumer, making it perfect for tasks like processing orders or sending out emails, as shown in Figure 9-4.

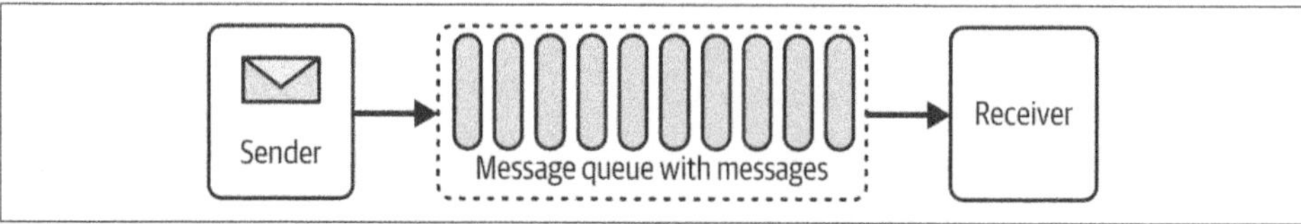

Figure 9-4. Azure Service Bus (queue)

Topics are used for publish/subscribe scenarios where a message needs to be sent to multiple consumers. When a message is sent to a topic, it can be delivered to multiple *subscriptions*, allowing different services to receive the same message and act on it independently.

Here's how you can set up a Service Bus namespace and a queue using Bicep:

```
resource serviceBusNamespace 'Microsoft.ServiceBus/namespaces@2021-06-01-preview' = {
  name: <service-bus-namespace>
  location: <location>
  sku: {
    name: <sku>
  }
}

resource serviceBusQueue 'Microsoft.ServiceBus/namespaces/queues@2021-06-01-preview' = {
  parent: <service-bus-namespace-reference>
  name: <service-bus-queue>
  properties: {
    enablePartitioning: true
  }
}
```

Here's how you can set up a Service Bus namespace and a queue using Azure CLI:

```
# Create a Service Bus namespace
$  az servicebus namespace create
    --resource-group <resource-group-name>
    --name <service-bus-namespace>
    --location <location>
    --sku <sku-name>
```

```
# Create a queue in the Service Bus namespace
$  az servicebus queue create
    --resource-group <resource-group-name>
    --namespace-name <service-bus-namespace>
    --name <service-bus-queue>
    --enable-partitioning true
```

Here's how you can set up a Service Bus namespace and a queue using PowerShell:

```
# Create a Service Bus namespace
New-AzServiceBusNamespace
    -ResourceGroupName <resource-group-name>
    -Name <service-bus-namespace>
    -SkuName <sku-name>
    -Location <location>

# Create a queue in the Service Bus namespace
New-AzServiceBusQueue
    -ResourceGroupName <resource-group-name>
    -NamespaceName <service-bus-namespace>
    -Name <service-bus-queue>
    -EnablePartitioning
```

You can also manage Service Bus resources using Azure CLI or PowerShell commands, such as updating or deleting queues and topics or checking the status of your resources.

Here are Azure CLI commands for updating and deleting the Service Bus queue:

```
# Update a queue (e.g., change max size)
$  az servicebus queue update
    --resource-group <resource-group-name>
    --namespace-name <service-bus-namespace>
    --name <service-bus-queue>
    --max-size 2048

# Delete a queue
$  az servicebus queue delete
    --resource-group <resource-group-name>
    --namespace-name <service-bus-namespace>
    --name <service-bus-queue>
```

Here are PowerShell commands for checking the status of a Service Bus namespace:

```
# Check the status of a Service Bus namespace
Get-AzServiceBusNamespace
    -ResourceGroupName <resource-group-name>
    -Name <service-bus-namespace>

# List all queues in a namespace
Get-AzServiceBusQueue
    -ResourceGroupName <resource-group-name>
    -NamespaceName <service-bus-namespace>
```

Designing Event-Driven Solutions on Azure

When designing event-driven applications on Azure, you will have to choose the right service for your use case and also integrate the service with your application. This involves understanding how the chosen service interacts with other Azure components and your application's architecture.

Choosing the Right Service for Your Use Case

When designing an event-driven system on Azure, the first step is to choose the right service based on your specific needs. Azure offers several services that support event-driven architectures, including Azure Event Grid, Azure Event Hubs, and Azure Service Bus. Each of these services has its strengths and is suited to different types of event handling.

Azure Event Grid is ideal for routing events from various sources to multiple destinations. It's best used for scenarios where you need to react to changes, such as file uploads, database changes, or resource modifications in Azure.

Azure Event Hubs, on the other hand, is designed for high-throughput data streaming. It's best suited for scenarios where you need to handle large volumes of data, such as telemetry from IoT devices, logs from applications, or streaming analytics. Event Hubs supports partitioning, which allows you to process data in parallel, making it highly scalable for real-time data processing.

Azure Service Bus is ideal for scenarios where you need guaranteed message delivery, such as order processing systems, booking systems, or financial transactions. Service Bus supports queues for point-to-point messaging and topics for publish/subscribe scenarios, so it has flexibility for different communication needs.

Choosing the right service depends on factors like the volume of events, the need for real-time processing, and the importance of message delivery guarantees. For instance, if you're building a solution that needs to process sensor data from thousands of devices in real time, Event Hubs would be the best fit. If you need to trigger workflows based on specific events, Event Grid would be more appropriate. And if you require reliable message delivery with complex routing logic, Service Bus would be the way to go.

Cost is another important factor to consider. Each of these services has different pricing models based on factors like the number of events processed, data retention, and throughput units. Analyzing your event volume and processing requirements can help you estimate costs and choose the most cost-effective service for your use case.

It's also important to consider integration with other Azure services. For example, if your solution relies heavily on serverless functions, Event Grid integrates seamlessly with Azure Functions. If you need advanced analytics, Event Hubs works well with

Azure Stream Analytics or Azure Data Explorer. Evaluating how each service fits within your overall architecture can guide your decision.

Designing Event Producers and Consumers

In an event-driven system, *event producers* are the components that generate events, while *event consumers* are the components that listen for and act on those events. Designing these producers and consumers effectively is key to building a responsive and scalable system.

Event producers can be anything that generates events, such as applications, devices, or cloud services. For example, an ecommerce application might generate events when an order is placed, a payment is processed, or inventory is updated. Producers should be designed to emit events consistently and reliably.

When designing event producers, it's important to minimize dependencies. Producers should not be tightly coupled with consumers, meaning they shouldn't need to know which consumers are handling the events. This decoupling is typically achieved by using an intermediary service like Azure Event Grid, Event Hubs, or Service Bus, which routes the events to the appropriate consumers.

For event consumers, the key is to design them to handle events efficiently and independently. Each consumer should be responsible for a specific task, such as processing an order, sending a notification, or updating a database. Consumers should be stateless where possible, meaning they don't rely on data from previous events, which makes them easier to scale and more resilient to failures.

Consumers need to be idempotent, which means they should handle events in a way that produces the same result even if the same event is processed multiple times. This is important because in distributed systems, events might be delivered more than once, and idempotent consumers prevent duplicate processing.

As referenced in "Azure Event Grid" on page 188, you can use Azure Event Grid as an intermediary for event-driven architecture. Here's a simple C# example showing how to publish an event to Event Grid as a producer and consume it using an Azure Function.

Event producer in C#:

```
using Azure.Messaging.EventGrid;
using System;
using System.Threading.Tasks;

class Program
{
    static async Task Main(string[] args)
    {
        string topicEndpoint = <your-event-grid-topic-endpoint>;
        string topicKey = "<your-topic-key>";
```

```
        var client = new EventGridPublisherClient(new Uri(topicEndpoint),
             new AzureKeyCredential(topicKey));

        var event = new EventGridEvent(
           subject: "OrderCreated",
           eventType: "Order.Created",
           dataVersion: "1.0",
           data: new { OrderId = 123, ProductName = "Laptop" }
        );

        await client.SendEventAsync(event);
        Console.WriteLine("Event published.");
    }
}
```

Event consumer in C#:

```
using Microsoft.Azure.WebJobs;
using Microsoft.Extensions.Logging;

public static class EventGridConsumer
{
   [Function(nameof(EventGridConsumer))]
    public static void Run([EventGridTrigger] JObject eventGridEvent,
    FunctionContext context)
    {
        var logger = context.GetLogger(nameof(EventGridConsumer));
        logger.LogInformation($"Event received: {eventGridEvent}");
        // Process the event, e.g., save to database, send notification, etc.
    }
}
```

Consumers should also handle errors gracefully. They should include retry logic, log errors for monitoring, and move failed events to a dead-letter queue if necessary. This ensures that errors don't disrupt the entire event processing pipeline.

Common Challenges and How to Overcome Them

As you are building your event-driven application, it's important to be proactive and prepare for failures or challenges that may come up in your system. Event-driven architectures can be powerful and flexible, but they also introduce complexities you need to handle carefully to ensure your application runs smoothly. In this section, we'll cover common challenges such as managing event storming and overloading, ensuring message delivery and handling duplicates, and debugging and troubleshooting event-driven systems. For each challenge, we'll discuss practical ways to overcome these issues.

Managing Event Storming and Overloading

Event storming occurs when a large number of events are generated in a short period, often overwhelming the system. This can lead to performance degradation, slow processing times, or even failures if the system can't keep up with the incoming load. Event storming is common in scenarios where there is a sudden spike in user activity.

To manage event storming and overloading, you need to implement strategies that help control the flow of events and ensure your system can handle bursts of activity without crashing. Here are some approaches to consider:

Rate limiting
: Rate limiting controls the number of events that are processed over a specific period. This can prevent your system from being overwhelmed by too many events at once. Azure Event Grid, for example, allows you to set up rate limits on event subscriptions to control the flow of events to consumers.

Throttling
: Throttling is another technique that temporarily slows down the processing rate when the system is under heavy load. Azure Functions automatically implements throttling based on the available resources, which helps manage overloads without requiring manual intervention.

Event batching
: Instead of processing events one by one, you can batch multiple events together and process them as a group. This reduces the overhead of processing each event individually and can significantly improve throughput. For example, Azure Event Hubs allows you to send events in batches, which is more efficient for high-throughput scenarios.

Scaling out consumers
: To handle increased loads, you can scale out your event consumers by adding more instances. Doing this ensures that more events can be processed in parallel because there are more consumers to process them, which helps with reducing the risk of backlog.

Circuit breaker pattern
: Implementing a circuit breaker pattern can help manage failures better. If a consumer is overwhelmed and starts failing, the circuit breaker temporarily stops sending events to that consumer until it recovers, preventing further overload and allowing the system to stabilize.

The right mix of these strategies creates an event processing pipeline that degrades gracefully under pressure rather than failing catastrophically.

Ensuring Message Delivery and Handling Duplicates

Ensuring messages are delivered reliably and handling duplicates are critical to maintaining data consistency and system integrity. Messages can sometimes be lost or delivered multiple times due to network issues, service interruptions, or retries.

Without proper handling, these issues can lead to data corruption, inconsistent states, or unexpected behaviors. Here are some strategies you can use:

Idempotent consumers
: One of the best ways to handle duplicate messages is to design idempotent consumers. An idempotent consumer processes the same message multiple times without changing the outcome. This means that even if a message is delivered more than once, the result remains consistent. For example, when updating a database, you can check if the operation has already been performed using unique identifiers and skip it if it has.

Retry policies
: Implementing retry policies for transient errors ensures your system makes additional attempts to process messages when temporary issues occur, like network interruptions or service unavailability. Azure SDKs typically provide configurable retry policies that allow you to set the number of retries, delay intervals, and error conditions.

Error handling and dead-letter queues
: Proper error handling is essential for managing messages that cannot be processed successfully. By configuring dead-letter queues, you can route problematic messages to a separate queue for further analysis. This prevents them from blocking the processing of other messages and allows you to handle failures more gracefully.

Testing for reliability
: Implementing test scenarios that simulate message loss or duplication can help you verify your system handles these conditions correctly. You can create automated tests that mimic real-world scenarios, such as network failures or service outages, to validate your system's resilience.

Message delivery problems become manageable engineering challenges when your system is designed with these reliability patterns from the start.

Debugging and Troubleshooting Event-Driven Systems

Debugging and troubleshooting event-driven systems can be more challenging compared to traditional architectures because of the asynchronous nature of events and the distributed components involved. Issues such as event delivery failures, processing errors, and unexpected behaviors need careful investigation to ensure the system runs reliably. Here are some strategies that you can use:

Centralized logging
: One of the most effective ways to debug event-driven systems is by implementing centralized logging. Tools like Azure Monitor and Application Insights can col-

lect logs from all of your event producers, consumers, and intermediary services, providing a complete view of the event flow. In Chapter 10, we will cover logging on Azure and you'll see how to do this. Centralized logging allows you to track the path of events, identify where failures occur, and analyze the root cause.

Correlation IDs
: To trace events across multiple services, use correlation IDs (also known as correlation vectors), as shown in Figure 9-5. A correlation ID is a unique identifier assigned to each event or transaction, allowing you to follow the event through various components of your system. By including the correlation ID in logs and error messages, you can easily trace the flow of an event from start to finish, making debugging much more manageable.

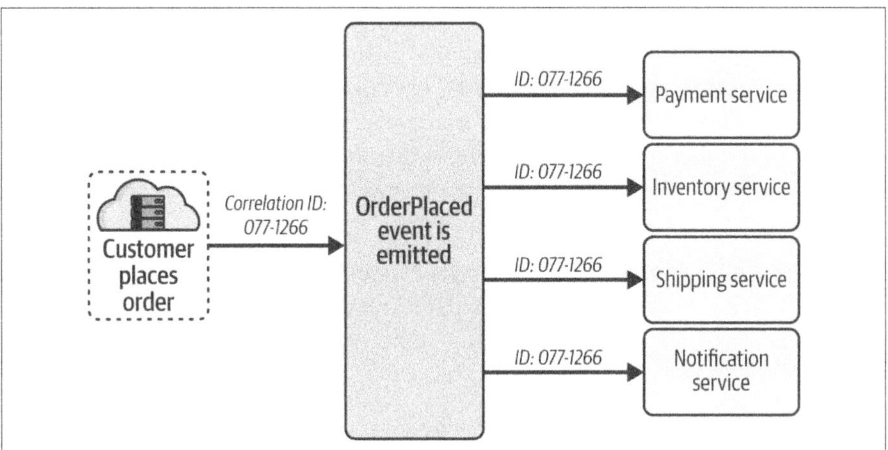

Figure 9-5. Correlation ID across services

Dead-letter queues
: As mentioned earlier, dead-letter queues store events that couldn't be processed successfully. Reviewing the contents of dead-letter queues can provide insights into what went wrong, such as malformed data or processing logic errors. Azure Service Bus and Event Grid both support dead-letter queues, making it easier to diagnose and resolve issues.

With comprehensive logging and tracing in place, troubleshooting becomes a matter of following the data rather than making educated guesses.

Other Event-Enabled Services in Azure

Beyond Azure Event Grid, Event Hubs, and Service Bus, Azure provides a range of other tools that can be used in event-driven scenarios. These services allow you to respond to events, process data in real time, and build applications that react to changes as they happen. Let's explore Azure Notification Hubs, Azure Cosmos DB change feed, Azure Stream Analytics, and Azure Data Factory. We'll go through what each service does, how it can be used, and provide examples and code snippets to help you get started.

Azure Notification Hubs

Azure Notification Hubs is a service that enables you to send push notifications to mobile devices like smartphones and tablets. It's useful for scenarios where you need to engage users with real-time updates, alerts, or messages directly on their devices. Notification Hubs can be used with event-driven architectures by triggering notifications in response to specific events, such as a new message in a chat app, an upcoming appointment, or a weather alert.

Notification Hubs supports major mobile platforms, including iOS, Android, and Windows, and integrates with various services like Event Grid, allowing you to set up workflows that trigger notifications based on events from different sources. For example, you can use Notification Hubs to send a push notification when a new file is uploaded to Azure Blob Storage or when a certain condition is met in your application.

A typical use case for Notification Hubs is a news app that sends breaking news alerts to users. When a news story is published, the backend system triggers an event, which is then handled by Azure Functions or Logic Apps to send a push notification via Notification Hubs.

To set up Azure Notification Hubs, you'll need to create a notification hub and configure it with the credentials of your chosen platform (e.g., Apple Push Notification service or Google Firebase). Here's how:

```
# Create a Notification Hub namespace
$  az notification-hub namespace create
    --resource-group <resource-group-name>
    --name <namespace>
    --location <location>

# Create a Notification Hub
az notification-hub create
    --resource-group <resource-group-name>
    --namespace-name <namespace-name>
    --name <notification-hub-name>
```

To send notifications, Notification Hubs require platform-specific credentials, such as API keys or certificates, to authenticate and authorize the sending of messages. We'll cover how to add credentials for Google Cloud Messaging (GCM), which is now Firebase Cloud Messaging (FCM). However, you can also manage credentials for other platforms like Amazon Device Messaging (ADM), Apple Push Notification service

(APNs), Baidu for Android in China, Microsoft Push Notification Service (MPNS) for Windows Phone, and Windows Notification Service (WNS).

To send notifications to Android devices using GCM/FCM, you'll need to provide an API key from Firebase. Here's how to add the GCM/FCM API key using Azure CLI:

```
$  az notification-hub credential gcm update
      --resource-group <resource-group-name>
      --namespace-name <namespace-name>
      --notification-hub-name <notification-hub-name>
      --google-api-key <gcm-fcm-api-key>
```

Here, `--google-api-key` is the API key obtained from the Firebase console.

After setting up the credentials for GCM/FCM with your notification hub, you can proceed to send a test notification to ensure everything is configured correctly. Sending a test notification allows you to verify that the platform-specific credentials are working and your notification setup is able to reach the intended devices.

You can use the `az notification-hub test-send` command in Azure CLI to send a test notification from your notification hub. This command allows you to send a sample payload to verify the notification delivery:

```
$ az notification-hub test-send
     --resource-group <resource-group-name>
     --namespace-name <namespace-name>
     --notification-hub-name <notification-hub-name>
     --notification-format gcm
     --message "test notification"
```

You can also programmatically send a notification using Azure Notification Hubs. To do this, you typically use the Notification Hubs SDK available for various programming languages like .NET, Java, Python, and others. I'll provide an example using C# with the .NET SDK, which is a common approach for sending notifications programmatically. This example will demonstrate how to send a notification to Android devices using FCM.

```
class Program
{
    // Connection string from your Notification Hub access policies (with Send permissions)
    private const string ConnectionString = "<Your_Notification_Hub_Connection_String>";
    // The name of your Notification Hub
    private const string HubPath = "<Your_Notification_Hub_Path>";

    static async Task Main(string[] args)
    {
        // Create a NotificationHubClient instance
        var hubClient =
          NotificationHubClient.CreateClientFromConnectionString(ConnectionString, HubPath);

        // Create the FCM notification payload
        var fcmPayload = "{ \"data\" : {\"message\":\"Hello from Azure Notification
              Hubs!\"}}";

        try
```

```
        {
            // Send the notification to all registered devices
            var result = await hubClient.SendFcmNativeNotificationAsync(fcmPayload);
            Console.WriteLine($"Notification sent successfully: {result.State}");
        }
        catch (Exception ex)
        {
            Console.WriteLine($"Error sending notification: {ex.Message}");
        }
    }
}
```

To send notifications to specific devices, you can use tags. They allow you to categorize devices and send targeted notifications:

```
// Send a notification to devices with a specific tag
await hubClient.SendFcmNativeNotificationAsync(fcmPayload, "myTag");
```

Azure Cosmos DB Change Feed

One powerful feature of Cosmos DB (discussed in more detail in Chapter 5) is the change feed, which provides a way to track changes (inserts and updates) to items in a container in real time. This makes it a great fit for event-driven scenarios where you need to respond to data changes as they happen.

The change feed works by capturing every change made to the data in a Cosmos DB container. Applications can then consume these changes to trigger actions like updating other systems, processing data in real time, or synchronizing data across multiple services. For example, you could use the change feed to automatically update a search index whenever new documents are added to your database.

Another use case is a personalized music app that curates playlists based on user preferences and current trends. Imagine a feature where users can subscribe to playlists themed around their favorite genres, moods, or even specific artists. As new songs that match these criteria are added to the database, the change feed triggers updates to automatically refresh the playlists in real time. This way, users get the latest hits and trending songs in their curated lists without having to manually update anything. For example, if a new Afrobeats song is added to the database, it instantly appears in the user's *Top Afrobeats* playlist, keeping their music experience fresh and personalized.

To use the change feed, you need to set up a processor that listens to the feed and handles the changes. This can be done using Azure Functions, Azure Stream Analytics, or custom code. For example, you can use an Azure Function with a Cosmos DB trigger to automatically handle new or updated items in a container:

```
public static class UpdatePlaylistFunction
{
    [FunctionName("UpdatePlaylistFunction")]
    public static void Run(
        [CosmosDBTrigger(
```

```
            databaseName: "MusicDatabase",
            collectionName: "Songs",
            ConnectionStringSetting = "<cosmosdb-connection-string>",
            LeaseCollectionName = "leases",
            CreateLeaseCollectionIfNotExists = true)] IReadOnlyList<Document> input,
        ILogger log)
    {
        if (input != null && input.Count > 0)
        {
            log.LogInformation($"New songs added: {input.Count}");
            foreach (var song in input)
            {
                UpdatePlaylistsWithNewSong(song);
            }
        }
    }
}
```

The previous code defines an Azure Function named `UpdatePlaylistFunction` that triggers whenever there are changes (inserts or updates) in the `Songs` container of the `MusicDatabase` Cosmos DB. The function uses a `[CosmosDBTrigger]` attribute to automatically monitor the specified database and container, using a lease collection named `leases` to keep track of the processed changes. When new songs are detected, the function calls an arbitrary method `UpdatePlaylistsWithNewSong` to update relevant playlists, ensuring that new songs are appropriately added to users' playlists based on their preferences or other criteria. This approach allows the application to respond to data changes in real time, keeping playlists current with the latest music additions.

You can configure the function app with the appropriate connection strings and set up the trigger to listen to the specific container and partition you are interested in. By doing so, you can build an efficient and reactive system that responds immediately to data changes in Cosmos DB.

Azure Stream Analytics

Azure Stream Analytics is a real-time analytics service designed to process and analyze large volumes of data streams from sources like Azure Event Hubs, Azure IoT Hub, and Azure Blob Storage. It's a powerful tool for event-driven architectures that need to perform real-time data processing, such as filtering, aggregating, or transforming incoming data on the fly.

With Azure Stream Analytics, you can define queries using a SQL-like language to analyze data as it arrives and output the results to various destinations such as Azure SQL Database, Azure Blob Storage, Power BI, or other data stores. This makes it easy to create real-time dashboards, detect patterns, or trigger alerts based on the data.

A typical use case for Azure Stream Analytics is monitoring sensor data from IoT devices. For example, you might have an array of temperature sensors sending data to

Azure Event Hubs. Stream Analytics can process this data in real time, checking for temperature anomalies and sending alerts if readings go outside of safe ranges.

Stream Analytics supports complex event processing (CEP) capabilities, which allow you to identify patterns across multiple events, such as detecting a sequence of events that occur within a specific time window. This is useful in scenarios like fraud detection, where you might want to detect unusual behavior based on a series of actions.

To set up Azure Stream Analytics, you'll need to define inputs (e.g., Event Hubs or IoT Hub), outputs (e.g., Azure SQL Database or Blob Storage), and the query that specifies how to process the data. Stream Analytics jobs can be managed through the Azure portal, Azure CLI, or programmatically via the SDK.

Here's sample code to create a Stream Analytics job using Azure CLI:

```
# Create a Stream Analytics job
$  az stream-analytics job create
    --resource-group <resource-group-name>
    --job-name  <job-name>
    --location <location>
    --output-error-policy Drop

# Add a stream blob input with CSV serialization
$  az stream-analytics input create
    --properties "{\"type\":\"Stream\",\"datasource\":{\"type\":\"Microsoft.Storage/Blob\",
    \"properties\":{\"container\":\"state\",\"dateFormat\":\"yyyy/MM/dd\",\"pathPattern\":
    \"{date}/{time}\",\"sourcePartitionCount\":16,\"storageAccounts\":[{\"accountKey\":
    \"someAccountKey==\",\"accountName\":\"someAccountName\"}],\"timeFormat\":\"HH\"}},
    \"serialization\":{\"type\":\"Csv\",\"properties\":{\"encoding\":\"UTF8\",
    \"fieldDelimiter\":\",\"}}}"
    --input-name <input-name>
    --job-name <job-name>
    --resource-group <resource-group-name>

# Add a DocumentDB output
$  az stream-analytics output create
    --job-name <job-name>
    --datasource "{\"type\":\"Microsoft.Storage/DocumentDB\",\"properties\":
    {\"accountId\":\"someAccountId\",\"accountKey\":\"accountKey==\"
    ,\"collectionNamePattern\":\"collection\",\"database\":\"db01\",
    \"documentId\":\"documentId\",\"partitionKey\":\"key\"}}"
    --output-name <output-name>
    --resource-group <resource-group-name>

# Define a query for the job
az stream-analytics transformation create
    --resource-group MyResourceGroup
    --job-name MyStreamAnalyticsJob
    --name MyTransformation
    --streaming-units 3
    --saql "SELECT * FROM MyInput WHERE Temperature > 30"
```

This section demonstrated how Azure Stream Analytics can be a powerful tool for processing and analyzing real-time data streams in event-driven architectures. The service allows you to define SQL-like queries to filter, aggregate, and transform data on the fly, making it ideal for use cases like monitoring sensor data, detecting patterns, and triggering actions based on real-time inputs.

The provided code snippet illustrates how to set up a Stream Analytics job using Azure CLI, defining inputs from sources like Azure Blob Storage, configuring outputs to destinations such as Azure Cosmos DB (formerly DocumentDB), and specifying the query that processes the data. In the example, a Stream Analytics job is created, an input stream is defined with Comma-Separated Values (CSV) serialization, an output is configured to Azure Cosmos DB, and a query is set up to filter data where the temperature exceeds a certain threshold.

Azure Data Factory

Azure Data Factory (ADF) is a cloud-based data integration service that allows you to create, schedule, and orchestrate data workflows. It helps you move data between different data stores, process and transform data, and load it into target destinations. ADF is highly flexible and can connect to a wide range of data sources, including cloud services, on-premises databases, and file systems. It's ideal for building complex data pipelines that automate the movement and transformation of data across various environments.

In event-driven scenarios, ADF can be triggered by specific events, such as the arrival of new data, changes in data sources, or scheduled times. This makes it a valuable tool for automating data workflows that need to respond in real time to changes. For example, you can set up a pipeline that starts processing data as soon as a new file is uploaded to Azure Blob Storage, transforming the data and loading it into a data warehouse for analysis.

A common use case for ADF is in ETL (extract, transform, load) processes, where data is extracted from one or more sources, transformed according to business rules, and loaded into a target system. With event triggers, ADF can start ETL jobs automatically whenever new data is available, reducing the need for manual intervention and speeding up the data processing pipeline.

ADF uses pipelines to define workflows. A pipeline is a series of activities, each of which performs a specific task, like copying data, running a stored procedure, or calling a web service. Pipelines can include conditional logic, allowing you to control the flow of data processing based on certain conditions. For example, you can set up a pipeline that checks the quality of incoming data and only proceeds if the data meets certain standards.

Let's set up a pipeline that triggers when a new file is uploaded to Azure Blob Storage. The pipeline will copy the file to another storage location and then log the event. First, you'll need to create a pipeline that copies data from one location to another. In the ADF UI, you can use the Copy Data activity to define the source and destination of your data.

```
$ az datafactory pipeline create
    --factory-name <factory-name>
    --pipeline <copy-data-json-template>
    --name <name>
    --resource-group <resource-group-name>
```

Now, create an event trigger that starts the pipeline when a new file is uploaded to a specific container in Azure Blob Storage. Here's an example of how you can set up an event trigger using Azure CLI:

```
$ az datafactory trigger create
    --factory-name <factory-name>
    --resource-group <resource-group-name>
    --properties <event-trigger-json>
    --name <name>
```

Summary

This chapter covered event-driven architectures with Azure. We explored how event-driven systems enable distributed components to interact in real time by responding to events such as user actions or system changes. Key components of these architectures include event producers, event consumers, and event brokers, which together allow for loosely coupled, scalable, and responsive systems. You learned how Azure services like Event Grid, Event Hubs, and Service Bus facilitate the implementation of event-driven architectures, each suited for different types of event handling and processing requirements.

We discussed common patterns like publish/subscribe, event sourcing, and CQRS that help manage events effectively within these systems. Additionally, you learned about Azure tools like Stream Analytics for processing data streams, Notification Hubs for push notifications, and Cosmos DB's change feed for tracking data changes, providing practical examples and code snippets for implementing these solutions.

We also covered the strategies for overcoming common challenges in event-driven systems, such as managing event storming, ensuring reliable message delivery, and debugging asynchronous workflows. In the next chapter, you will learn about monitoring and observability on Azure.

CHAPTER 10

Monitoring and Observability on Azure

After building your application and deploying it to Azure, the work doesn't stop there. You want to constantly make sure your application is reliable, available, and performing well for your users. Monitoring and observability are essential to keep an eye on your application's health, catch problems early, and understand how your system behaves. Without proper monitoring, you could miss important issues like slow performance or even outages that impact your users.

In this chapter, we will go over the key Azure services that help you monitor and manage your applications effectively. We'll start with Azure Monitor, which provides a unified platform for collecting and analyzing data from your applications and resources. You'll learn about Azure Application Insights, a tool that helps you track how your application performs, find errors, and get insights into user activities.

We'll also look at Azure Log Analytics, which lets you gather and search through log data from different sources, using powerful queries to find patterns and solve problems. We'll explore Azure Data Explorer, which is great for analyzing large amounts of data in real time, making it useful for tracking system performance and diagnosing issues.

Additionally, we'll cover Azure Service Health and Azure Resource Health, which give you information about the health of Azure services and your resources, helping you stay ahead of potential problems. We'll discuss how Azure Automation can help you set up automatic actions and alerts so you're always informed when something needs your attention.

We'll also talk about Azure Network Watcher, which helps you monitor and troubleshoot network issues, and Azure Cost Management and Billing, which lets you keep track of your cloud spending and set budgets to avoid unexpected costs. Finally, we'll share best practices for building a strong monitoring strategy, picking the right tools, and continuously improving your approach to observability on Azure.

By the end of this chapter, you'll have a clear understanding of how to set up effective monitoring and observability for your Azure applications, making sure they run smoothly, meet user needs, and are ready to handle any challenges that come your way.

Overview of Monitoring and Observability

Imagine Instagram being down on Christmas Day so you can't post your favorite family pajama photo. Frustrating, right? This is why monitoring and observability are important. They are like the eyes and ears of any application, especially in cloud environments like Azure.

Monitoring is all about collecting data from your application and infrastructure to track how things are running. This includes tracking performance metrics, checking for errors, and watching resource usage. Monitoring tools alert you when something goes wrong, like when a server goes down or when the app starts running slow, so you can fix issues before they impact your users.

Observability takes things a step further. It's not just about seeing what's wrong, but understanding why it happened. It involves collecting and analyzing detailed data from your system, such as logs, metrics, and traces, to get a complete picture of your application's behavior. This helps you find the root cause of issues faster and even predict potential problems before they occur.

In cloud environments, monitoring is important because your applications run on shared resources that can change dynamically. Servers may be scaled up or down, moved, or even temporarily go offline. Without monitoring, you might not know when your application is struggling due to resource limits, unexpected traffic spikes, or other issues.

Monitoring helps you keep your cloud applications reliable and available. It allows you to detect performance bottlenecks, manage resource costs, and ensure that your app meets user expectations. With proper monitoring, you can set up automatic alerts and even automated actions, like scaling out additional servers when traffic increases, to maintain seamless operations.

In monitoring and observability, it's important to know about metrics, logs, traces, alerts, and dashboards:

Metrics
: Metrics are measurements that track the performance and health of your system. For example, CPU usage, memory consumption, response time, and request rates

are all metrics. Metrics are usually numerical data that can be collected in real time, helping you quickly spot trends or abnormal behavior.

Logs
: Logs are detailed records of events that occur in your application. They can include error messages, system events, user actions, or any custom information developers choose to include. This flexibility makes logs essential for troubleshooting, as they can be tailored to capture the specific context needed to trace issues back to their source.

Traces
: Traces follow the flow of a request as it moves through different parts of your application. They are particularly useful in microservices architectures where a single request might touch multiple services. Traces help you see the entire journey of a request, from start to finish, and identify where delays or errors are occurring.

Alerts
: Alerts notify you when something goes wrong. You can set up alerts to trigger when metrics exceed certain thresholds, like when CPU usage is too high, or when specific errors appear in logs. Alerts are essential for catching issues early and ensuring you can respond quickly to fix problems.

Dashboards
: Dashboards provide a visual overview of your monitoring data. They display key metrics, logs, and traces in a way that's easy to understand, using charts, graphs, and other visuals. Dashboards help you get a quick snapshot of your system's health and performance, making it easier to monitor everything at a glance.

Collectively, each of these features provide insight into the health and performance of your application.

Azure Monitor

Azure Monitor is a monitoring service that provides full-stack observability across your applications, infrastructure, and network. It helps you maximize the performance and availability of your applications by collecting, analyzing, and acting on telemetry data from Azure and on-premises resources.

Azure Monitor is a tool that helps you track and optimize the performance of your Azure resources. It collects data from various sources like applications, VMs, and network resources to provide insights into their health and performance. This data includes metrics and logs, which are stored in a time-series database for analysis.

Querying Metrics with Azure Monitor

In Azure Monitor, metrics are simply numbers that show how well a resource is performing or what state it's in over time. These numbers help you understand how your applications and infrastructure are behaving, letting you keep an eye on important performance indicators, recognize patterns, and catch any unusual activity. In this section, we'll walk through how to pull these metrics and use them to make informed decisions about your operations.

It's essential to understand the following key elements in Azure Monitor's metrics data model:

Time
: This is the exact timestamp indicating when the metric value was recorded.

Resource
: This refers to the specific resource associated with that metric.

Namespace
: Think of this as a grouping label that organizes related metrics together, making it easier to filter and manage your data.

Metric name
: This is the identifier for the measurement you're looking at—examples might include *Percentage CPU* or *Network In*.

Metric value
: This is the actual number that tells you the performance or state of the resource at the time it was recorded.

Dimensions (optional)
: These are extra details that can further break down the metric, allowing you to analyze the data more deeply. Keep in mind that custom metrics can have up to 10 dimensions.

One of the simplest ways to fetch metrics through code is by using the Azure CLI with the `az monitor metrics` command. This command lets you pull performance data for your Azure resources right from the command line, making it easy to automate tasks and integrate with other monitoring tools.

The basic syntax to query metrics looks like this:

```
$ az monitor metrics list
    --resource <resource-id>
    --metric <metric-name>
    --dimension <dimension>
```

Let's look at an example. To monitor the CPU usage of a VM, start by identifying the resource ID for your VM. Then, run the following command to retrieve the CPU usage metric:

```
$   az monitor metrics list
      --resource "/subscriptions/<id>/…/virtualMachines/<vm-name>"
      --metric "Percentage CPU"
      --interval PT1M
      --aggregation Average
      --start-time "2025-02-04T14:00:00Z"
      --end-time "2025-02-04T15:00:00Z"
```

In the preceding code snippet, the command retrieves the CPU usage metric for a VM by specifying its resource ID (which you should replace with your actual resource ID) and the `Percentage CPU` metric. The metric is sampled every minute using the interval parameter set to `PT1M`, with the average calculated for each interval. Instead of using a time span, the command specifies the time range by setting the `--start-time` and `--end-time` parameters, ensuring you capture data for a one-hour period.

Let's look at a more complicated example. Imagine you're trying to understand how a VM's CPU is behaving over time, not only by reviewing its average, minimum, and maximum values, but also by filtering the data based on a particular dimension. In this case, let's assume the metric supports a custom dimension (such as a tag or a category) that segments the CPU usage data. This combined query allows you to gain a comprehensive view of performance trends over time with additional granularity.

Here's an example of how you might do this using the Azure CLI:

```
$   az monitor metrics list
     --resource "/subscriptions/<id>/…/virtualMachines/<vm-name>"
     --metric "Percentage CPU"
     --dimension "CustomDimensionName"
     --interval PT5M
     --aggregation Average Minimum Maximum
     --start-time "2025-02-04T14:00:00Z"
     --end-time "2025-02-04T15:00:00Z"
```

This command queries the `Percentage CPU` metric for a specified VM, filtering and segmenting the data by a custom dimension (`CustomDimensionName`) in five-minute intervals (`PT5M`), and calculates the average, minimum, and maximum CPU usage between 14:00 and 15:00 UTC on February 4, 2025. When you run this command, Azure returns a JSON file. This file contains a series of time-stamped entries, each showing the average, minimum, and maximum CPU usage, neatly segmented by your chosen category.

You can also list the available metric definitions and namespaces for your resource using commands such as `az monitor metrics list-namespaces` and `az monitor metrics list-definitions`. To explore metrics at the subscription level, use `az monitor metrics list-sub` and `az monitor metrics list-sub-definitions` to see the detailed data and definitions available. Now that you have seen how to query and list your metrics, we can move forward to creating and managing alerts with Azure Monitor to stay on top of your system's performance.

Creating and Managing Alerts with Azure Monitor

When certain conditions are met, Azure Monitor can automatically trigger alerts to warn you about potential problems or even start fixing them right away. This proactive setup helps you address issues before they become bigger problems, which ensures your applications and resources remain healthy and responsive. Azure Monitor supports various alert types designed for different situations and data sources.

Azure Monitor alerts fall into four main categories: metric alerts, log search alerts, activity log alerts, and Prometheus alerts.

Metric alerts

Metric alerts are triggered by pre-computed metric data, making them ideal when the data you need is already available as metrics and requires little to no additional processing. For example, the following command creates an alert named `HighCPUAlert` that keeps an eye on a VM's CPU usage and triggers when the average usage goes over 80% during a 15-minute period (with the condition checked every 5 minutes).

```
$  az monitor metrics alert create
     --name "HighCPUAlert"
     --resource-group "<resource-group>"
     --scopes "/subscriptions/<id>/.../virtualMachines/<vm-name>"
     --condition "avg Percentage CPU > 80"
     --description "Alert when CPU usage exceeds 80%"
     --evaluation-frequency "PT5M"
     --window-size "PT15M"
     --action "/subscriptions/<id>/.../actionGroups/<group>"
```

In this command, the `--name` parameter sets the alert's name, while the `--scopes` parameter specifies the exact resource to monitor (in this case, a VM). The `--condition` parameter defines the threshold. Here, it's checking if the average of `Percentage CPU` exceeds 80. The `--evaluation-frequency` and `--window-size` parameters control how often the alert evaluates the data and over what time period the data is aggregated, respectively, and finally, the `--action` parameter designates the action group that will be notified or triggered when the alert fires. In Azure Monitor, an action group is a collection of notification and action preferences (such as emails, SMS messages, webhooks, or logic apps) that define what happens when an alert is triggered. Before referencing an action group in an alert, you need to configure it to specify how you want to be notified or what actions should be taken automatically.

Azure Monitor also has additional commands for managing your alerts. You can delete a metrics-based alert rule using `az monitor metrics alert delete`, manage near-real-time metric alert rule dimensions with `az monitor metrics alert` `dimension` or build one using `az monitor metrics alert dimension create`, list your metric-based alert rules with `az monitor metrics alert list`, display details of a specific alert with `az monitor metrics alert show`, and update an existing alert using `az monitor metrics alert update`.

After working with metric alerts to monitor pre-computed data, let's explore how to create alerts based on detailed log information.

Log search alerts

These alerts enable you to perform advanced logic and filtering on your data by using the Kusto Query Language (KQL) to analyze logs. For example, to create an alert that triggers when error events occur in the logs over the past 30 minutes, you can use the following Azure CLI command, which uses the scheduled query functionality:

```
$ az monitor scheduled-query create
        --name "ErrorEventAlert"
        --resource-group "<resource-group>"
        --scopes "/subscriptions/<id>/resourceGroups/<group>"
        --query "Event | where Level == 'Error' | where Time > ago(30m)"
        --description "Alert when errors happen in the last 30 minutes"
        --evaluation-frequency "PT5M"
        --time-window "PT30M"
        --action-groups "/subscriptions/<id>/…/actionGroups/<group>"
```

In this command, the `--query` parameter holds the KQL statement that filters your log data for error events occurring in the last 30 minutes. The `--evaluation-frequency` option sets how often the query is executed (every five minutes), while the `--time-window` option defines the period over which the logs are aggregated. The `--action-groups` parameter also specifies the action group that will be notified or triggered when the alert condition is met.

Activity log alerts

These alerts monitor the Azure Activity Log, which records every action taken on your resources, making them very useful for auditing events such as resource creation, deletion, or configuration changes. For instance, to create an alert that notifies you when a resource deployment occurs, you might run:

```
$ az monitor activity-log alert create
    --activity-log-alert-name "ResourceChangeAlert"
    --resource-group "<resource-group>"
    --scope "/subscriptions/<subscription-id>"
    --condition "category='Administrative' and
operationName='Microsoft.Resources/deployments/write'"
    --description "Alert when a resource deployment occurs"
    --action-group "/subscriptions/<id>/.../actionGroups/<group>"
```

This command creates an activity log alert that monitors events recorded in the Azure Activity Log. It is designed to capture administrative operations across the subscription. Specifically, it triggers when a resource deployment occurs, as defined by the condition that filters for events in the `Administrative` category and with an operation name of `Microsoft.Resources/deployments/write`. The `--scope` parameter is set at the subscription level to cover all resources, while the `--action` parameter specifies the action group that will be notified or triggered when the alert fires.

Prometheus alerts

These alerts are designed for environments that use Prometheus metrics stored in Azure Monitor managed services for Prometheus, and they utilize the PromQL query language to evaluate time-series data. For example, the following command creates an alert named `PrometheusHighLatencyAlert` that triggers when the average value of the Prometheus metric `prometheus_metric_latency_seconds` exceeds 0.5 seconds. This alert is applied to a managed Kubernetes cluster, evaluates the metric every minute over a five-minute window, and notifies the specified action group if the condition is met:

```
$ az monitor metrics alert create
    --name "PrometheusHighLatencyAlert"
    --resource-group "<resource-group>"
    --scopes "/subscriptions/<id>/.../managedClusters/<cluster-name>"
    --condition "avg(prometheus_metric_latency_seconds) > 0.5"
    --description "Alert when Prometheus latency exceeds 0.5 seconds"
    --evaluation-frequency "PT1M"
    --window-size "PT5M"
    --action "/subscriptions/<id>/.../actionGroups/<action-group>"
```

The `--condition` parameter uses PromQL to specify the alert condition (for example, average latency greater than 0.5 seconds), while the `--evaluation-frequency` and `--window-size` parameters define how often the metric is evaluated and over what period data is aggregated. The `--action` parameter connects the alert to an action group, enabling notifications or automation.

Azure Application Insights

Multiple Azure services work together to simplify the monitoring and management of applications, and Azure Application Insights is a key part of this ecosystem. Application Insights is an Application Performance Management (APM) tool that continuously monitors live applications across all platforms and languages.

Some advantages of using Application Insights are effective error tracking, comprehensive performance monitoring, and detailed analysis of user behavior. Application Insights collects detailed telemetry, such as data on failed requests, slow response times, and unhandled exceptions, to help identify potential issues early, preventing them from affecting users. It also records metrics like page views, session durations, and custom events, which provide the data needed to optimize application performance and user engagement. To get started, you begin by creating an Application

Insights resource using the Azure CLI. For example, to create a new resource for a web application in the East US region, you can run:

```
$  az monitor app-insights component create
    --app "MySampleWebAppInsights"
    --location "EastUS"
    --resource-group "test-resource-group"
    --application-type web
```

In this command, the `--app` parameter sets the name of your resource, `--location` specifies the region, and `--resource-group` shows where the resource is managed. The `--application-type` tells Application Insights what kind of application you are monitoring. This resource is where all your application's data will be sent for analysis.

Additionally, using Application Insights through the Azure portal provides powerful tools for visualizing the results of your KQL queries. These visualizations help you to quickly interpret your data, identify trends, and diagnose issues, making it easier to optimize your application's performance and user experience.

Once you have your Application Insights resource, you can connect your web app to it. To collect telemetry from your web application, you need this step, and here's how you do it in the Azure CLI:

```
$  az monitor app-insights component connect-webapp
    --app "MySampleWebAppInsights"
    --web-app "MyTestWebApp"
    --resource-group "test-resource-group"
```

Here, the `--web-app` parameter identifies the web app you want to monitor.

Once you have connected your application to your Application Insights resource, you can start working with your telemetry data. For example, to see all the error events from the past hour, you can use this command:

```
$ az monitor app-insights query
    --app "MySampleWebAppInsights"
    --analytics-query "exceptions | where timestamp > ago(1h) | sort by timestamp desc"
    --output table
```

This command uses KQL to search through your data. It looks in the *exceptions* table, filters for events from the last hour, and sorts them by time in descending order. The `--output table` option makes the results easy to read.

How Did the Exceptions Table Get Created?

Application Insights automatically organizes your application's telemetry data into default tables like requests, exceptions, traces, and dependencies. When you set up your app with an SDK or agent and send data to Application Insights, the exceptions table is created on its own to store any exception events your app logs. You don't need to create this table manually; it's part of the standard setup once telemetry is enabled.

You can also secure your log data by creating API keys. API keys are like special passwords that allow specific people or tools to access your telemetry data without exposing your main account credentials. This way, you can share necessary information securely while keeping your main account safe.

For example, if you have a team member who needs to analyze your application's performance data, you can create an API key that grants them read-only access to the telemetry data. This ensures they can access the necessary information without having full control over your Application Insights resource.

To create such an API key, you can use the following command:

```
$ az monitor app-insights api-key create
    --app "MyWebAppInsights"
    --api-key "ReadOnlyAPIKey"
    --read-properties ReadTelemetry
    --write-properties WriteAnnotations
```

This command creates an API key named "ReadOnlyAPIKey" for the Application Insights resource `MyWebAppInsights`. The `--read-properties` parameter assigns the `ReadTelemetry` role, granting read access to telemetry data. The `--write-properties` parameter assigns the `WriteAnnotations` role, allowing the API key to add annotations to your Application Insights data.

How Can I Send Data to Application Insights from My API?

You can send data to Application Insights from your API in two ways. First, you can use an SDK. If you're using .NET, for example, you add the Application Insights package to your project, set your instrumentation key, and then call functions like TrackEvent or TrackException to send data. Second, you can send data directly using the REST API by creating a JSON message with your telemetry data (like errors or custom events) and posting it to the Application Insights endpoint with an HTTP POST request. Both methods help you collect information about how your API is performing.

Ensuring your application's availability is important for maintaining user satisfaction and trust. One effective way to achieve this is by setting up web tests, also known as synthetic tests, which proactively monitor your site's performance from various global locations. These tests simulate user interactions, allowing you to detect potential issues before real users are affected.

For example, to create a web test that pings your website every five minutes, you can use the following Azure CLI command:

```
$ az monitor app-insights web-test create \
    --location "South Central US" \
    --resource-group "my-resource-group" \
```

```
--name "my-webtest-my-component" \
--web-test '
<WebTest Name="my-webtest" Enabled="True" Timeout="120">
  <Items>
    <Request Method="GET"
Url="http://my-component.azurewebsites.net" ExpectedHttpStatusCode="200" />
  </Items>
</WebTest>'
--description "Ping web test alert for mytestwebapp"
--enabled true
--frequency 300
--web-test-kind "ping"
--locations "Id=us-fl-mia-edge"
--retry-enabled true
--synthetic-monitor-id "my-webtest-my-component"
--timeout 120
--tags hidden-link:XX=XX
```

Setting up web tests, also known as synthetic monitoring, is like having automated scouts checking your website's health from various parts of the world. Here's how they help:

Regularly check if your website is accessible from different regions
: Web tests simulate user visits to your site from multiple global locations. This ensures that people everywhere can access your site without problems. By running these tests, you can spot and fix access issues before real users encounter them.

Gather data on response times and detect latency issues that could affect user experience
: These tests measure how quickly your website responds to user actions. If parts of your site are slow, the tests will highlight these areas, allowing you to improve speed and ensure a smooth experience for visitors.

Set up notifications to inform you promptly if the test detects downtime or performance degradation
: If your website goes down or starts running slowly, web tests can immediately alert you. This prompt notice lets you address issues quickly, minimizing disruptions for your users.

The result is faster issue resolution and improved application reliability, along with the confidence that comes from knowing your application is being monitored continuously from multiple perspectives.

Azure Log Analytics

Another tool for gathering and analyzing logs is Azure Log Analytics, a key part of Azure Monitor. It collects different kinds of log data and stores it all in one central location. This makes it easier for you to search through your logs, see what's happening in your application, and find issues quickly.

The benefits of using Log Analytics include having all your log data in one place, which simplifies troubleshooting and performance monitoring. With the query tools from Log Analytics, you can easily filter, sort, and analyze your logs to spot trends and diagnose problems.

Data Collection and Ingestion

Logs are like records that capture what's happening across your computing environment. They can originate from various sources, including Azure resources like VMs, web apps, and storage accounts; custom applications you've developed; and even on-premises systems where you manage your own servers. Imagine trying to troubleshoot a current issue in your system that is affecting your operations. Without centralized logging, identifying the root cause can be challenging.

To effectively monitor and analyze all this information, it's essential to centralize these logs. In Azure, you achieve this by configuring diagnostic settings for each resource and directing their logs to a Log Analytics workspace, a centralized repository for log data.

For instance, to set up diagnostic settings on a VM using the Azure CLI, you can use the following command:

```
$ az monitor diagnostic-settings create
    --resource "/subscriptions/<id>/.../virtualMachines/<vm-name>"
    --name "sendlogs"
    --workspace "<workspace-id>"
    --logs '[{"category": "AuditEvent", "enabled": true}]'
```

This command tells the specified resource to send logs from the `AuditEvent` category to your Log Analytics workspace. The following is an example of how you can configure diagnostic settings for a VM using C#. This snippet uses the Azure Management Libraries for .NET to create or update diagnostic settings, sending `AuditEvent` logs to a Log Analytics workspace with a retention policy of 30 days:

```
static async Task Main(string[] args)
{
    string tenantId = "tenant-id";
    string clientId = "client-id";
    string clientSecret = "client-secret";
    string subscriptionId = "subscription-id";
    string resourceId = "/subscriptions/id/.../virtualMachines/vm-name";
    string workspaceId = "workspace-id";

    // Authenticate and create a MonitorManagementClient
    var serviceCreds = await ApplicationTokenProvider.LoginSilentAsync(
          tenantId, clientId, clientSecret);
    var monitorClient = new MonitorManagementClient(serviceCreds)
    {
        SubscriptionId = subscriptionId
    };

    // Define diagnostic settings parameters
```

```
        var diagnosticSettingsParameters = new DiagnosticSettingsResource
        {
            WorkspaceId = workspaceId,
            Logs = new[]
            {
                new LogSettings
                {
                    Category = "AuditEvent",
                    Enabled = true,
                    RetentionPolicy = new RetentionPolicy
                    {
                        Days = 30,
                        Enabled = true
                    }
                }
            }
        };

        var result = await monitorClient.DiagnosticSettings.CreateOrUpdateAsync(
              resourceId, "sendlogs", diagnosticSettingsParameters);
        Console.WriteLine("Diagnostic Settings Created: " + result.Id);
    }
```

When you use Azure Log Analytics, you need to decide how long to keep your log data before it gets deleted. This is called *data retention*. When setting up diagnostic settings, you can choose a retention period, like 30 days. That means any logs collected, such as system events or application errors, will stay in your workspace for 30 days before being removed automatically.

Keeping logs for the right amount of time is important. If you store them too long, they take up space and increase storage costs. If you delete them too soon, you might not have enough data to investigate problems or analyze trends. Finding the right balance helps keep your system efficient. If you need logs for a longer time, such as for compliance or audits, you can extend the retention period. If cost is a bigger concern, you can set a shorter period to save space and reduce expenses.

Querying and Analyzing Log Data

The KQL is a powerful tool designed for querying and analyzing large volumes of data in Azure Log Analytics and other Azure services. KQL is a read-only query language that operates on a data-flow model, which is both easy to read and author. It is optimized for querying telemetry, metrics, and logs, and it has deep support for text search, time-series analysis, and various other data analysis functions. KQL has different operators and functions to analyze data effectively. Here are some common queries.

Counting rows

If you want to determine the number of records in a table, you use the `count` keyword. When you write the query, it will look similar to this:

```
ConnectionEvents
| count
```

This query returns the total number of entries in the ConnectionEvents table.

Sampling data

If you want to view a subset of the data in a table as opposed to all the records, you use the `take` keyword. When you write the query, it will look similar to the following code snippet:

```
ConnectionEvents
| take 5
```

This retrieves five random records from the ConnectionEvents table, which provides a quick glimpse into the data structure and content.

Filtering data

If you want to find specific records that meet a condition from data in a table as opposed to all the records, you use the `where` keyword. Combining multiple conditions can be achieved using logical operators like `and` and `or`. When you write the query, it will look similar to this code snippet:

```
ConnectionEvents
| where Type == "Friendship" and Medium == "SocialMedia"
```

This filters the data to show only friendship connections from social media.

Aggregating data

If you want to summarize information in a particular way, you use the `summarize` keyword. With the `summarize` keyword, you can group data and perform calculations such as `count`, `average`, `min`, and `max`. Grouping can be done by one or more columns depending on what you need to do to structure the query that provides meaningful information. When you write the query, it will look similar to this code snippet:

```
ConnectionEvents
| summarize Count = count() by Type
```

This provides the number of connection events recorded for each connection type (let's assume types can be friendship, family, work colleague, etc.).

Visualizing data

To create visualizations such as time series, pie charts, or bar charts, you'll need to use the Azure portal. You can write your KQL query in the portal then use the built-in visualization tools to render your results. For instance, consider this query that creates a time-series chart:

```
ConnectionEvents
| summarize ConnectionCount = count() by bin(StartTime, 1d)
| render timechart
```

When you run this query in the Azure portal, it will generate a time-series chart showing the number of events per day. Note the visualization capabilities, including the use of the `render` keyword, are available through the portal and cannot be executed directly from the CLI.

Writing complex queries

Let's explore a more complex query that builds upon the foundational KQL operations you've been working with, such as counting rows, sampling data, filtering, aggregating, and visualizing. This advanced query will demonstrate how to combine these operations to gain deeper insights from your data.

Consider the following scenario: Suppose you have a table named ConnectionEvents that logs various types of user connections, including their types (e.g., friendship, family, work colleague) and the medium through which they occur (e.g., social media, email, in person). You want to analyze the daily trends of these connection events over the past month to understand user engagement patterns. See the following query:

```
ConnectionEvents
| where Timestamp >= startofday(ago(30d))
| summarize DailyCount = count() by Type, Medium, bin(Timestamp, 1d)
| extend Day = format_datetime(Timestamp, 'yyyy-MM-dd')
| project Day, Type, Medium, DailyCount
| order by Day asc, Type asc, Medium asc
```

In this query, we start by filtering the ConnectionEvents table to include only records from the past 30 days, beginning from the start of each day using the helper function `startofday(ago(30d))`. KQL offers a large collection of helper functions like this one for date and time manipulation, string operations, and more, which can simplify complex queries. We then group the data by `Type`, `Medium`, and each day (using `bin(Timestamp, 1d)`), calculating the total number of events (`count()`) for each combination. Next, we create a new column, `Day`, that formats the Timestamp into a `YYYY-MM-DD` string for better readability. We then select only the columns of interest: `Day`, `Type`, `Medium`, and `DailyCount`. Finally, we sort the results in ascending order by `Day`, `Type`, and `Medium` to organize the output chronologically and categorically.

This query provides a daily breakdown of connection events over the past month, categorized by their type and medium. By analyzing this data, you can identify trends, such as which types of connections are most common on specific days or which mediums are most frequently used. With this insight, you can now decide to come up with strategies to enhance user engagement and optimize the features on your application.

Azure Data Explorer

Azure Data Explorer (ADX) is a service from Microsoft that helps you collect and analyze large amounts of data quickly. It's designed to handle different types of data, like logs from your applications, information from websites, or streams from Internet of Things (IoT) devices. This makes it useful for tasks like monitoring systems, diagnosing problems, and gaining insights from data.

One of the key features of ADX is its ability to process and analyze data in real time. This means you can work with data as it's being generated, which is crucial for applications that require immediate insights. ADX achieves this by separating storage and compute resources, allowing for independent scaling and efficient data processing. It also uses KQL to interact with your data.

In terms of data ingestion, ADX is versatile. It supports various methods to bring data into the system, including batch uploads, streaming, and direct pushes via APIs or SDKs. This flexibility allows you to work with structured data (like tables), semistructured data (like JSON), and unstructured data (like plain text). In "Ingesting Data into Azure Data Explorer" on page 224, you will see what makes this possible.

Integration with other Azure services is another strength of ADX. For example, you can use it with Power BI to create visualizations of your data, or with Azure Data Factory to manage data workflows. This makes it easier to build comprehensive data solutions that leverage the strengths of multiple Azure services.

Cost management is also a consideration with ADX. The service is designed to optimize both storage and query performance, helping you control costs even when dealing with large volumes of data. This means you can scale your data operations without worrying about excessive expenses.

Now that you know some of the benefits of using ADX, let's see how we can use it.

Creating an Azure Data Explorer Cluster and Database

An ADX cluster is a collection of computing resources that provides the foundation for running your data analytics workloads. Once the cluster is set up, you can create databases within it to organize and store your data. In this section, you will see how to create your ADX cluster and database using the Azure CLI and Bicep.

Creating an ADX cluster with Azure CLI

Before you can start using ADX, the first step is to get your cluster set up:

```
$ az kusto cluster create
    --resource-group MyResourceGroup
    --name MyADXCluster
    --location WestUS
    --sku name="Standard_D13_v2" capacity=2
```

In this command, `--resource-group` specifies the Azure resource group where the cluster will reside, `--name` sets the name of your new ADX cluster, `--location` determines the Azure region for deployment, and `--sku` defines the cluster's SKU, including the instance type and the number of instances (capacity).

Creating a Kusto database within the cluster

After the cluster is operational, you can create a database using the Azure CLI:

```
$  az kusto database create
    --resource-group MyResourceGroup
    --cluster-name MyADXCluster
    --database-name MyDatabase
    --read-write-database soft-delete-period=P365D hot-cache-period=P7D
```

Here, `--cluster-name` specifies the name of the cluster where the database will be created, `--database-name` sets the name of the new database, and `--read-write-database` configures the database properties: `soft-delete-period` determines how long deleted data is retained (in this case, 365 days), and `hot-cache-period` sets the duration for which data is kept in the hot cache for faster queries (here, 7 days).

Deploying an ADX cluster and database using Bicep

You can also use Bicep to create your Kusto resources, and I'd strongly recommend you do this through IaC so your deployments are consistent and repeatable. We talked about Bicep in Chapter 4, but as a refresher, Bicep is a domain-specific language (DSL) that simplifies the process of defining and deploying Azure resources.

Here's how you can define an ADX cluster and a database using Bicep:

```
param location string = 'WestUS'
param clusterName string = 'MyADXCluster'
param databaseName string = 'MyDatabase'
param skuName string = 'Standard_D13_v2'
param capacity int = 2

resource adxCluster 'Microsoft.Kusto/clusters@2022-01-01' = {
  name: clusterName
  location: location
  sku: {
    name: skuName
    capacity: capacity
  }
}
```

```
resource adxDatabase 'Microsoft.Kusto/clusters/databases@2022-01-01' = {
  name: '${adxCluster.name}/${databaseName}'
  properties: {
    softDeletePeriod: 'P365D'
    hotCachePeriod: 'P7D'
  }
}
```

In this Bicep file, we start by defining parameters for the location, cluster name, database name, SKU name, and capacity. These parameters make the template flexible and reusable across different environments. The `adxCluster` resource defines the ADX cluster with the specified SKU and capacity. The `adxDatabase` resource creates a database within the cluster, setting properties like `softDeletePeriod` and `hotCachePeriod` to manage data retention and caching.

Ingesting Data into Azure Data Explorer

As mentioned at the beginning of this section, ADX supports several ingestion methods:

Batch ingestion
: You can upload files stored in Azure Blob Storage into ADX.

Streaming ingestion
: For real-time scenarios, ADX can ingest streaming data using Event Hubs or IoT Hub.

Direct ingestion via REST API or SDK
: You can push data directly to ADX using the Kusto SDK available across programming languages, or using `HTTP POST` requests with JSON payloads.

For example, to ingest data from a blob storage container, you might set up an ingestion mapping that tells ADX how to parse your data. The ingestion can be triggered via Azure Data Factory or directly using ADX's REST API. Although there isn't a direct az CLI command for data ingestion, you can script this process using REST calls or SDKs in your preferred programming language.

Let's see how you could ingest data into ADX in a real-world scenario. The next section contains an example of a complete logging pipeline written in C#. In this example, log events are written to a local file as they are emitted, and a background timer periodically triggers the ingestion of the batched logs into an ADX cluster. This approach avoids calling the ingestion client every time a log is emitted by batching logs and processing them in intervals.

Main method

This method sets up the logging system. It creates an ingest client for ADX, sets up a timer to trigger every five minutes, and simulates the emission of log events by calling the logging method repeatedly. This is where the pipeline starts and runs until you stop the program.

```
// These are initialized in the class (outside the Main method)
static IKustoQueuedIngestClient ingestClient;
static Timer ingestionTimer;
static string logFilePath = "logs.txt";

// The Main method
static async Task Main(string[] args)
{
    var url = "https://ingest-mycluster.eastus.kusto.windows.net";
    ingestClient = KustoIngestFactory.CreateQueuedIngestClient(url);
    ingestionTimer = new Timer(300000);
    ingestionTimer.Elapsed += IngestionTimer_Elapsed;
    ingestionTimer.Start();
    for (int i = 0; i < 10; i++)
    {
        EmitLog($"Log entry {i}: {DateTime.UtcNow}");
        await Task.Delay(1000);
    }
    Console.WriteLine("Logs have been emitted...");
    Console.ReadKey();
    ingestionTimer.Stop();
}
```

In the `Main` method, we first create the ingest client with the endpoint URL for our ADX cluster. We then set up a timer that fires every 300,000 milliseconds (5 minutes) and attach the `IngestionTimer_Elapsed` method to handle the timer events. A loop simulates log generation, writing 10 log entries with a one-second delay between each. The program waits for a key press before stopping the timer and ending.

EmitLog method

This method handles writing each log event to a local file. Every time a log is generated, it is appended to a file named *logs.txt*.

```
static void EmitLog(string logEntry)
{
    File.AppendAllText(logFilePath, logEntry + Environment.NewLine);
    Console.WriteLine("Emitted log: " + logEntry);
}
```

The `EmitLog` method takes a log message as input and appends it to *logs.txt* along with a new line. This simple approach allows the program to collect log data over time without immediately sending it to ADX.

IngestionTimer_Elapsed method

This method is called automatically by the timer. It checks if the log file exists, renames it to prevent reprocessing, and sends the batch of logs to ADX. After the logs are successfully ingested, the temporary file is removed.

```
static async void IngestionTimer_Elapsed(object sender, ElapsedEventArgs e)
{
    if (File.Exists(logFilePath))
    {
        string originalFilePath = logFilePath;
        string tempFilePath = originalFilePath + ".ingest";
        File.Move(originalFilePath, tempFilePath);
        var props = new KustoIngestionProperties("MyDB", "MyTable");
        await ingestClient.IngestFromFileAsync(tempFilePath, props);
        File.Delete(tempFilePath);
        Console.WriteLine("Logs ingested & temp file deleted.");
    }
}
```

When the timer fires, `IngestionTimer_Elapsed` checks if *logs.txt* exists. If it does, it renames the file to avoid duplicating data during the ingestion process. The method then sets up the ingestion properties (targeting a specific database and table in ADX) and calls `IngestFromFileAsync` to send the log data. Once the data is ingested, the temporary file is deleted, keeping the storage clean.

Querying Data in Azure Data Explorer

Once your data is ingested, you can use KQL to query and analyze it. Here's a basic example that shows how to query the data:

```
MyTable
| take 10
```

The previous code snippet is a query to list 10 records in a table called MyTable. In "Querying and Analyzing Log Data" on page 219, we covered more ways to query data in ADX. You can run such queries in the ADX web UI or in Power BI.

Azure Service Health

Azure Service Health is a tool within Azure that keeps you informed about service issues, planned maintenance, and other health advisories that can affect your resources. It provides personalized alerts and guidance to help you prepare for and respond to Azure service incidents. This service is especially important for maintaining high availability and reliability in your applications by ensuring you know when issues or changes in Azure might impact your workloads.

Azure Service Health is made up of three main parts:

Azure status
: This shows a global view of the health of Azure services across all regions. It's useful for checking if there's a widespread issue affecting many users.

Service Health
: This offers a personalized view tailored to the services and regions you're using. It provides details about outages, planned maintenance, and other advisories that specifically impact your resources. Setting up alerts here ensures you're notified about issues that matter to you.

Resource Health
: This focuses on the health of your individual resources, like specific VMs or databases. It helps you determine if a problem is due to an issue on Azure's side or something within your own setup. You can also set up alerts to stay informed about the availability of your resources.

> **Example of Service Health in Action**
>
> Imagine you're running a critical application on Azure, and Microsoft schedules maintenance that could temporarily affect your services. With Service Health alerts set up, you'd receive a notification about this planned maintenance. This allows you to prepare in advance, perhaps by informing your users or adjusting your application's operations to minimize disruption. Being proactive in this way helps maintain the reliability and availability of your applications.

Here's an example of a Bicep file that creates an activity log alert for Service Health notifications. This alert monitors the activity log for events categorized under `ServiceHealth` and triggers an alert when such events are detected. Additionally, it sets up an action group to send email notifications to specified recipients.

```
param actionGroupName string = 'ServiceHealthActionGroup'
param alertRuleName string = 'ServiceHealthActivityLogAlert'
param emailAddress string

var alertScope = subscription().id

resource actionGroup 'Microsoft.Insights/actionGroups@2022-06-01' = {
  name: actionGroupName
  location: 'Global'
  properties: {
    groupShortName: 'SvcHealthAG'
    enabled: true
    emailReceivers: [
      {
        name: 'PrimaryContact'
        emailAddress: emailAddress
```

```
                useCommonAlertSchema: true
            }
        ]
    }
}

resource activityLogAlert 'Microsoft.Insights/activityLogAlerts@2022-06-01' = {
  name: alertRuleName
  location: 'Global'
  properties: {
    scopes: [
      alertScope
    ]
    enabled: true
    condition: {
      allOf: [
        {
          field: 'category'
          equals: 'ServiceHealth'
        }
      ]
    }
    actions: {
      actionGroups: [
        {
          actionGroupId: actionGroup.id
        }
      ]
    }
  }
}
```

In this Bicep template, two things are happening:

- The `actionGroup` resource defines an action group named "ServiceHealthActionGroup" with an email receiver. Replace the `emailAddress` parameter with the desired recipient's email address.
- The `activityLogAlert` resource creates an alert rule named "ServiceHealthActivityLogAlert" that monitors the subscription's activity log for events where the category is `ServiceHealth`. When such an event is detected, the alert triggers and sends a notification via the specified action group.

With this configuration in place, you'll receive timely notifications about service health events, allowing you to respond proactively to potential disruptions and keep your applications running smoothly.

Azure Network Watcher

Azure Network Watcher is a tool to help monitor and diagnose your Azure network. It has features like packet capture, connection monitoring, and network topology monitoring. These tools assist in identifying and resolving network issues, and this, in turn, makes sure your applications run smoothly.

Before using Network Watcher, ensure it's enabled in the region where your resources are located. To enable it using the Azure CLI, run:

```
$ az network watcher configure
    --locations <region>
    --enabled true
```

Replace `<region>` with your Azure region, such as `eastus` or `westeurope`. For example, to enable Network Watcher in the East US region, run:

```
$ az network watcher configure
    --locations eastus
    --enabled true
```

To monitor the connection between a VM and another resource, use the connection monitor feature. This helps ensure your VM can communicate with other services. Here's how to set it up:

```
$ az network watcher connection-monitor create
    --name test-connection-monitor
    --endpoint-source-name test-vm001
    --endpoint-source-resource-id resource-id
    --endpoint-dest-name adoranwodo
    --endpoint-dest-address adoranwodo.com
    --test-config-name TCPSiteConfig
    --protocol Tcp
    --tcp-port 2048
```

In the code snippet, the Azure CLI command `az network watcher connection-monitor create` is used to establish a connection monitor named `test-connection-monitor`. This monitor assesses the connectivity between a source VM, identified as `test-vm001` with the resource ID `resource-id`, and a destination endpoint named `adoranwodo`, corresponding to the address `adoranwodo.com`. The test configuration, labeled `TCPSiteConfig`, specifies the use of the `Tcp` protocol targeting port `2048`. When you set up this connection monitor, you can regularly evaluate the network performance and reliability between your specified source VM and the destination address. As a result, connectivity issues will be promptly detected and addressed as a result of the integration.

If you need to capture and analyze network traffic to or from a VM, use the packet capture feature:

```
$ az network watcher packet-capture create
    --resource-group test-resource-group
    --vm test-vm001
    --name test-packet-capture
    --storage-account samplestorage
    --time-limit 300
```

This command starts a packet capture session on `test-vm001` for up to 300 seconds (5 minutes) and stores the capture in `samplestorage`.

Building a Strong Monitoring Strategy

"The most difficult part of software is maintenance" is a quote I first encountered during my bachelor's degree and has stayed with me throughout my career. Now, as technology has evolved into the era of site reliability engineers (SREs), observability, monitoring, platform engineering, and autonomous teams, this insight remains pertinent. The complexity and scale of modern systems have amplified the challenges of maintenance, making comprehensive monitoring more critical than ever. Each of the following elements are necessary when creating a complete observability strategy.

Defining Objectives and Key Performance Indicators

A strong monitoring strategy begins with establishing clear goals and objectives that provide direction for monitoring efforts. These objectives should align with the organization's mission and strategic aims because monitoring activities must contribute to overarching goals (at the end of the day, we are serving customers). Once objectives are defined, identifying relevant key performance indicators (KPIs) becomes essential. KPIs are quantifiable measures that gauge an organization's performance against set targets, objectives, or industry peers. They serve as benchmarks for success, enabling organizations to track progress and make informed decisions.

Establishing Clear Goals and Objectives

The foundation of an effective monitoring strategy lies in setting specific, measurable, achievable, relevant, and time-bound (SMART) objectives. This approach ensures goals are well defined and attainable within a specified timeframe. For instance, an objective might be to reduce system downtime by 20% over the next quarter. Another objective could be to have an uptime of 99.99% throughout the quarter. Such clarity provides a focused direction for monitoring efforts and facilitates the assessment of progress.

Identifying Relevant KPIs

With objectives in place, the next step is to determine KPIs that align with these goals. KPIs should be directly related to the objectives and provide measurable evidence of progress. For example, if the objective is to enhance system reliability, relevant KPIs might include mean time between failures (MTBF) and mean time to repair (MTTR). Selecting appropriate KPIs ensures monitoring efforts are focused on critical aspects of performance that impact organizational success.

Regular Review and Adaptation of KPIs

After the KPIs have been defined and aligned with all organizational goals, they need to be reassessed to ensure continued relevance and effectiveness as things evolve over time (Figure 10-1). This continuous reassessment helps maintain a connection between monitoring efforts and the company's strategic direction. Frequent reviews support a monitoring approach that remains strong and ready to handle new challenges and opportunities.

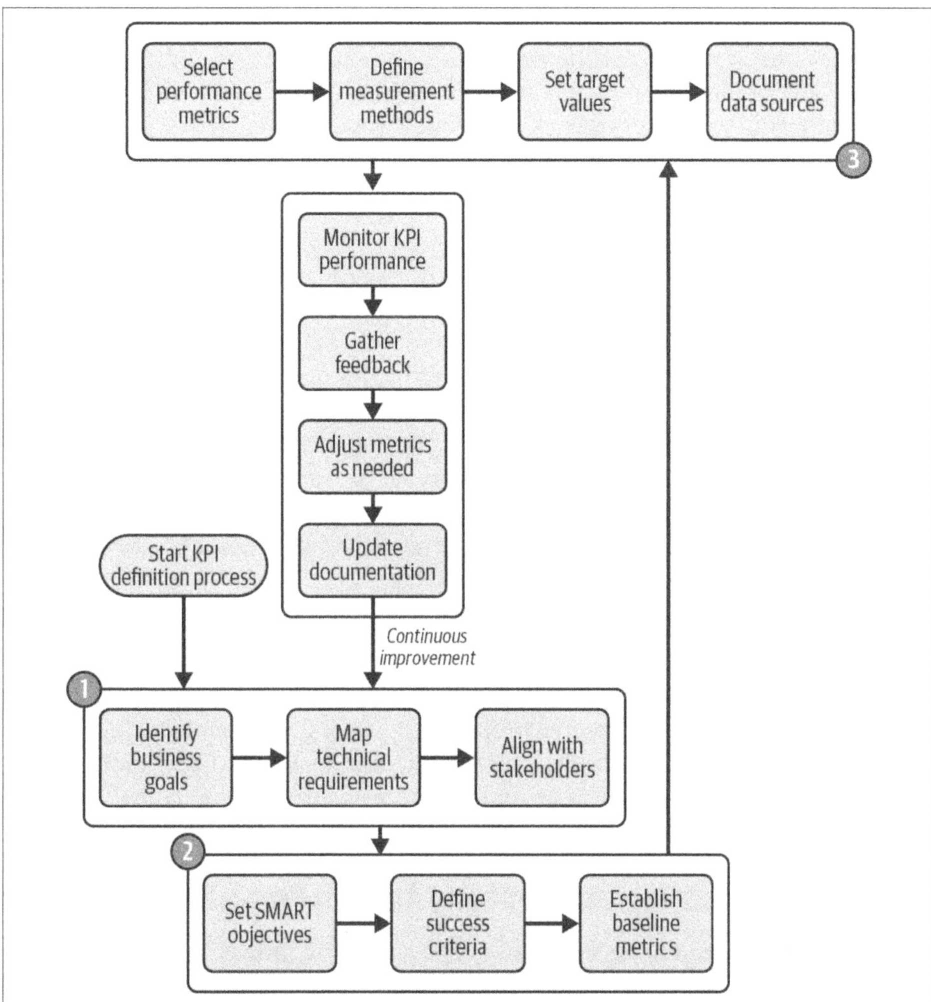

Figure 10-1. Flow chart for defining KPIs

Once the KPIs have been defined, the next critical step is ensuring that data is collected, managed, analyzed, and reported in a structured and reliable manner. This requires designing efficient data collection methods, implementing strong data management and analysis processes, clearly assigning roles and responsibilities, and establishing effective reporting and feedback mechanisms. These elements form the backbone of a successful monitoring strategy, ensuring that relevant insights are extracted and acted upon.

Designing Data Collection Methods and Tools

The foundation of effective monitoring is selecting appropriate data collection techniques for your application. Different monitoring objectives require different data collection approaches. For example, user experience monitoring may involve feedback surveys and session recordings, while infrastructure monitoring relies on automated logging and real-time telemetry. Choosing the right tools, such as API logs, system performance metrics, or network monitoring solutions, ensures that the collected data is accurate, timely, and relevant.

It's important that the data collection process is reliable and collects valid data. To do this, you'll need to standardize procedures, which means leveraging structured logging formats, consistent sampling intervals, and well-defined data schemas, as these help maintain data integrity. Without these safeguards, inconsistencies in data could lead to inaccurate analysis and misinformed decision making. For the data collection process, you can use a tool like OpenTelemetry (OTel). OTel is an open source framework that provides a standardized approach to instrumenting, generating, collecting, and exporting telemetry data, including metrics, logs, and traces. It has vendor-agnostic APIs, SDKs, and tools to facilitate effective observability across various systems.

OTel has the OpenTelemetry Collector, a standalone service designed to receive, process, and export telemetry data. The Collector supports multiple data formats and protocols, which allows it to integrate seamlessly with various data sources and backends. Implementing OTel in your environment involves instrumenting your applications with OTel SDKs to generate telemetry data, configuring the Collector to receive this data, and setting up exporters to send the processed data to your chosen observability platforms.

Implementing Data Management and Analysis Processes

After data is collected, it needs to be stored in a structured format, secured, and made available for analysis using Azure monitoring services. Data storage protocols in Azure ensure information is organized and retained in solutions like Azure Storage, Log Analytics workspaces, or data lakes. Security measures, including encryption, RBAC, and audit logging, protect sensitive data and prevent unauthorized access.

To gain insights from the stored data, you can use the tools within the Azure observability system we discussed in this chapter. Azure Monitor and Log Analytics have powerful query capabilities and visualization tools to identify trends, detect anomalies, and understand correlations.

Assigning Roles and Responsibilities

For a monitoring strategy to work well, it's important to assign roles for every part of the process clearly. When roles are defined, everyone knows what they are accountable for, which helps prevent any gaps in monitoring. SREs, platform engineers, and operations teams need to work together on tasks like observability, incident response, and system maintenance.

Providing proper training and resources gives team members the skills and tools they need to do their jobs effectively. This might include onboarding sessions for monitoring tools, regular technical workshops, and access to detailed documentation outlining best practices. Teams need to define on-call rotations so people have an idea of when they're required to be on call. Teams should also create incident response playbooks or troubleshooting guides so teams understand exactly how to react when alerts or anomalies occur.

Establishing Reporting and Feedback Mechanisms

Monitoring efforts should lead to clear, actionable improvements. When regular reporting schedules are established, the insights from incidents will reach everyone who needs them, whether that's engineering teams, leaders, or compliance officers. Automated dashboards can help show real-time system health metrics or regular summaries that highlight performance trends and incidents, and this ensures the data is always up to date and easily accessible.

It's also important to create feedback loops, as it helps with continuous improvement. Observability is not fixed; it changes as systems grow and user needs evolve. Teams need processes in place to review monitoring results, adjust thresholds, and refine KPIs based on actual performance. Regular incident postmortems, retrospectives, and iterative updates to monitoring objectives all help build a flexible and resilient observability strategy.

Summary

This chapter covered monitoring and observability and the different Azure services that make it possible. We walked through how monitoring helps track application performance, detect issues, and ensure reliability, while observability provides deeper insights into system behavior. I introduced Azure Monitor, which collects and analyzes data from applications and resources, and showed how to query metrics and set up alerts to detect problems early. You saw how teams can use Azure Application Insights to track application performance and how Azure Log Analytics helps to collect and analyze logs. We also created and queried an ADX cluster for handling large-scale data, and you set up Azure Service Health to monitor outages and planned maintenance and used Azure Network Watcher to diagnose network issues. Finally, we covered how to build a strong monitoring strategy by setting clear goals, tracking KPIs, and using the right tools to ensure smooth application performance. In the next chapter, you will learn about caching on Azure.

CHAPTER 11
Caching Strategies in Azure

The more we build distributed systems that are read-heavy, the more important it becomes to ensure that frequently accessed data is delivered with lightning speed, and caching stands at the forefront of that effort. As we innovate with technology and scale our products consistently to meet the increasing volume of simultaneous requests while keeping costs in check, effective caching has become a necessity. This chapter lays out a comprehensive roadmap for understanding and implementing caching within Azure's ecosystem.

In this chapter, we will cover the fundamentals of caching, including its definition, key performance metrics, and the various types (local, distributed, and session caching), and then dive into essential caching patterns such as cache-aside, read-through/write-through, and write-behind caching, along with strategies for cache invalidation. We will explore Azure's caching services with a focus on Azure Cache for Redis, and we'll also look at Azure's content delivery network (CDN) offerings.

Introduction to Caching

Let's define caching and talk about its importance by considering an example. Let's use a hypothetical learning management system (LMS) that your team is working on as our application. Imagine an LMS with two million daily active users, where most of these users, primarily students, are consuming content (reading or watching lectures) far more often than educators are creating or uploading new material. In such a system, caching plays a crucial role by storing frequently accessed content (like course materials, video thumbnails, and user profiles) in a fast, temporary storage layer. This ensures the system can deliver content quickly without having to repeatedly query the primary database for every user request.

In cloud applications, caching is a strategy that dramatically improves performance and scalability. By placing a cache layer, whether it is a local in-memory cache or a distributed cache like Azure Cache for Redis, between the application and its data source, the system can serve repeated requests from this high-speed layer. The benefits are clear: users experience lower latency as data is retrieved quickly from the cache, and the load on the database is significantly reduced. This reduction in database calls not only boosts performance but also minimizes operational costs and improves the overall responsiveness of the application.

Business benefits extend well beyond performance enhancements. In our hypothetical LMS, lower latency means that students can access course materials instantly, leading to a better user experience and increased engagement. With reduced database load, the system can handle a higher volume of concurrent requests without the need to scale the backend infrastructure dramatically. This cost optimization is essential in cloud environments where compute and storage resources are billed based on usage. By strategically caching data, companies can keep operational expenses in check while ensuring a seamless experience for users.

When considering why caching matters specifically in the Azure ecosystem, it's important to understand the challenges inherent to cloud-based data access. Unlike traditional on-premises environments, cloud applications often operate over distributed networks with varying degrees of latency and potential bottlenecks. Azure environments, while highly scalable, also need to contend with network variability, transient faults, and the overhead of accessing remote databases. Caching mitigates these challenges by providing a local (or near-local) repository of data that can be accessed rapidly, ensuring the application remains responsive despite the complexities of cloud connectivity, as shown in Figure 11-1.

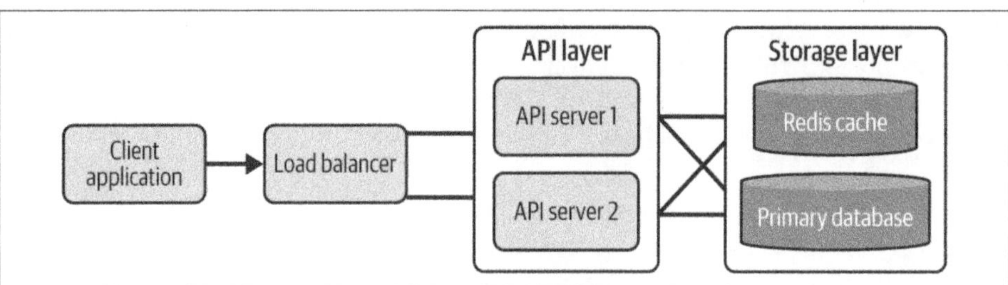

Figure 11-1. Simple system architecture using a cache

Beyond the fundamentals and benefits of caching, let's examine some key performance measures and different ways to use caching. In simple terms, caching is a method of keeping a copy of data in a fast, temporary storage area. This means when your system needs that data again, it can fetch it quickly instead of going back to a slower main database every time.

One important goal of caching is to improve the speed of your application. To see if your caching is working well, you look at measures like the cache hit ratio (how often the data is found in the cache), the cache miss ratio (how often it isn't), the delay in getting data (latency), and the number of operations the cache can handle in a given time (throughput). These are the performance measures to help you know if your cache is making things faster. Figure 11-2 is an illustration of these different caching performance metrics.

There are different ways to set up caching, and the first is local, in-memory caching. This kind of caching stores data directly in the memory of your application. For example, using .NET's IMemoryCache, you can quickly access data stored on the same server. It's very fast because there is no network delay, but its scope is limited to one application instance. Figure 11-3 illustrates this.

Another type is distributed caching. This means you use a separate service that all parts of your application can access. Azure Cache for Redis is a popular option for this. Distributed caching is useful when your application runs on many servers, as it provides a shared pool of cached data for all of them, ensuring that everyone sees the same information.

It is also important to know the difference between session caching and data caching. Session caching is used to store information specific to a user, like a login session or shopping cart, and it only needs to be kept for a short time. Data caching, on the other hand, holds general data that many users need to see, such as a product list or course details, and is kept for longer periods.

Choosing between local and distributed caching often depends on the needs of your system. Local caching is great for very fast access in a simple setup, while distributed caching works better for larger systems with many servers. Your decision will affect how you manage your cache and how you refresh or remove data when it becomes outdated.

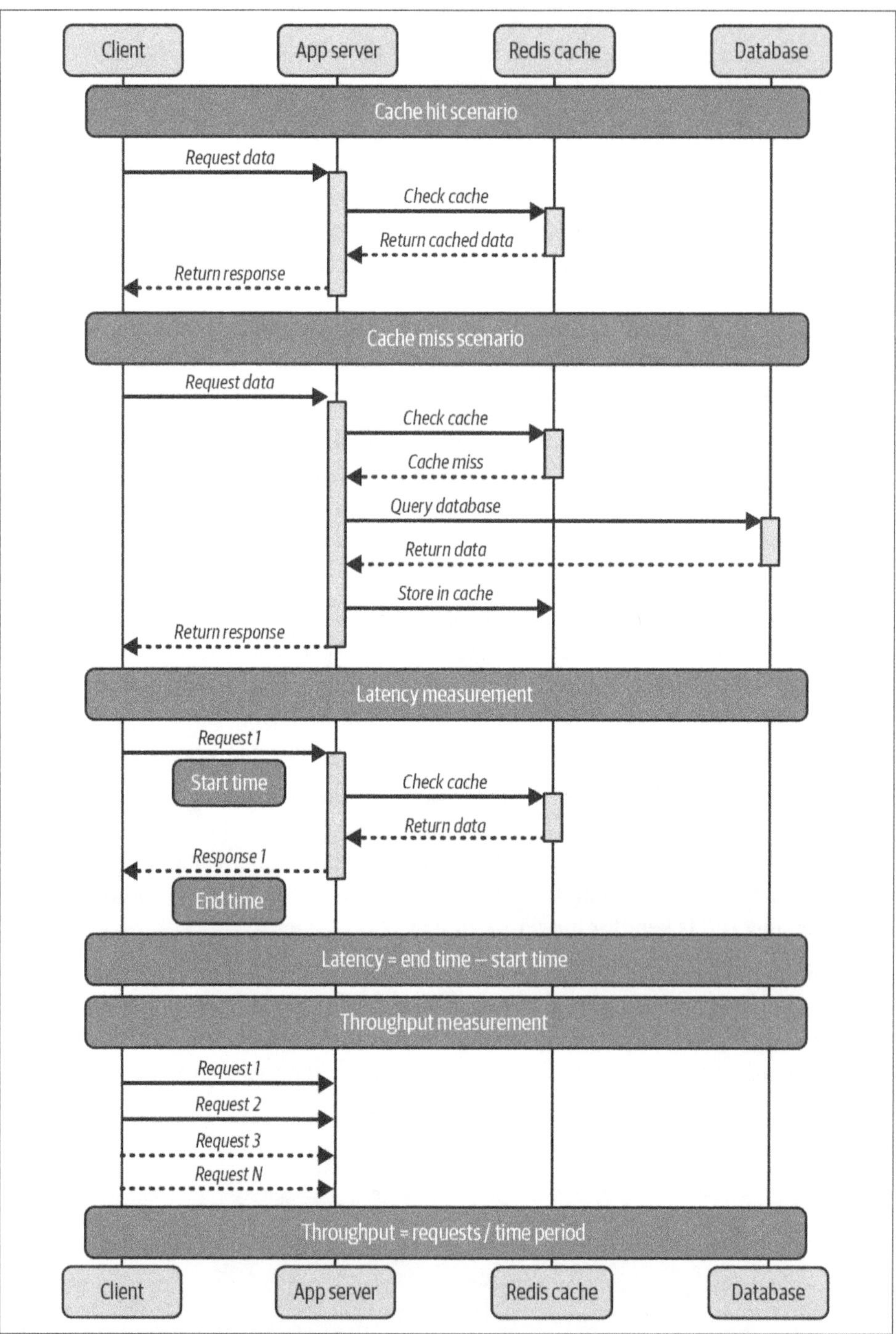

Figure 11-2. Cache operations and metrics

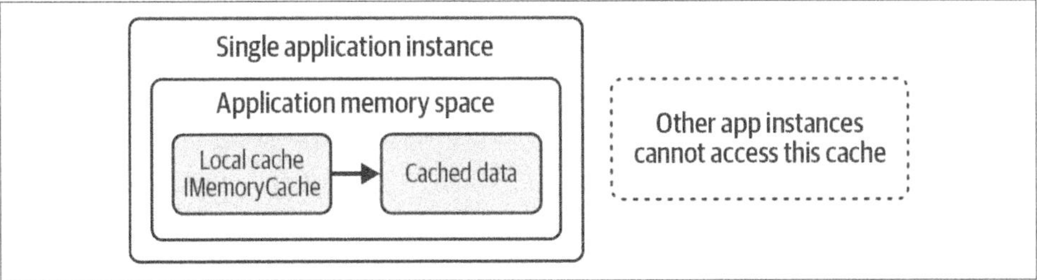

Figure 11-3. Local cache

Caching Patterns and Strategies

There are different caching strategies you can use to boost performance and reduce database load. One common method is the cache-aside pattern, where the application checks the cache first and then retrieves and stores data from the database if it's missing. Other strategies, such as read-through/write-through and write-behind caching, automate the process of keeping the cache and database in sync. Finally, we will discuss cache invalidation techniques, like setting expiration times and using notifications, to ensure that the cached data remains fresh and accurate.

Cache-Aside (Lazy Loading) Pattern

The cache-aside, or lazy loading, pattern is a popular approach to caching that lets your application load data into the cache only when it is needed. In this pattern, your code first checks if the required data is already in the cache; if it is, the data is returned immediately, saving time and reducing load on your database. However, if the data is not found (a cache miss), your application then retrieves the data from the database, returns it to the caller, and writes it into the cache so that subsequent requests can be served faster.

Here's a simple C# example to illustrate the process:

```
var data = cache.Get(key);
if (data == null)
{
    // Fetch data from the database
    data = database.ReadData(key);

    // Store in cache with an expiration time
    cache.Set(key, data, TimeSpan.FromMinutes(10));
}

return data;
```

This example shows the lazy loading mechanism in action: the cache is populated only when needed, which helps to keep the cache lean and focused on frequently accessed items. One major benefit is that it minimizes unnecessary caching; only data that is actually requested gets stored, which can save memory and processing power.

It also reduces the number of direct calls to the database, which improves overall system performance and scalability.

On the downside, the cache-aside pattern can introduce challenges. For instance, if the data changes, the cache might hold outdated information unless you have a strategy for cache invalidation that can withstand this. Also, if many requests for the same missing data occur simultaneously, they can all trigger database calls (a problem sometimes called the *thundering herd* issue) unless you implement locking or another concurrency control mechanism.

Read-Through/Write-Through Caching

Read-through/write-through caching is a pattern where the cache handles data fetching and updates automatically so you don't have to write extra code to manage it (Figure 11-4). With read-through caching, when your application requests data, it first checks the cache. If the data isn't there (a cache miss), the cache automatically fetches the data from the database, stores it, and then returns it to the caller. This means subsequent requests for the same data can be served directly from the cache, reducing load on the database and improving response times.

In write-through caching, every time data is updated, the change is written both to the cache and the underlying database simultaneously. This keeps the two data stores in sync, which is crucial for applications that need strong consistency. For instance, in a financial or ecommerce system, ensuring that every update is immediately reflected in both the cache and the database helps prevent discrepancies and stale data issues.

One key benefit of this approach is that it abstracts much of the caching logic from your application. The cache itself becomes responsible for keeping its contents fresh, which simplifies the application code. It also provides a reliable way to maintain data integrity, as every write operation automatically propagates to the database, which reduces the risk of data inconsistencies.

This pattern works best in scenarios where data is frequently read and must always be accurate. For example, if you have an application where users constantly view product information or account details, using read-through caching ensures that popular data is quickly available. Similarly, write-through caching is useful when updates need to be immediately reflected across all layers of the system, such as in real-time dashboards or inventory management systems.

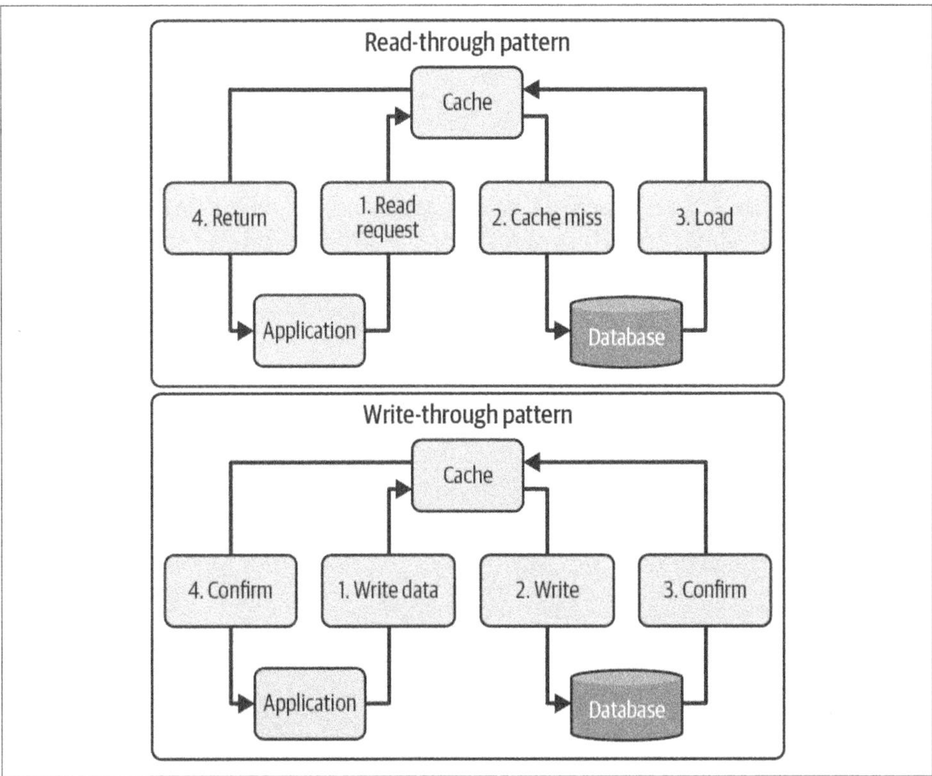

Figure 11-4. Read-through/write-through caching

Write-Behind (Write-Back) Caching

Write-behind caching, also known as write-back caching, is a pattern where your application writes changes to the cache first and then updates the underlying data store asynchronously. In this pattern, when data is updated, the cache reflects the change immediately and later writes the update to the database in the background. This method can greatly improve the write performance of your application, as it reduces the wait time for database operations. However, it also introduces trade-offs regarding consistency and the potential for data loss if the cache fails before the data is written back.

With write-behind caching, database writes are batched since they don't happen synchronously. This batching can reduce the number of database writes and lower the overall load. A common scenario for write-behind caching is when handling user activity or engagement on social media platforms. For example, instead of updating the database every time a user likes or comments on a post, the system can immediately record these interactions in the cache. Then, at regular intervals, a background process can aggregate these actions and update the database in a single, consolidated write. This helps reduce database load during periods of high user activity while still ensuring metrics like post-like counts and comment totals eventually stay consistent.

The main technical trade-off with write-behind caching is that it can lead to data consistency issues. Since updates are delayed, there is a window of time during which the cache contains data that hasn't been committed to the database. If the cache crashes or loses its contents before the data is flushed, you might lose some updates. This makes the write-behind caching pattern best suited for applications where occasional temporary inconsistencies are acceptable, or where high throughput is more important than immediate consistency.

Cache Invalidation Strategies

Cache invalidation is key to keeping your cached data fresh and consistent with the underlying data store. One of the simplest strategies is to set an expiration time (time to live [TTL]) on cached items. This means that when you store an item, you specify a duration after which the item is automatically removed. For example, in C#, using a Redis client you might write:

```
cache.StringSet("user:123", userData, TimeSpan.FromMinutes(15));
```

This code sets the cache entry for a user to expire in 15 minutes.

Another approach is sliding expiration. Instead of a fixed timeout, the expiration timer resets every time the cached item is accessed. This way, frequently used data stays in the cache, while rarely accessed data expires automatically. Implementing sliding expiration might require additional logic in your caching layer to update the expiration time on each access.

Explicit cache flushing is another strategy where the application manually clears cache entries when it knows the underlying data has changed. For instance, after an update operation, you can call a method to remove the outdated cache entry:

```
cache.KeyDelete("user:123");
```

This immediate invalidation ensures that the next time the data is requested, it is reloaded from the primary data store. Now that the fundamentals are out of the way, it's time to look into Azure caching services.

Azure Caching Services

Azure primarily uses Azure Cache for Redis, a fast service that keeps data in memory so it can be quickly accessed. It comes with different plans that can grow with your needs and offers features like backup options and data replication across regions. You can also cache data using Azure SQL Database or store data locally on VMs or within App Service. This section explains these options and helps you choose the best one for your application.

Azure Cache for Redis

Azure Cache for Redis is a cloud-based, in-memory data store that helps applications run faster by reducing the need to fetch data from slower storage. Azure's Redis service is based on the popular open source Redis database, but with built-in security, scalability, and high availability. It supports different pricing tiers, including Basic, Standard, and Premium, with features like clustering, geo-replication, and enterprise security in higher tiers.

Creating and managing your Redis instance

Before using Redis, you need to create an instance of it in your Azure subscription. To create a Redis instance using the Azure CLI, run the following command:

```
$ az redis create
    --name mysampleredis
    --resource-group testrg
    --location eastus
    --sku Standard
    --vm-size c1
```

In the preceding code snippet, the Azure CLI command creates a Redis instance with specific parameters. The `--name` flag sets the instance name as `mysampleredis`, while the `--resource-group` flag designates `testrg` as the resource group where the instance will be deployed. The `--location` flag specifies `eastus` as the chosen Azure region for the deployment. The `--sku` flag selects the `Standard` pricing tier, and the `--vm-size` flag sets the cache size to `C1`, which represents a small instance.

Once the command is executed, Azure will deploy the Redis instance. You can view its details in the Azure portal under the Azure Cache for Redis section.

You can also create and manage a Redis instance in Bicep. To do so, add the following code to your Bicep file:

```
resource myRedis 'Microsoft.Cache/Redis@2023-08-01' = {
  name: 'mysampleredis'
  location: 'eastus'
  sku: {
    name: 'Standard'
    family: 'C'
    capacity: 1
  }
  properties: {}
}
```

Once you successfully run the appropriate `az` deployment command to deploy this to Azure, you should see the instance in the Azure portal under the Azure Cache for Redis section. Once Redis is created, applications need to connect to it. In C#, we use the StackExchange.Redis library. The library can be installed using the command `dotnet add package StackExchange.Redis`, but there are other ways to install it, such as adding the dependency directly to the .csproj file or using NuGet Package Manager in Visual Studio. Once the dependency is added, you can add the following code to connect to Redis:

```
using StackExchange.Redis;
using System;

class Program
{
    static void Main()
    {
        string connectionString =
            "mysampleredis.redis.cache.windows.net:6380,password=abcd,ssl=True";
        var redis = ConnectionMultiplexer.Connect(connectionString);
        IDatabase db = redis.GetDatabase();

        db.StringSet("message", "Hello reader!");
        string value = db.StringGet("message");

        Console.WriteLine(value);
    }
}
```

In the previous code snippet, the StackExchange.Redis library connects to an Azure Cache for Redis instance using `ConnectionMultiplexer.Connect`. The `GetDatabase()` method retrieves the Redis database, allowing operations like `StringSet` to store a key-value pair and `StringGet` to retrieve it. Finally, the value is printed to the console, displaying "Hello reader!"

Sometimes, you may need to modify the configuration of an existing Redis instance, whether to scale resources, change pricing tiers, or adjust settings for performance and security. To make updates using the Azure CLI, you can run the `az redis update` command. For example, to upgrade a Redis instance to the Premium tier, use the following command:

```
$ az redis update
    --name mysampleredis
    --resource-group testrg
    --sku Premium
    --vm-size p1
```

This command updates the SKU to Premium and sets the instance size to P1, unlocking advanced features such as VNet support, better security, and improved performance. The `update` command can also modify other configurations, such as enabling clustering or adjusting persistence settings.

For Bicep, you only need to update the `sku` section in your code to reflect the new tier and size:

```
sku: {
  name: 'Premium'
  family: 'P'
  capacity: 1
}
```

After making this change, redeploying the template will apply the updated configuration automatically.

Managing access control in Redis

By default, Azure Cache for Redis is secured with firewalls and access control rules to restrict unauthorized access. These security measures help ensure that only trusted clients can connect to the Redis instance. Azure allows you to configure firewall rules to define which IP addresses or address ranges are permitted to access Redis.

To allow a specific IP address to connect to Azure Cache for Redis, use the following command in Azure CLI:

```
$  az redis firewall-rules create
     --name mysampleredis
     --resource-group testrg
     --rule-name AllowMyIP
     --start-ip 192.168.1.1
     --end-ip 192.168.1.1
```

This command creates a firewall rule named `AllowMyIP`, which allows access only from `192.168.1.1`. If other IPs attempt to connect, they will be blocked. You can also specify a range of IP addresses by modifying the `--start-ip` and `--end-ip` values.

To list all configured firewall rules for a Redis instance, run:

```
$  az redis firewall-rules list
     --name <name>
     --resource-group <resource-group>
```

This command returns a list of all firewall rules, including their names and allowed IP ranges.

You can also remove a firewall rule and revoke access for a specific IP. To do that, use the following command:

```
$  az redis firewall-rules delete
     --name <name>
     --resource-group <resource-group>
     --rule-name <rule-name>
```

Once deleted, that IP address will no longer be able to connect to Redis.

Access control is an important part of securing a Redis instance. If Redis is not properly protected, unauthorized users could gain access, change data, or even disrupt services. To keep Redis safe, it is important to follow best practices when setting up access control.

One of the most important steps is to limit IP access. This means allowing only specific IP addresses to connect to Redis instead of leaving it open to all users. If possible, avoid using public IP addresses and restrict access to only trusted machines. Allowing only necessary IPs reduces the risk of unwanted connections.

Another key practice is to use private networking. Instead of exposing Redis to the public internet, it is safer to place it inside an Azure VNet. This ensures only machines within the same private network can communicate with Redis, making it much harder for outsiders to gain access. Don't worry if you don't know what a VNet is, we will cover it in Chapter 12.

Instead of relying only on IP addresses for access, it is recommended to use managed identities such as Entra ID (formerly Azure AD) authentication where possible. Managed identities are a more secure and flexible way for applications to connect to Redis without needing to hardcode passwords or store credentials in configuration files.

Managing Redis patch schedules

Redis needs regular updates to keep the service running smoothly. These updates are applied by Azure, but you can choose when they happen to avoid interruptions during busy hours. To control when updates happen, you can set a patch schedule. This allows you to pick a specific day and time for maintenance so it does not affect your application's performance during peak hours.

For example, to schedule maintenance on Sunday at 3 A.M. UTC, run the following command:

```
$ az redis patch-schedule create
    --name testcache
    --resource-group testrg
    --schedule-entries '[{"dayOfWeek": "Sunday", "startHourUtc": 3}]'
```

This tells Azure to apply updates only on Sundays at 3 A.M. UTC. Choosing a time when traffic is low helps reduce any impact on users. If you need to check when updates are scheduled, you can use the following command:

```
$ az redis patch-schedule show
    --name testcache
    --resource-group testrg
```

This will display the current patch schedule, showing which day and time Redis maintenance will take place. Reviewing the schedule from time to time ensures that updates happen at a convenient time for your system.

Managing Redis server links

In the Premium tier, Redis supports geo-replication, allowing multiple Redis instances to be linked together. This helps with disaster recovery, improves performance by placing replicas closer to users, and ensures high availability. A replica Redis instance is a read-only copy that mirrors data from the primary instance.

To set up geo-replication, you need to create a link between your primary Redis instance and a secondary instance. This ensures that the secondary instance continuously receives updates from the primary.

Use the following command to link a secondary Redis instance to a primary one:

```
$ az redis server-link create
    --name <primary-cache-name>
    --resource-group <resource-group>
    --server-to-link <replica-cache-name>
    --replication-role Secondary
```

In this command, `--name` specifies the primary Redis instance, while `--server-to-link` designates the secondary Redis instance that will act as a read-only replica. The `--replication-role Secondary` flag ensures that the linked Redis instance only mirrors the data from the primary without modifying it. Once the link is created, any updates to the primary cache are automatically replicated to the replica cache; this ensures data remains consistent across both instances.

If a replica is no longer needed or you want to stop replication, you can remove the link between the primary and secondary instances. The following command deletes the link between the two servers:

```
$ az redis server-link delete
    --name <primary-cache-name>
    --resource-group <resource-group>
    --linked-server-name <replica-cache-name>
```

Here, `--name` identifies the primary Redis instance, and `--linked-server-name` specifies the replica Redis instance being removed. Once the link is deleted, the replica cache will stop receiving updates from the primary cache and will no longer function as a synchronized replica.

Other Azure Caching Options

While Azure Cache for Redis is the most commonly used caching solution, there are other alternatives that may be more suitable depending on the specific workload. These include query caching in Azure SQL Database and in-memory caching within VMs or Azure App Service. Understanding these options can help in selecting the right approach based on the factors you may be optimizing for.

Azure SQL Database caching

Databases often slow down applications, especially when the same queries are executed repeatedly. Instead of running identical queries over and over, Azure SQL Database provides several caching techniques to improve query performance. One such feature is the Query Store, which tracks query execution plans and caches frequently used queries for reuse. This eliminates the need for redundant computation, reducing response times and improving overall performance. To enable the Query Store, the following command can be executed:

```
ALTER DATABASE MyDatabase SET QUERY_STORE = ON;
```

Another useful caching technique is indexed views, which precompute and store the results of frequently executed queries as a virtual table. This allows queries to retrieve precomputed results rather than recomputing them each time. For example, a query that frequently counts orders per customer can be turned into an indexed view:

```
CREATE VIEW CachedOrders WITH SCHEMABINDING AS
SELECT CustomerID, COUNT(*) AS OrderCount FROM Orders GROUP BY CustomerID;
```

Result set caching is another technique that allows Azure SQL Database to cache the output of frequently executed queries. When a query is run multiple times, instead of fetching fresh data from disk, the cached result is returned. This improves performance for read-heavy workloads. Enabling it requires running:

```
ALTER DATABASE MyDatabase SET RESULT_SET_CACHING ON;
```

While database caching improves efficiency by reducing redundant queries, it is best suited for read-heavy applications. For write-intensive applications where data changes frequently, cached query results may become stale, leading to inconsistencies. In such cases, combining database caching with an external caching layer, such as Redis, may be a better approach.

Local in-memory caching on VMs or Azure App Service

For applications running in Azure VMs or Azure App Service, in-memory caching is a fast and simple way to store frequently accessed data. We talked about this briefly in "Introduction to Caching" on page 235. Unlike distributed caching solutions like Redis, in-memory caching stores data directly within the application's memory, avoiding network latency.

When running applications on Azure VMs, in-memory caching can be implemented within the application itself. For example, in C#, caching data in RAM can be done using the `MemoryCache` class:

```
var memoryCache = new MemoryCache(new MemoryCacheOptions());
memoryCache.Set("user123", "Cached Data", TimeSpan.FromMinutes(10));
```

To be able to use this, you need to add the cache service to your dependency injection (DI) container like this:

```
services.AddMemoryCache();
```

This method is useful when working with small datasets that need to be accessed frequently. It is also the fastest caching approach since data is retrieved from RAM instead of a database. However, one major downside is that the cache does not persist after a machine restart. If the machine shuts down or crashes, all cached data is lost. Additionally, in-memory caching on a single machine is not ideal for distributed applications, as different instances cannot share the same cache.

CDN Integration for Content Delivery

Remember our LMS from the previous sections? Imagine if we had different students in various parts of the world, and they all wanted to watch the same lecture video at the same time. If our system stored the video on a single server, every student would need to pull the file from that one location. This would create a huge problem—slow load times, buffering, and maybe even total system failure if too many students tried to access the video at once. This is why we need content delivery networks (CDNs).

A CDN is a system of servers spread across different locations that work together to quickly deliver content like images, videos, scripts, and web pages to users. Instead of every student in our LMS pulling the lecture video from a single server, a CDN stores copies of that video on multiple servers worldwide. When a student clicks "play," the video loads from the nearest server instead of a faraway origin server, making everything faster.

> ### How CDNs Complement Caching Strategies
>
> CDNs and caching go hand in hand. While in-memory caches like Redis store frequently used application data (like user sessions or search results), CDNs store website and app content to reduce load on origin servers. In other words, a cache speeds up backend requests, while a CDN speeds up content delivery to the user.
>
> If our LMS only used Azure Cache for Redis, we could reduce database queries by caching frequently requested data, like student profiles or course progress. But every time a student wanted to watch a video, the request would still go to our main storage (like Azure Blob Storage). With a CDN, that content is already cached at the edge servers, so users get instant access.

Latency is the delay that happens when data travels from the server to the user. If our LMS hosted videos on a single server in the US, students in Europe, Africa, or Asia would experience longer load times because the data has to travel a greater distance. A CDN reduces latency by storing cached copies of the video in different locations (called edge servers) around the world.

When a student in Lagos, for example, tries to watch the video, they don't have to stream it all the way from the US. Instead, the CDN finds the closest edge server, maybe one in West Africa, and delivers the video from there. This makes the experience much smoother with less buffering and lag.

CDNs don't just speed up videos, they also improve the delivery of other types of content. They cache and serve static content such as images, stylesheets (CSS), JavaScript files, and fonts, reducing the load on origin servers and ensuring faster page loads. They also help with dynamic content, including API responses and personalized web pages, by optimizing delivery and reducing latency. They are also widely used for software downloads, such as app updates and game patches, to ensure large files are distributed efficiently to users worldwide. For live streaming, CDNs make it possible for thousands or even millions of viewers to watch events without overwhelming the origin server, balancing traffic across multiple edge locations to prevent slowdowns or crashes.

Azure has two major solutions for speeding up content delivery across the globe: Azure CDN and Azure Front Door. Both serve as CDNs; however, they serve different purposes and are optimized for different use cases.

Azure CDN

Azure CDN is designed to cache static content at multiple edge locations worldwide. It helps reduce the time it takes to load websites, apps, and media files by serving content from the nearest CDN location instead of fetching it from the origin every time.

This is useful for scenarios like:

- Serving images, videos, and large assets faster
- Reducing bandwidth costs by offloading traffic from storage services like Azure Blob Storage
- Handling sudden spikes in traffic, such as a product launch or Black Friday sale, without overwhelming the origin server

For Azure CDN, when a user requests content (e.g., an image from a website), Azure CDN checks if the file already exists in a nearby edge server. If the file exists in the CDN cache, it is served instantly from that location. If the file does not exist, Azure CDN fetches it from the origin server (such as Azure Blob Storage), stores a copy, and serves it to the user. The next time someone requests the same file, it will be available from the cache instead of the origin. This process is called *cache warming* because the CDN gradually stores content based on demand.

To create an Azure CDN profile and endpoint that caches content from an Azure storage account, use:

```
$ az cdn profile create
    --name <cdn-profile-name>
    --resource-group <resource-group>
    --sku Standard_Microsoft

$ az cdn endpoint create
    --name <cdn-endpoint-name>
    --profile-name <cdn-profile-name>
    --resource-group <resource-group>
    --origin <storage>.blob.core.windows.net
```

This sets up an Azure CDN profile, creates an endpoint, and links it to a storage account where content is served. If deploying via Bicep, the script would look like this:

```
resource cdnProfile 'Microsoft.Cdn/profiles@2023-04-01' = {
  name: <cdn-profile-name>
  location: 'global'
  sku: { name: 'Standard_Microsoft' }
}

resource cdnEndpoint 'Microsoft.Cdn/profiles/endpoints@2023-04-01' = {
  name: <cdn-endpoint-name>
  parent: cdnProfile
  properties: {
    origins: [{
      name: 'MyOrigin'
      properties: { hostName: '<storage>.blob.core.windows.net' }
    }]
  }
}
```

Once deployed, the CDN will start caching and serving content from Azure Blob Storage. Azure CDN is great for static content but does not handle dynamic content well. If an API or web application needs real-time processing, CDN alone isn't enough. In such cases, Azure Front Door has a better solution for handling dynamic traffic and ensuring low-latency, intelligent routing.

Azure Front Door

Azure Front Door is a global application delivery network that combines content caching with intelligent traffic routing, security, and load balancing.

Unlike Azure CDN, which focuses only on static content, Front Door can accelerate dynamic content and route user traffic across multiple backend services. It ensures that users get the fastest and most reliable response, even if servers are distributed across multiple regions.

Azure Front Door is the right choice when the following exist:

- An application has users in multiple regions and needs a fast and reliable experience worldwide.
- Traffic needs to be intelligently routed to the best-performing or healthiest backend service.
- Security features like DDoS protection and WAF are required.
- APIs or dynamic websites need to be accelerated, not just static files.

When a user makes a request (e.g., accessing a website), Azure Front Door determines the best backend to handle it. If the content is cacheable, it serves it from an edge location, just like Azure CDN. If the request requires real-time processing, it routes the user to the closest and most responsive backend (e.g., a web app or API in Azure). If a backend becomes unhealthy or slow, Front Door automatically redirects traffic to another available backend.

To create an Azure Front Door with an endpoint and backend:

```
$  az afd profile create
     --resource-group <resource-group>
     --name <front-door-profile-name>
     --sku Premium_AzureFrontDoor

$  az afd endpoint create
     --resource-group <resource-group>
     --profile-name <front-door-profile-name>
     --endpoint-name <front-door-endpoint-name>

$  az afd origin-group create
     --resource-group <resource-group>
     --profile-name <front-door-profile-name>
     --origin-group-name <origin-group-name>
```

The first command creates an Azure Front Door profile, which defines the configuration and capabilities of the service. The second command sets up an endpoint, which acts as the publicly accessible entry point where users or applications send requests. The third command creates an origin group, which is a collection of backend servers that handle requests coming through the Front Door endpoint.

What Is an Origin Group?

An origin group is responsible for routing traffic to one or more backend origins, such as web apps, APIs, or storage accounts. It helps distribute traffic based on health checks, failover rules, and load-balancing policies. For example, if one backend server becomes unresponsive, Azure Front Door automatically directs traffic to a healthy server within the origin group so the web app can stay up.

To create an Azure Front Door profile, endpoint, and origin group in Bicep, add the following code snippet to your main Bicep file:

```
resource afdProfile 'Microsoft.Cdn/profiles@2023-04-01' = {
  name: <front-door-profile-name>
  location: 'global'
  sku: { name: 'Premium_AzureFrontDoor' }
}

resource afdEndpoint 'Microsoft.Cdn/profiles/endpoints@2023-04-01' = {
  name: <front-door-endpoint-name>
  parent: afdProfile
  properties: {}
}

resource afdOriginGroup 'Microsoft.Cdn/profiles/originGroups@2023-04-01' = {
  name: 'MyFDOriginGroup'
```

```
    parent: afdProfile
    properties: {
      sessionAffinityEnabledState: 'Enabled'
      healthProbeSettings: {
        probePath: '/'
        probeProtocol: 'Https'
        probeIntervalInSeconds: 120
      }
    }
  }
```

In the preceding code snippet, an Azure Front Door profile, endpoint, and origin group are created using Bicep. The `afdProfile` resource sets up the Front Door profile with the Premium SKU, allowing global traffic distribution. The `afdEndpoint` resource defines an endpoint linked to the profile, acting as the public entry point for users. The `afdOriginGroup` resource creates an origin group to manage backend servers. It enables session affinity, ensuring requests from the same user go to the same backend, and configures health probes to check backend availability every 120 seconds. This setup ensures efficient traffic routing, load balancing, and high availability.

Summary

This chapter covered caching in Azure, which helps applications run faster by storing frequently used data in a quick-access storage layer instead of always fetching it from a database. We covered different types of caching, like storing data in local memory, using a shared cache across multiple servers, and keeping temporary user sessions. The chapter also covered key caching methods, such as checking the cache first before going to the database (cache-aside), automatically fetching and updating data in the cache (read-through/write-through), and delaying database updates to improve performance (write-behind). It focused on Azure Cache for Redis, explaining how to set it up, manage security, and keep it updated. Additionally, other caching options, like Azure SQL Database caching and in-memory caching on VMs, were also discussed. The chapter ended with CDNs, like Azure CDN and Azure Front Door, which store copies of files like images and videos in different locations worldwide to load them faster for users. In the next chapter, you will learn about networking in Azure.

CHAPTER 12

Networking in Azure

Networking connects everything, allowing resources, apps, and users to communicate smoothly. In the cloud, networking is important because it controls how information moves, how different parts of a system connect, and how secure those connections are. Azure has powerful networking tools that help create, manage, and secure these connections.

In this chapter, we will start with Azure VNets, which allow cloud resources to connect with each other. We will explore subnets, which help organize networks and improve security, and discuss how IP addresses are used in Azure. We will also look at different ways resources can connect, such as VPN gateway, ExpressRoute, and Private Link. Next, we will cover load balancing with Azure Load Balancer and Azure Traffic Manager. Finally, we will discuss Azure DNS and how to configure custom domain names on Azure. By the end of this chapter, you will have a strong understanding of how Azure networking works and how to use it effectively.

Introduction to Azure Networking

Computer networks in cloud computing work like huge digital highways that connect different machines and services. In traditional networks, you deal with physical cables and routers, but cloud networking creates these connections through software. This means you can set up and change network structures without touching any hardware. When you're working with Azure, this becomes really powerful because you can build entire networks with just a few clicks or commands.

The backbone of Azure networking is something called a virtual network, or VNet for short. Think of a VNet as your own private piece of Azure's cloud. It's like having your own isolated network floating in Microsoft's data centers. Inside this network, you can put all sorts of things: VMs that act as servers, databases that store your data, and web applications your customers use. Each of these gets its own IP address, just like devices in your home network have their own addresses.

Speaking of addresses, Azure uses two types: private ones for things talking to each other inside your network, and public ones for anything that needs to be reachable from the rest of the internet. It's similar to how your home router gives your devices local addresses but shows a different address to the outside world. This system helps keep things organized and secure, while making sure everything can still communicate when it needs to.

To make networks even more manageable, Azure lets you create subnets, which are smaller sections within your VNet. It's like dividing a large office building into departments. You might put all your database servers in one subnet, web servers in another, and perhaps keep a separate subnet for tools that help you manage everything. This separation helps control traffic flow and keeps things secure by letting you set different rules for different areas.

When it comes to network connectivity on Azure, there are a few options. You can set up private connections that never touch the public internet. This is great for linking to your company's existing network or other cloud resources. You can also use public connections when you need to make things available to users around the world. Azure gives you tools to secure both types, letting you control exactly who can access what.

The next few sections will go deeper into these tools and show examples using Azure Bicep and the Azure CLI.

Azure Virtual Networks

At its core, a VNet is your private network in Azure's cloud environment, and it provides the fundamental infrastructure necessary for your resources to communicate securely. When you deploy a VNet in Azure, you're essentially carving out your own isolated section of Azure's cloud. This isolation gives you complete control over your network environment, including IP address ranges, routing tables, and security policies. Think of it as having your own private data center but without the physical hardware constraints.

Let's explore how to create a basic VNet using Azure CLI. This command establishes the foundation of your network infrastructure:

```
$  az network vnet create
    --name myVNet
    --resource-group myResourceGroup
    --location eastus
    --address-prefix 10.0.0.0/16
    --subnet-name mySubnet
    --subnet-prefix 10.0.1.0/24
```

If you choose to use IaC, the same network can be defined using Bicep:

```
resource virtualNetwork 'Microsoft.Network/virtualNetworks@2021-05-01' = {
  name: 'myVNet'
  location: resourceGroup().location
  properties: {
    addressSpace: {
      addressPrefixes: [
        '10.0.0.0/16'
      ]
    }
    subnets: [
      {
        name: 'mySubnet'
        properties: {
          addressPrefix: '10.0.1.0/24'
          privateEndpointNetworkPolicies: 'Enabled'
          privateLinkServiceNetworkPolicies: 'Enabled'
        }
      }
    ]
  }
}
```

VNets have so many benefits when it comes to communication and security in Azure's cloud infrastructure. One of the most powerful aspects of VNet communication is its flexibility. Resources within the same VNet can talk to each other by default through private IP addresses, and this removes the need for complex routing configurations. This native communication capability extends across subnets within the VNet, allowing you to create sophisticated multitier applications. For example, you can place your web servers in one subnet, application servers in another, and databases in a third, all communicating securely through internal network paths.

The security benefits of VNets are particularly noteworthy. NSGs serve as built-in firewalls, allowing you to control inbound and outbound traffic at both the subnet and individual resource level. You can create detailed security rules that specify exactly which types of traffic are allowed or denied, based on source and destination IP addresses, ports, and protocols. This granular control ensures your resources are protected against unauthorized access while still allowing legitimate traffic to flow.

VNets also excel at hybrid connectivity scenarios. Through site-to-site VPN connections or ExpressRoute circuits, you can securely extend your on-premises network into Azure. This hybrid networking capability is crucial for organizations that need to maintain some workloads on premises while leveraging cloud resources. The connection is secure and private, ensuring sensitive data remains protected as it travels between your data center and Azure.

When it comes to service integration, VNets provide special features like service endpoints and private links. These allow you to access Azure services like storage accounts, SQL databases, and Key Vault through private IP addresses, keeping traffic within Azure's backbone network. This enhances security by eliminating exposure to the public internet, and it also reduces data transfer costs since traffic stays within Azure's network.

Subnets and IP Addressing in Azure

Think of subnets as smaller, organized sections within your VNet. Each subnet gets its own portion of the VNet's IP address space, which enables organized and secure resource placement.

Let's start by creating a VNet with multiple subnets using Azure CLI:

```
# Create the parent virtual network
az network vnet create
  --name enterpriseVNet
  --resource-group myRG
  --location eastus
  --address-prefix 172.16.0.0/16

# Create subnets for different workloads
az network vnet subnet create
  --name frontendSubnet
  --resource-group myRG
  --vnet-name enterpriseVNet
  --address-prefixes 172.16.1.0/24

az network vnet subnet create
  --name backendSubnet
  --resource-group myRG
  --vnet-name enterpriseVNet
  --address-prefixes 172.16.2.0/24
```

This Azure CLI code creates a VNet with two distinct subnets. The first command establishes our main network space with a generous address range of `172.16.0.0/16`, providing us with thousands of possible IP addresses. We then carve out two subnets: a frontend subnet for web-facing resources and a backend subnet for internal processing and databases. Each subnet gets a `/24` address space, allowing for up to 254 usable IP addresses per subnet.

If you choose to use IaC, the same network segmentation can be achieved using Bicep. Here's how we can declare our network infrastructure:

```
// Assuming that frontendNsg and backendNsg were defined earlier
resource enterpriseVNet 'Microsoft.Network/virtualNetworks@2021-05-01' = {
  name: 'enterpriseVNet'
  location: resourceGroup().location
  properties: {
    addressSpace: {
      addressPrefixes: [
        '172.16.0.0/16'
      ]
    }
    subnets: [
      {
        name: 'frontendSubnet'
```

```
          properties: {
            addressPrefix: '172.16.1.0/24'
            networkSecurityGroup: {
              id: frontendNsg.id
            }
          }
        }
        {
          name: 'backendSubnet'
          properties: {
            addressPrefix: '172.16.2.0/24'
            networkSecurityGroup: {
              id: backendNsg.id
            }
          }
        }
      ]
    }
  }
```

IP addressing in Azure follows the industry-standard CIDR (Classless Inter-Domain Routing) notation, a method that efficiently represents IP address ranges. When we specify an address range like `172.16.0.0/16`, the `/16` indicates that the first 16 bits of the address are fixed for the network portion, leaving the remaining bits for host addresses. This gives us a theoretical maximum of 65,536 IP addresses in our VNet. Let's examine how we arrived at this number. In a `/16` network, we have 16 bits that are fixed for the network portion (in this case, `172.16`) and 16 bits that can vary for host addresses. In binary, this means the first two octets are set (`10101100.00010000`), while the last two octets can contain any combination of ones and zeros. Since each bit can be either zero or one, and we have 16 bits that can vary, we calculate the total number of possible combinations as 2 raised to the power of 16 (2^16). This calculation gives us exactly 65,536 possible unique IP addresses within this network range. These addresses span from `172.16.0.0` to `172.16.255.255`, providing ample addressing space for most VNet deployments. Figure 12-1 illustrates this.

To manage address ranges effectively in Azure, you can use several key Azure CLI commands. To view your current IP address space usage, use:

```
$  az network vnet show
     --name myVNet
     --resource-group <resource-group>
     --query "addressSpace.addressPrefixes"
```

This command retrieves the configured address spaces for your VNet and displays all CIDR ranges assigned to it. It's particularly useful when you need to verify your network's address space configuration or plan for network expansion, as it shows both primary and any additional address ranges you've configured.

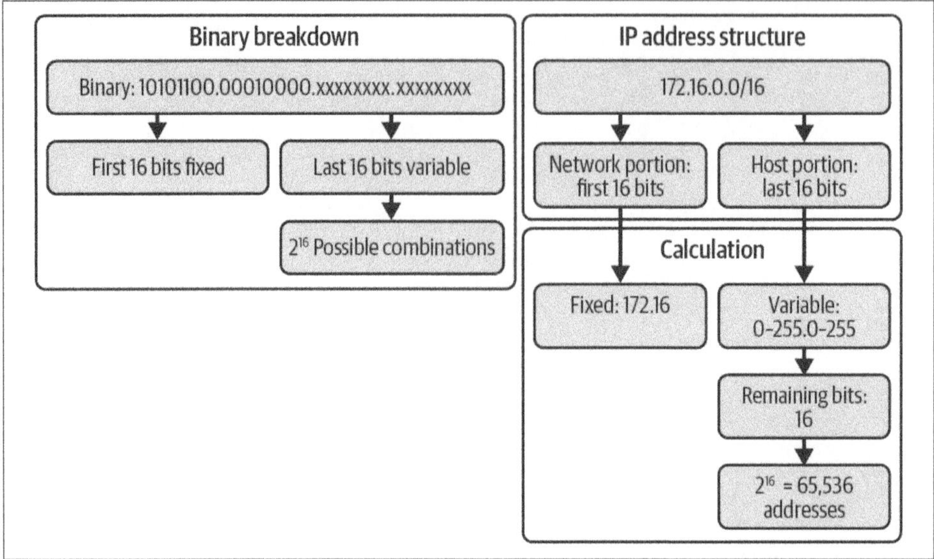

Figure 12-1. IP address calculation

For monitoring IP utilization within subnets, use:

```
$  az network vnet subnet list
     --resource-group <resource-group>
     --vnet-name <vnet-name>
     --output table
```

This command shows all subnets within your VNet and displays each subnet's address prefix, security group associations, and other key properties in a tabular format. This helps you understand how your address space is segmented and identify available ranges for new subnets.

When you need to track specific IP assignments within a subnet, use:

```
$  az network nic list
      --resource-group myResourceGroup
      --query "[].ipConfigurations[].{PrivateIP:privateIPAddress,
              "Name:name, Subnet:subnet.id}"
      --output table
```

This command lists all network interface configurations in your resource group, showing which IP addresses are currently assigned to resources. The output includes the private IP address of each network interface, its name, and the subnet it belongs to, which is helpful for tracking IP utilization and troubleshooting network connectivity issues.

In Azure, you'll work with both public and private IP addresses. Private IP addresses enable internal communication within your VNet and with connected on-premises networks, while public IPs allow resources to communicate with the internet. Here's how to create both types:

```
# Create a public IP address
$  az network public-ip create
     --name <name>
     --resource-group <resource-group>
     --allocation-method Static
     --sku Standard
     --version IPv4

# Create a network interface with both private and public IPs
$  az network nic create
     --name <name>
     --resource-group <resource-group>
     --vnet-name productionVNet
     --subnet frontendSubnet
     --private-ip-address 172.16.1.10
     --public-ip-address webServerPublicIP
```

When working with private IP addresses in Azure, you should use these ranges as defined in RFC 1918 (*https://oreil.ly/rfc1918*):

- 10.0.0.0/8 (10.0.0.0–10.255.255.255)
- 172.16.0.0/12 (172.16.0.0–172.31.255.255)
- 192.168.0.0/16 (192.168.0.0–192.168.255.255)

Here's a Bicep example showing how to implement both public and private IP addressing in your infrastructure:

```
resource publicIP 'Microsoft.Network/publicIPAddresses@2021-05-01' = {
  name: 'webServerPublicIP'
  location: resourceGroup().location
  sku: {
    name: 'Standard'
  }
  properties: {
    publicIPAllocationMethod: 'Static'
    publicIPAddressVersion: 'IPv4'
    dnsSettings: {
      domainNameLabel: 'mywebserver'
    }
  }
}

resource networkInterface 'Microsoft.Network/networkInterfaces@2021-05-01' = {
  name: 'webServerNIC'
  location: resourceGroup().location
  properties: {
    ipConfigurations: [
      {
        name: 'ipconfig1'
        properties: {
          subnet: {
            id: resourceId('Microsoft.Network/virtualNetworks/subnets',
                  'productionVNet', 'frontendSubnet')
```

```
            }
            privateIPAddress: '172.16.1.10'
            privateIPAllocationMethod: 'Static'
            publicIPAddress: {
              id: publicIP.id
            }
          }
        }
      ]
    }
  }
```

This Bicep configuration shows the relationship between public and private IP addresses. The network interface gets a static private IP (`172.16.1.10`) and is associated with a public IP address. This setup is common for resources like web servers that need both internal network access and internet connectivity.

Connectivity Between Resources

In Azure's networking infrastructure, connecting resources requires understanding several key technologies that enable secure and efficient communication. Let's start with VNet peering, which is Azure's native solution for connecting VNets within the cloud platform.

VNet peering establishes a low-latency, high-bandwidth connection between two virtual networks using Microsoft's backbone infrastructure. When implementing peering, you're creating a two-way communication channel that operates at the network layer, which allows for seamless IP-based communication between resources. Here's the technical implementation:

```
$ az network vnet peering create
    --name VNet1-to-VNet2
    --resource-group <resource-group>
    --vnet-name VNet1
    --remote-vnet VNet2
    --allow-vnet-access
    --allow-forwarded-traffic
    --allow-gateway-transit
```

This command establishes the initial peering connection between `VNet1` and `VNet2`. The `allow-forwarded-traffic` parameter enables traffic that originates from outside the VNet but is forwarded by a network virtual appliance, while `allow-gateway-transit` permits the peered network to utilize the local network's VPN gateway. After execution, resources can communicate using private IP addresses, maintaining security by keeping traffic off the public internet.

Here's the equivalent Bicep configuration for VNet peering:

```
resource vnetPeering 'Microsoft.Network/virtualNetworks/virtualNetworkPeerings@2021-05-01'=
{
  name: '${vnet1.name}/VNet1-to-VNet2'
  properties: {
```

```
      allowVirtualNetworkAccess: true
      allowForwardedTraffic: true
      allowGatewayTransit: true
      useRemoteGateways: false
      remoteVirtualNetwork: {
        id: vnet2.id
      }
    }
  }
```

When dealing with hybrid connectivity scenarios, a VPN gateway is also very useful. A VPN gateway serves as the endpoint for encrypted *IPsec/IKE* connections from your on-premises network.

What Do IPsec/IKE Do?

Internet Protocol Security (IPsec) and Internet Key Exchange (IKE) work together as a protocol suite to secure network communications, particularly in the context of VPNs. IPsec provides the encryption and authentication mechanisms for securing data packets, while IKE handles the complex task of establishing and managing secure connections. Think of IPsec as the security guard that protects your data packets, while IKE is the key master who decides who gets access and manages the exchange of encryption keys.

When two networks need to communicate securely, they first engage in what's called the *IKE handshake*. During Phase 1 of this handshake, the two endpoints authenticate each other and establish a secure channel for negotiating the IPsec security parameters. This initial exchange is like two security systems verifying each other's credentials before allowing any data to pass through. Phase 1 can operate in two modes: *main mode*, which provides increased security through six messages exchanged between peers, or *aggressive mode*, which is faster but slightly less secure, using only three messages.

Once Phase 1 is complete, Phase 2 (also called *quick mode*) begins. Here, the endpoints negotiate the specific security parameters that will protect the actual data traffic. This includes agreeing on encryption algorithms (like AES), hash functions (like SHA-256), and perfect forward secrecy parameters. The result is what's called a Security Association (SA)—essentially a contract between the two endpoints about how they'll protect the data flowing between them.

IPsec then uses these negotiated parameters to protect the data in one of two ways: Authentication Header (AH), which provides integrity and authentication but not confidentiality, or Encapsulating Security Payload (ESP), which provides confidentiality through encryption in addition to integrity and authentication. ESP is more commonly used today because it offers more comprehensive protection. These protocols can operate in either *transport mode*, which only encrypts the payload of IP packets, or *tunnel mode*, which encrypts the entire IP packet and is used in VPN deployments.

To implement the VPN gateway for hybrid connectivity, the process begins with creating the necessary networking components:

```
# Create the Gateway Subnet - must be named 'GatewaySubnet'
$  az network vnet subnet create
    --name GatewaySubnet
    --resource-group <resource-group>
    --vnet-name VNet1
    --address-prefix 10.0.255.0/27

# Create the public IP for the gateway
$  az network public-ip create
    --name VPNGatewayIP
    --resource-group <resource-group>
    --allocation-method Static
    --sku Standard
```

The gateway subnet requires careful planning—the /27 subnet provides 32 IP addresses, which is Microsoft's recommended minimum size. This subnet houses the gateway instances and must be named `GatewaySubnet` for Azure to recognize its purpose. The public IP uses static allocation to ensure the address doesn't change after gateway reboots or maintenance.

Next, create the VPN gateway itself:

```
$  az network vnet-gateway create
    --name <name>
    --resource-group <resource-group>
    --vnet VNet1
    --gateway-type Vpn
    --sku VpnGw1
    --vpn-type RouteBased
    --public-ip-address VPNGatewayIP
    --no-wait
```

The `VpnGw1` SKU provides up to 650 Mbps aggregate throughput with support for basic features like point-to-site VPN and Border Gateway Protocol (BGP) routing. The `RouteBased` VPN type enables more flexible routing options compared to policy-based VPNs.

ExpressRoute is another service that can be used for connectivity. It provides a dedicated private connection to Azure, bypassing the public internet entirely. Think of it as having your own fiberoptic cable directly to Microsoft's network. This connection happens through a connectivity provider (like Equinix or Megaport) at speeds ranging from 50 Mbps to 100 Gbps. Here's how to establish an ExpressRoute circuit:

```
$  az network express-route create
    --name production-circuit
    --resource-group test-rg
    --location eastus
    --bandwidth 100
    --peering-location "New York"
    --provider Equinix
    --sku-family MeteredData
    --sku-tier Premium
```

The previous command creates an ExpressRoute circuit with premium features enabled. The SKU tier `Premium` allows for global connectivity across geopolitical regions and supports more BGP routes. After creating the circuit, you'll receive a service key your connectivity provider uses to establish the physical connection.

Here's the same configuration in Bicep, showing the relationship between different ExpressRoute components:

```
resource expressRouteCircuit 'Microsoft.Network/expressRouteCircuits@2021-05-01' = {
  name: 'production-circuit'
  location: resourceGroup().location
  sku: {
    name: 'Premium_MeteredData'
    tier: 'Premium'
    family: 'MeteredData'
  }
  properties: {
    serviceProviderProperties: {
      serviceProviderName: 'Equinix'
      peeringLocation: 'New York'
      bandwidthInMbps: 100
    }
    allowClassicOperations: false
    peerings: [
      {
        name: 'AzurePrivatePeering'
        properties: {
          peeringType: 'AzurePrivate'
          peerASN: 65001
          primaryPeerAddressPrefix: '172.16.0.0/30'
          secondaryPeerAddressPrefix: '172.16.0.4/30'
          vlanId: 100
        }
      }
    ]
  }
}
```

Once your ExpressRoute circuit is active, you'll need to connect it to your VNet using an ExpressRoute gateway:

```
$ az network vnet-gateway create
    --name expressRouteGW
    --resource-group <resource-group>
    --location eastus
    --vnet myVNet
    --gateway-type ExpressRoute
    --sku ErGw1AZ
    --no-wait
```

Moving on to Private Link, this service enables you to access Azure PaaS services over a private endpoint in your VNet. Instead of exposing your services to the public internet, Private Link provides private IP connectivity. Here's how to set up a private endpoint for an Azure Storage account:

```
$  az network private-dns zone create
    --name "privatelink.blob.core.windows.net"
```

```
    --resource-group <resource-group>

$ az network private-dns link vnet create
    --name <name>
    --resource-group <resource-group>
    --zone-name "privatelink.blob.core.windows.net"
    --virtual-network <virtual-network>
    --registration-enabled false

$  az network private-endpoint create
    --name <name>
    --resource-group <resource-group>
    --vnet-name <vnet-name>
    --subnet dataSubnet
    --private-connection-resource-id $(az storage account show -g test-resourcegroup -n
        storageacc --query id -o tsv) \
    --group-id blob
    --connection-name <connection-name>
```

Here's the equivalent Bicep configuration for Private Link setup:

```
resource privateEndpoint 'Microsoft.Network/privateEndpoints@2021-05-01' = {
  name: 'myStorageEndpoint'
  location: resourceGroup().location
  properties: {
    privateLinkServiceConnections: [
      {
        name: 'myStorageConnection'
        properties: {
          privateLinkServiceId: storageAccount.id
          groupIds: [
            'blob'
          ]
        }
      }
    ]
    subnet: {
      id: subnet.id
    }
  }
}

resource privateDnsZone 'Microsoft.Network/privateDnsZones@2020-06-01' = {
  name: 'privatelink.blob.core.windows.net'
  location: 'global'
  properties: {}
}

resource privateDnsZoneLink 'Microsoft.Network/privateDnsZones/
virtualNetworkLinks@2020-06-01' = {
  parent: privateDnsZone
  name: 'MyDNSLink'
  location: 'global'
  properties: {
    registrationEnabled: false
    virtualNetwork: {
      id: virtualNetwork.id
    }
  }
}
```

After setting up Private Link, clients within your VNet can access the storage account using its private endpoint IP address. The private DNS zone handles name resolution, ensuring that storage account names resolve to private IP addresses when accessed from the VNet.

Load Balancing and Traffic Management

There are multiple ways to do load balancing in Azure. Let's imagine you have four instances of your application, one deployed in West Europe, another in the Eastern US, a third in Southeast Asia, and a fourth in Australia East. Each instance has multiple VMs running your application. This setup requires careful consideration of how to distribute traffic effectively across these global resources. Load balancing services enable you successfully to manage this.

Azure Load Balancer

At the most basic level, Azure Load Balancer helps distribute traffic within a single region. For instance, in your West Europe deployment, you might have three virtual machines running your web application. Here's how to set this up:

```
# Create a load balancer with a public IP
$  az network lb create
    --resource-group <resource-group>
    --name europeLoadBalancer
    --sku Standard
    --public-ip-address europePIP
    --frontend-ip-name europeFrontend
    --backend-pool-name europeBackend
    --location westeurope
```

This command creates a Standard SKU load balancer in the West Europe region, configured with a public IP address. The frontend IP configuration is named `europeFrontend`, and it creates a backend pool named `europeBackend` where we'll later add our VMs. The Standard SKU provides enhanced security features and supports zone-redundant deployments.

Here's the equivalent Bicep code:

```
resource loadBalancer 'Microsoft.Network/loadBalancers@2021-05-01' = {
  name: 'europeLoadBalancer'
  location: 'westeurope'
  sku: {
    name: 'Standard'
  }
  properties: {
    frontendIPConfigurations: [
      {
        name: 'europeFrontend'
        properties: {
          publicIPAddress: {
            id: publicIP.id
```

```
            }
          }
        }
      ]
      backendAddressPools: [
        {
          name: 'europeBackend'
        }
      ]
    }
  }
```

Next, let's look at the health probe configuration:

```
# Add a health probe to check VM health
$  az network lb probe create
    --resource-group <resource-group>
    --lb-name europeLoadBalancer
    --name webProbe
    --protocol tcp
    --port 80
    --interval 30
    --threshold 2
```

This command sets up a health monitoring system that checks each backend VM every 30 seconds by attempting a TCP connection on port 80. If a VM fails to respond to two consecutive probes, it's considered unhealthy and removed from the load balancer's rotation. This ensures traffic is only directed to healthy instances.

Here's the Bicep equivalent for the health probe:

```
resource loadBalancer 'Microsoft.Network/loadBalancers@2021-05-01' = {
  // previous configuration ...
  properties: {
    // previous properties ...
    probes: [
      {
        name: 'webProbe'
        properties: {
          protocol: 'Tcp'
          port: 80
          intervalInSeconds: 30
          numberOfProbes: 2
        }
      }
    ]
  }
}
```

Finally, let's create the load balancing rule:

```
$  az network lb rule create
    --resource-group <resource-group>
    --lb-name europeLoadBalancer
    --name webRule
    --protocol tcp
    --frontend-port 80
    --backend-port 80
    --frontend-ip-name europeFrontend
```

```
    --backend-pool-name europeBackend
    --probe-name webProbe
    --idle-timeout 15
```

This rule defines how traffic is distributed to the backend pool. It listens for incoming TCP traffic on port 80 of the frontend IP and forwards it to port 80 on the backend VMs. The rule is associated with our health probe, ensuring traffic is only sent to healthy instances, and includes a 15-second idle timeout for connections.

Here's the Bicep equivalent for the load balancing rule:

```
resource loadBalancer 'Microsoft.Network/loadBalancers@2021-05-01' = {
  // previous configuration ...
  properties: {
    // previous properties ...
    loadBalancingRules: [
      {
        name: 'webRule'
        properties: {
          frontendIPConfiguration: {
            id: resourceId('Microsoft.Network/loadBalancers/frontendIPConfigurations',
                'europeLoadBalancer', 'europeFrontend')
          }
          backendAddressPool: {
            id: resourceId('Microsoft.Network/loadBalancers/backendAddressPools',
                'europeLoadBalancer', 'europeBackend')
          }
          probe: {
            id: resourceId('Microsoft.Network/loadBalancers/probes',
                'europeLoadBalancer', 'webProbe')
          }
          protocol: 'Tcp'
          frontendPort: 80
          backendPort: 80
          idleTimeoutInMinutes: 15
        }
      }
    ]
  }
}
```

This complete load balancer configuration creates a traffic distribution system in the West Europe region. The health probe actively monitors backend VMs every 30 seconds on port 80, and if any VM fails two consecutive checks, it's automatically removed from the traffic rotation.

Azure Application Gateway

For applications requiring more sophisticated routing capabilities, Application Gateway provides Layer 7 load balancing. This means it can make routing decisions based on URL paths and host headers. Here's how to set up an application gateway:

```
$ az network application-gateway create
    --name <app-gateway-name>
    --location westeurope
    --resource-group <resource-group>
```

```
--vnet-name <vnet-name>
--subnet <subnet>
--capacity 2
--sku Standard_v2
--http-settings-cookie-based-affinity Enabled
--frontend-port 80
--http-settings-port 80
--http-settings-protocol Http
--public-ip-address myAppGWPIP
--priority 1000
```

Let's break this down in Bicep:

```
resource applicationGateway 'Microsoft.Network/applicationGateways@2021-05-01' = {
  name: 'globalAppGateway'
  location: location
  properties: {
    sku: {
      name: 'Standard_v2'
      tier: 'Standard_v2'
    }
    gatewayIPConfigurations: [
      {
        name: 'appGatewayIpConfig'
        properties: {
          subnet: {
            id: appGatewaySubnet.id
          }
        }
      }
    ]
    frontendIPConfigurations: [
      {
        name: 'appGwPublicFrontendIp'
        properties: {
          publicIPAddress: {
            id: publicIP.id
          }
        }
      }
    ]
    frontendPorts: [
      {
        name: 'port_80'
        properties: {
          port: 80
        }
      }
    ]
    backendAddressPools: [
      {
        name: 'europePool'
        properties: {
          backendAddresses: [
            {
              ipAddress: '10.0.1.4'
            }
            {
              ipAddress: '10.0.1.5'
            }
```

```
          ]
        }
      }
    ]
    backendHttpSettingsCollection: [
      {
        name: 'HTTPSetting'
        properties: {
          port: 80
          protocol: 'Http'
          cookieBasedAffinity: 'Enabled'
          requestTimeout: 20
          probe: {
            id: resourceId('Microsoft.Network/applicationGateways/probes',
                'globalAppGateway', 'healthProbe')
          }
        }
      }
    ]
  }
}
```

This Bicep code creates an Azure application gateway named `globalAppGateway` using the `Standard_v2` tier. The configuration establishes the gateway's core networking components, starting with its placement in a specific subnet through the `gatewayIPConfigurations`. It sets up a public-facing frontend using a public IP address and configures it to listen on port 80 for incoming traffic. The backend pool, named `europePool`, is configured to distribute traffic to two specific backend servers with IP addresses `10.0.1.4` and `10.0.1.5`. The backend HTTP settings define how the gateway communicates with these servers, using HTTP protocol on port 80, with cookie-based session affinity enabled to ensure user requests consistently reach the same server, a 20-second request timeout for connections, and a health probe to monitor the backend servers' availability.

Application Gateway also supports WAF capabilities through its `WAF_v2` SKU, providing protection against common web exploits and vulnerabilities using OWASP core rule sets. Here's how to enable WAF protection:

```
# Create application gateway with WAF
az network application-gateway create
    --name globalAppGateway
    --resource-group <resource-group>
    --sku WAF_v2
    --capacity 2
    --subnet <subnet>
    --http-settings-cookie-based-affinity Enabled
    --public-ip-address <public-ip>

# Create WAF policy with OWASP rule set
az network application-gateway waf-policy create
    --name myWAFPolicy
    --resource-group <resource-group>
    --location eastus
    --type OWASP
```

```
    --version 3.2

# Configure policy settings (enable in Prevention mode)
az network application-gateway waf-policy policy-setting update
    --policy-name myWAFPolicy
    --resource-group <resource-group>
    --state Enabled
    --mode Prevention
    --request-body-check true
    --max-request-body-size 128

# Configure custom rules
az network application-gateway waf-policy custom-rule create
    --policy-name myWAFPolicy
    --resource-group <resource-group>
    --name BlockSpecificIPs
    --priority 1
    --rule-type MatchRule
    --action Block
    --match-conditions IPMatch Source_IP 192.168.1.0/24 192.168.2.0/24
```

Another powerful feature of Application Gateway is URL path-based routing, allowing you to route traffic to different backend pools based on the URL path. For example, sending */api/** requests to your API servers and */images/** to your storage servers:

```
resource applicationGateway 'Microsoft.Network/applicationGateways@2021-05-01' = {
  name: 'globalAppGateway'
  // ... other configuration
  properties: {
    urlPathMaps: [
      {
        name: 'pathBasedRouting'
        properties: {
          defaultBackendAddressPool: {
            id: defaultPool.id
          }
          defaultBackendHttpSettings: {
            id: defaultHttpSettings.id
          }
          pathRules: [
            {
              name: 'apiPath'
              properties: {
                paths: [
                  '/api/*'
                ]
                backendAddressPool: {
                  id: apiPool.id
                }
                backendHttpSettings: {
                  id: apiHttpSettings.id
                }
              }
             }
             // ... other paths
            }
          ]
        }
      }
```

```
    ]
  }
}
```

The URL path map configuration in this Application Gateway setup (shown in the code snippet) enables intelligent routing based on URL patterns, where any requests matching */api/** are directed to a specific backend pool and HTTP settings dedicated to API handling. All other requests that don't match the specified path patterns are automatically routed to the default backend pool and HTTP settings, providing a flexible way to handle different types of traffic within the same application gateway.

Azure Front Door

Azure Front Door is a CDN solution operating at Microsoft's edge locations worldwide, functioning as a global load balancer that intelligently distributes traffic across multiple regions. Unlike traditional load balancers that operate within a single region, Front Door routes users to the nearest edge location using anycast networking, then makes intelligent routing decisions based on various metrics to determine the optimal backend (called an origin) to handle each request.

To set up Front Door with load balancing capabilities, let's first create a Front Door profile and endpoint:

```
# Create Front Door profile
$  az afd profile create
    --profile-name <profile-name>
    --resource-group <resource-group>
    --sku Standard_AzureFrontDoor

# Add an endpoint
$  az afd endpoint create
    --endpoint-name <endpoint-name>
    --profile-name <profile-name>
    --resource-group <resource-group>
```

The equivalent Bicep configuration would be:

```
resource frontDoorProfile 'Microsoft.Cdn/profiles@2021-06-01' = {
  name: <profile-name>
  location: 'global'
  sku: {
    name: 'Standard_AzureFrontDoor'
  }
}

resource endpoint 'Microsoft.Cdn/profiles/afdEndpoints@2021-06-01' = {
  parent: frontDoorProfile
  name: <endpoint-name>
  location: 'global'
  properties: {
    enabledState: 'Enabled'
  }
}
```

Next, we'll create an origin group and add our backend origins. The origin group configuration includes health probe settings that check each backend's health every 120 seconds:

```
# Create origin group
$  az afd origin-group create
    --origin-group-name myOriginGroup
    --profile-name myFrontDoor
    --resource-group myRG
    --probe-request-type GET
    --probe-protocol Http
    --probe-interval-in-seconds 120
    --probe-path /health

# Add origins
$  az afd origin create
    --origin-name europeOrigin
    --origin-group-name myOriginGroup
    --profile-name myFrontDoor
    --resource-group myRG
    --host-name europe-app.azurewebsites.net
    --priority 1
    --weight 1000

$  az afd origin create
    --origin-name usOrigin
    --origin-group-name myOriginGroup
    --profile-name myFrontDoor
    --resource-group myRG
    --host-name us-app.azurewebsites.net
    --priority 1
    --weight 1000
```

Here's the corresponding Bicep configuration:

```
resource originGroup 'Microsoft.Cdn/profiles/originGroups@2021-06-01' = {
  parent: frontDoorProfile
  name: 'myOriginGroup'
  properties: {
    loadBalancingSettings: {
      sampleSize: 4
      successfulSamplesRequired: 3
    }
    healthProbeSettings: {
      probePath: '/health'
      probeRequestType: 'GET'
      probeProtocol: 'Http'
      probeIntervalInSeconds: 120
    }
  }
}

resource europeOrigin 'Microsoft.Cdn/profiles/originGroups/origins@2021-06-01' = {
  parent: originGroup
  name: 'europeOrigin'
  properties: {
    hostName: 'europe-app.azurewebsites.net'
    priority: 1
    weight: 1000
```

```
    enabledState: 'Enabled'
  }
}

resource usOrigin 'Microsoft.Cdn/profiles/originGroups/origins@2021-06-01' = {
  parent: originGroup
  name: 'usOrigin'
  properties: {
    hostName: 'us-app.azurewebsites.net'
    priority: 1
    weight: 1000
    enabledState: 'Enabled'
  }
}
```

In this configuration, both origins have equal priority (`1`) and weight (`1000`), meaning Front Door will distribute traffic evenly between them when both are healthy. The health probe checks the */health* endpoint every 120 seconds using `HTTP GET` requests. When Front Door detects an origin is slow or unhealthy, it automatically routes more traffic to healthy origins, ensuring optimal application performance and availability.

What sets Front Door apart is its integration with Microsoft's global network. It can detect and route around internet problems by using Microsoft's private backbone network, which provides more reliable connections than public internet routing alone.

Azure Traffic Manager

Azure Traffic Manager is a DNS-based traffic load balancer that enables distribution of traffic across global Azure regions. Unlike Front Door, which operates at Layer 7 (HTTP/S), Traffic Manager works at the DNS level, making it suitable for non-HTTP/S protocols as well.

Let's configure Traffic Manager to distribute traffic across our global application endpoints:

```
# Create Traffic Manager profile
az network traffic-manager profile create
  --name myTrafficManager
  --resource-group test-rg
  --routing-method Performance
  --unique-dns-name myapp-global
  --ttl 30
  --monitor-protocol HTTP
  --monitor-port 80
  --monitor-path "/health"

# Add endpoints for different regions
az network traffic-manager endpoint create
  --name europeEndpoint
  --profile-name myTrafficManager
  --resource-group test-rg
  --type azureEndpoints
  --target-resource-id "/subscriptions/xxx/.../sites/europe-app"
  --endpoint-location westeurope
```

```
az network traffic-manager endpoint create
  --name usEndpoint
  --profile-name myTrafficManager
  --resource-group test-rg
  --type azureEndpoints
  --target-resource-id "/subscriptions/xxx/…/sites/us-app"
  --endpoint-location eastus
```

Here's the equivalent Bicep configuration:

```
resource trafficManagerProfile 'Microsoft.Network/trafficManagerProfiles@2021-05-01' = {
  name: 'myTrafficManager'
  location: 'global'
  properties: {
    profileStatus: 'Enabled'
    trafficRoutingMethod: 'Performance'
    dnsConfig: {
      relativeName: 'myapp-global'
      ttl: 30
    }
    monitorConfig: {
      protocol: 'HTTP'
      port: 80
      path: '/health'
      intervalInSeconds: 30
      toleratedNumberOfFailures: 3
      timeoutInSeconds: 10
    }
  }
}

resource europeEndpoint 'Microsoft.Network/trafficManagerProfiles/endpoints@2021-05-01' = {
  parent: trafficManagerProfile
  name: 'europeEndpoint'
  properties: {
    target: 'europe-app.azurewebsites.net'
    endpointLocation: 'westeurope'
    endpointStatus: 'Enabled'
    priority: 1
  }
}

resource usEndpoint 'Microsoft.Network/trafficManagerProfiles/endpoints@2021-05-01' = {
  parent: trafficManagerProfile
  name: 'usEndpoint'
  properties: {
    target: 'us-app.azurewebsites.net'
    endpointLocation: 'eastus'
    endpointStatus: 'Enabled'
    priority: 1
  }
}
```

Traffic Manager operates by responding to DNS queries based on the configured routing method. In this example, we're using the `Performance` routing method, where Traffic Manager will return the IP address of the endpoint with the lowest latency for the requesting client. When a client requests *myapp-global.trafficmanager.net*, Traffic

Manager measures the latency from the client's local DNS resolver to each Azure region and returns the IP address of the fastest responding endpoint.

The service monitors endpoint health by regularly checking the specified path (*/health*) on port 80. If an endpoint fails to respond to health checks, Traffic Manager automatically routes users to the next best performing healthy endpoint. The TTL value of 30 seconds ensures that DNS records are refreshed frequently, allowing Traffic Manager to respond quickly to changes in endpoint health or performance.

Unlike Azure Front Door, Traffic Manager doesn't terminate SSL/TLS connections or provide WAF capabilities since it operates purely at the DNS level. However, this DNS-based approach makes it more versatile for scenarios involving non-HTTP protocols or when you need to route traffic to on-premises endpoints.

The service also provides detailed monitoring and diagnostics through Azure Monitor, allowing you to track metrics such as endpoint health status, query volumes, and routing efficiency. You can configure alerts based on these metrics to proactively respond to changes in traffic patterns or endpoint health as follows:

```
resource trafficManagerDiagnostics 'Microsoft.Insights/diagnosticSettings@2021-05-01-preview'
= {
  name: 'tmDiagnostics'
  scope: trafficManagerProfile
  properties: {
    workspaceId: logAnalyticsWorkspace.id
    logs: [
      {
        category: 'ProbeHealthStatusEvents'
        enabled: true
      }
    ]
    metrics: [
      {
        category: 'AllMetrics'
        enabled: true
      }
    ]
  }
}
```

The preceding code snippet sets up diagnostic settings for Traffic Manager, sending both probe health status events and all metrics to a Log Analytics workspace. This enables you to track critical information about your global routing performance. The `ProbeHealthStatusEvents` category captures all endpoint health check results, while `AllMetrics` includes data about query volumes, endpoint latency, and routing decisions.

To complement this monitoring setup, you can create alert rules that notify you when specific conditions occur. Here's how to configure an alert for endpoint health:

```
resource healthAlert 'Microsoft.Insights/metricAlerts@2018-03-01' = {
  name: 'EndpointHealthAlert'
```

```
    location: 'global'
    properties: {
      description: 'Alert when any endpoint becomes degraded or inactive'
      severity: 2
      enabled: true
      scopes: [
        trafficManagerProfile.id
      ]
      evaluationFrequency: 'PT1M'
      windowSize: 'PT5M'
      criteria: {
        'odata.type': 'Microsoft.Azure.Monitor.SingleResourceMultipleMetricCriteria'
        allOf: [
          {
            name: 'Endpoint Health'
            metricNamespace: 'Microsoft.Network/trafficManagerProfiles'
            metricName: 'ProbeAgentCurrentEndpointStateByProfileResourceId'
            operator: 'LessThan'
            threshold: 1
            timeAggregation: 'Average'
            criterionType: 'StaticThresholdCriterion'
          }
        ]
      }
      actions: [
        {
          actionGroupId: actionGroup.id
        }
      ]
    }
  }
```

This monitoring and alerting configuration ensures you have visibility into your global traffic routing performance and can respond quickly to any issues that arise. The alert will trigger if any endpoint's health check fails, allowing you to take corrective action before user experience is significantly impacted.

Azure DNS

Azure DNS is the cloud-based domain name system (DNS) hosting service powered by Azure. Think of it as a phone book for the internet. When someone types *www.myfantasticwebsite.com* into their browser, Azure DNS is responsible for converting that name into an IP address that computers can understand (like `23.55.10.1`). What makes Azure DNS special is its integration with other Azure services and its global network of name servers that help ensure fast responses no matter where your users are located.

Let's start by creating a public DNS zone in Azure, which is essentially declaring "I want to manage the DNS records for this domain in Azure":

```
# Create a DNS zone
az network dns zone create
  --name myfantasticwebsite.com
  --resource-group test-rg
```

```
  --tags environment=production

# Add an A record pointing to your web app
az network dns record-set a add-record
  --resource-group test-rg
  --zone-name myfantasticwebsite.com
  --record-set-name www
  --ipv4-address 23.55.10.1
```

Here's the equivalent Bicep code:

```
resource dnsZone 'Microsoft.Network/dnsZones@2018-05-01' = {
  name: 'myfantasticwebsite.com'
  location: 'global'
  tags: {
    environment: 'production'
  }
}

resource wwwRecord 'Microsoft.Network/dnsZones/A@2018-05-01' = {
  parent: dnsZone
  name: 'www'
  properties: {
    TTL: 3600
    ARecords: [
      {
        ipv4Address: '23.55.10.1'
      }
    ]
  }
}
```

When you create a DNS zone in Azure, it automatically creates four name servers for your domain. These name servers are geographically distributed to provide high availability and fast response times. You'll need to update your domain registrar (like GoDaddy or Namecheap) to use these Azure name servers. This process, called *delegating* your domain to Azure DNS, tells the internet, "For this domain, ask Azure's name servers where everything is."

Now, let's talk about private DNS zones, which are different from public DNS zones. Private DNS zones work only within your Azure VNets, making them perfect for internal applications. They let you use custom domain names (like *app.internal*) that only work inside your Azure environment:

```
# Create a private DNS zone
az network private-dns zone create
  --resource-group test-rg
  --name internal.myfantasticwebsite.com

# Link the private DNS zone to your virtual network
az network private-dns link vnet create
  --resource-group test-rg
  --zone-name internal.myfantasticwebsite.com
  --name myVNetLink
  --virtual-network myVNet
  --registration-enabled true
```

The Bicep equivalent shows how to create a private DNS zone and link it to your VNet:

```
resource privateDnsZone 'Microsoft.Network/privateDnsZones@2020-06-01' = {
  name: 'internal.myfantasticwebsite.com'
  location: 'global'
}

resource vnetLink 'Microsoft.Network/privateDnsZones/virtualNetworkLinks@2020-06-01' = {
  parent: privateDnsZone
  name: 'myVNetLink'
  location: 'global'
  properties: {
    registrationEnabled: true
    virtualNetwork: {
      id: virtualNetwork.id
    }
  }
}
```

When you enable auto-registration in a private DNS zone (that's what registration-enabled true does), any VM you create in the linked VNet automatically gets a DNS record created for it. For example, if you create a VM named "appserver," it automatically gets registered as *appserver.internal.contoso.com*. This makes it easy for your resources to find each other using friendly names instead of IP addresses.

You can also add custom records to your private DNS zone. This is useful for pointing to internal load balancers, databases, or other resources:

```
az network private-dns record-set a add-record
  --resource-group test-rg
  --zone-name internal.myfantasticwebsite.com
  --record-set-name database
  --ipv4-address 10.0.0.4
```

And here's how you'd do it in Bicep:

```
resource privateARecord 'Microsoft.Network/privateDnsZones/A@2020-06-01' = {
  parent: privateDnsZone
  name: 'database'
  properties: {
    ttl: 3600
    aRecords: [
      {
        ipv4Address: '10.0.0.4'
      }
    ]
  }
}
```

Records you create in your private DNS zone are only visible inside the VNets linked to the zone. This is great for security because it means your internal domain names and IP addresses aren't exposed to the public internet.

When you're setting up DNS in Azure, there's also the concept of DNS forwarders. These come into play when you need your on-premises systems to resolve names in your private DNS zones, or vice versa. You can set up a DNS forwarder using Azure Firewall or a custom DNS server VM to handle these scenarios, creating a seamless naming experience across your hybrid environment.

Remember that DNS changes can take time to propagate due to caching. When you create or update DNS records, the TTL value determines how long other DNS servers will cache your records. A lower TTL means changes propagate faster but generate more DNS queries; a higher TTL reduces query load but means changes take longer to take effect.

Summary

This chapter covered networking in Azure, explaining how resources, applications, and users communicate securely in the cloud. It introduced Azure VNets as the foundation of Azure networking, along with subnets for organizing resources and IP addressing for managing communication. Different connectivity options were explored, including VPN gateway, ExpressRoute, and Private Link, which enable secure and efficient connections between resources. The chapter also covered load balancing and traffic management, highlighting Azure Load Balancer, Application Gateway, Front Door, and Traffic Manager for distributing traffic efficiently. I wrapped up the chapter by explaining Azure DNS, which translates domain names into IP addresses, supporting both public and private networking. The next chapter will cover some developer practices in Azure.

CHAPTER 13

Developer Practices in Azure

As developers, writing code is just one part of the job. We also need to think about how applications are built, deployed, and maintained in the cloud. The AZ-204 exam focuses on developing solutions in Azure, and understanding developer practices is key to building efficient, scalable, and secure applications. Azure provides a wide range of tools and services that help developers automate tasks, monitor performance, and secure workloads. Whether you're working with web apps, APIs, or serverless functions, knowing how to use these services effectively is essential for cloud development.

In this chapter, we'll explore the developer tools and services relevant to AZ-204. We'll start with Azure CLI, PowerShell, and SDKs for managing cloud resources. After this, I'll introduce an app called Zuta and use it as a foundation for talking about Azure App Service, Functions, and Logic Apps for application development. The goal is to give you a practical feel for all the theoretical concepts you've picked up throughout this book so you get an idea on how they all tie together. We'll dive into CI/CD solutions like Azure Pipelines and GitHub Actions and discuss monitoring with Azure Monitor and Log Analytics. Security best practices, including Azure Key Vault and Entra ID, will also be highlighted. By the end of this chapter, you'll have a strong understanding of Azure developer practices, which will help you prepare for the AZ-204 exam and apply these concepts in real-world development.

Introduction

Cloud development has fundamentally changed how we build and deploy applications. Azure, as a cloud platform, brings a unique set of tools, services, and best practices that developers need to understand to create effective cloud native applications. When we talk about developer practices in Azure, we're not just discussing coding standards—we're looking at a complete approach to building applications that can scale, remain secure, and adapt to changing business needs.

Let's start with why best practices matter in cloud development. Unlike traditional on-premises applications, cloud applications need to handle automatic scaling, be resilient to failures, and manage costs effectively. A simple example of this is how we handle application configuration. Instead of the traditional approach of storing configuration in files, Azure encourages the use of services like Azure App Configuration and Key Vault. Here's a basic setup that demonstrates this modern approach:

```
# Create a simple development environment
$  az group create
    --name sample-resource-group
    --location eastus

# Set up basic application infrastructure
$  az appconfig create
    --name sample-app-config
    --resource-group sample-resource-group
    --location eastus
    --sku free
```

This simple configuration setup demonstrates how Azure supports modern development practices. Rather than managing configuration files across multiple servers, developers can centrally manage their application settings and feature flags.

Azure supports developers through various integrated tools and services that work together to create a comprehensive development environment. Think of it as a toolbox where each tool has a specific purpose but works seamlessly with others. Examples include the Visual Studio integration, Azure DevOps pipelines, managed Kubernetes services, serverless functions, and more. These tools help developers focus on writing code rather than managing infrastructure.

Azure also emphasizes security and compliance throughout the development lifecycle. Rather than treating security as an afterthought, Azure has tools and services that make it easier to build secure applications from the ground up. This includes everything from managed identities for accessing services to built-in DDoS protection.

Understanding these developer practices is important because they form the foundation for everything else you'll do in Azure. It could be building a simple web application or a complex microservices architecture, but these practices will help you make better decisions about how to structure your applications, manage your code, and deploy your solutions.

Choosing the Right Development Tools

Azure has several developer tools that help with creating, deploying, and managing cloud applications. These tools include Azure CLI, Azure PowerShell, Azure SDKs, Azure DevOps, GitHub, and integrated development environments (IDEs) like Visual

Studio and Visual Studio Code. Each of these tools serves a specific purpose, and knowing when to use them can improve productivity and make cloud development more efficient.

The Azure CLI is a lightweight and scriptable tool that allows developers to interact with Azure services directly from a terminal or command prompt. It supports multiple operating systems, including Windows, macOS, and Linux. Developers use Azure CLI to create and manage resources without needing to navigate the Azure portal. For example, you can create a VM using a single command:

```
$  az vm create
     --resource-group <resource-group>
     --name <name>
     --image UbuntuLTS
     --admin-username azureuser
     --generate-ssh-keys
```

Azure CLI is commonly used in automation scripts and CI/CD pipelines because it allows developers to perform tasks quickly without manual intervention. It supports JSON and table outputs, making it easy to integrate with other tools.

Azure PowerShell has similar functionality to Azure CLI but is built for users who prefer PowerShell scripting. It is useful for Windows administrators and developers working in a Windows environment. Unlike Azure CLI, which is optimized for single command execution, Azure PowerShell works well for handling complex automation workflows that require looping, conditionals, and object manipulation. For example, let's say you need to create a resource group, deploy a storage account, then create a container inside that storage account for storing files. Instead of running three separate commands, you can achieve all of this in one PowerShell script:

```
# Define variables
$resourceGroupName = "MyResourceGroup"
$location = "EastUS"
$storageAccountName = "mystorageaccount$(Get-Random)" # Randomized to avoid name conflicts
$containerName = "mycontainer"

# Create a resource group
New-AzResourceGroup -Name $resourceGroupName -Location $location

# Create a storage account inside the resource group
New-AzStorageAccount -ResourceGroupName $resourceGroupName `
    -Name $storageAccountName `
    -Location $location `
    -SkuName "Standard_LRS" `
    -Kind "StorageV2"

# Retrieve the storage account key
$storageKey = (Get-AzStorageAccountKey -ResourceGroupName $resourceGroupName -Name
      $storageAccountName)[0].Value

# Create a storage context using the retrieved key
$storageContext = New-AzStorageContext -StorageAccountName $storageAccountName
      -StorageAccountKey $storageKey
```

```
# Create a container inside the storage account
New-AzStorageContainer -Name $containerName -Context $storageContext -Permission Blob

# Output storage account and container details
Write-Output "Storage account '$storageAccountName'
            "created in resource group '$resourceGroupName'"
Write-Output "Blob container '$containerName' created successfully."
```

Since Azure PowerShell integrates deeply with the Windows ecosystem, it is often the preferred choice for automating Azure tasks in enterprise environments.

For application development, Azure SDKs provide libraries and APIs developers can use to interact with Azure services directly from their code. These SDKs are available for multiple programming languages, including .NET, Python, Java, JavaScript, and Go. They simplify tasks like working with Azure Blob Storage, managing databases, or authenticating users with Azure Entra ID. Instead of making raw HTTP calls to Azure APIs, developers can use these SDKs to work with cloud services using familiar programming constructs. For example, in C#, uploading a file to Azure Blob Storage using the SDK looks like this:

```
using Azure.Storage.Blobs;
using System;
using System.IO;
using System.Threading.Tasks;

class Program
{
    static async Task Main()
    {
        // Define the connection string and blob details
        string connectionString = "your_connection_string";
        string container = "mycontainer";
        string blobName = "myfile.txt";
        string localFilePath = "myfile.txt";

        // Create a BlobServiceClient
        var client = new BlobServiceClient(connectionString);

        // Get container reference (create if it doesn't exist)
        var cClient = client.GetBlobContainerClient(container);
        await cClient.CreateIfNotExistsAsync();

        // Get a reference to the blob
        BlobClient blobClient = cClient.GetBlobClient(blobName);

        // Upload the file to Blob Storage
        using FileStream fileStream = File.OpenRead(localFilePath);
        await blobClient.UploadAsync(fileStream, overwrite: true);

        Console.WriteLine($"File '{blobName}' uploaded to Storage.");
    }
}
```

Using SDKs improves code maintainability and makes it easier to integrate Azure services into applications.

For source control and CI/CD, developers rely on Azure DevOps and GitHub. Azure DevOps is an enterprise-grade platform that provides tools for source code management, automated builds, release pipelines, and project tracking. Teams using Azure DevOps can manage repositories using Azure Repos (which supports Git and Team Foundation Version Control [TFVC]), automate deployments with Azure Pipelines, and plan sprints using Azure Boards. A simple CI/CD pipeline in Azure DevOps might include steps to pull the latest code, build the application, run tests, and deploy it to an Azure app service.

On the other hand, GitHub, which is also owned by Microsoft, is a widely used platform for hosting Git repositories and managing open source and enterprise software projects. GitHub Actions enables developers to automate workflows directly within their repositories. A GitHub Actions workflow for deploying an application to Azure might look like this:

```
name: Deploy to Azure
on: [push]
jobs:
  build-and-deploy:
    runs-on: ubuntu-latest
    steps:
      - name: Checkout code
        uses: actions/checkout@v2
      - name: Login to Azure
        uses: azure/login@v1
        with:
          creds: ${{ secrets.AZURE_CREDENTIALS }}
      - name: Deploy to App Service
        run: az webapp up
--name myapp
--resource-group MyResourceGroup
--location eastus
```

Developers often choose between Azure DevOps and GitHub based on their project requirements. Azure DevOps is ideal for enterprises that require detailed tracking and governance, while GitHub is widely preferred for open source and lightweight CI/CD automation.

For coding and debugging, Visual Studio and VS Code are the primary tools used by Azure developers. Visual Studio is a full-featured IDE designed for large-scale .NET development. It comes with built-in support for Azure, allowing developers to create, deploy, and debug cloud applications with minimal setup. It integrates with Azure Functions, Kubernetes, and Azure SQL, making it ideal for enterprise-grade applications.

For those who prefer a lightweight, cross-platform editor, VS Code is a powerful option. It supports extensions that enable seamless integration with Azure services.

The Azure Tools extension for VS Code allows developers to manage resources, deploy applications, and run Azure Functions without leaving the editor. A developer using VS Code can deploy an application to Azure App Service with just a few clicks, thanks to its deep integration with Azure CLI and Git.

Application Development in Azure

To make the concepts discussed in this book clearer, let's assume we are developing a cloud-based ecommerce app with the fictional name Zuta. This app will consist of the following:

- A web app for the frontend and API layer using Azure App Service
- A serverless backend for event-driven actions using Azure Functions
- Automated workflows using Azure Logic Apps
- A managed API gateway using Azure API Management
- A database layer using Azure Cosmos DB for handling product listings, orders, and user data
- Containerized microservices for processing payments using AKS

The goal is to ensure that Zuta is scalable, highly available, and fully managed in Azure. Each component is optimized for cloud development, and by the end of this section, you will have a complete understanding of how to build and deploy applications using Azure's compute solutions.

Building Applications with Azure App Service

For Zuta, we will use Azure App Service to deploy both our frontend (a React-based single-page application) and backend (a Python Flask API). This ensures our ecommerce app is always online, scalable, and integrates seamlessly with Azure's managed services.

First, we create a resource group to manage all resources in one place:

```
$ az group create
    --name ZutaResourceGroup
    --location eastus
```

Next, we set up an App Service plan to define the hosting environment:

```
$ az appservice plan create
    --name ZutaAppPlan
    --resource-group ZutaResourceGroup
    --sku B1
    --is-linux
```

Now, we create the web app:

```
$ az webapp create
    --resource-group ZutaResourceGroup
    --plan ZutaAppPlan
    --name ZutaWebApp
    --runtime "PYTHON|3.9"
```

This command provisions a Python 3.9 environment for our Flask API backend. Azure App Service allows deployment slots, which let us test new versions of the application before rolling them out to production. For Zuta, we need a staging slot to test new releases before going live.

To create a staging slot, use:

```
$ az webapp deployment slot create
    --resource-group ZutaResourceGroup
    --name ZutaWebApp
    --slot staging
```

For the React-based frontend, we create another web app within the same App Service plan. Although React applications are typically static, you can deploy them in a Node.js environment, if server-side rendering is needed, or simply serve static files:

```
$ az webapp create
    --resource-group ZutaResourceGroup
    --plan ZutaAppPlan
    --name ZutaFrontend
    --runtime "NODE|14-lts"
```

Note: While Azure Static Web Apps is an alternative for deploying purely static sites, in this example, we use Azure App Service for both the backend and frontend for consistency.

With this setup, we can deploy the latest changes to staging, verify everything is working correctly, and then swap it into production seamlessly. In Bicep, this would be:

```
resource zutaApp 'Microsoft.Web/sites@2021-02-01' = {
  name: 'ZutaWebApp'
  location: 'eastus'
  properties: {
    serverFarmId: appServicePlan.id
    ... //other configurations
  }
}

resource stagingSlot 'Microsoft.Web/sites/slots@2021-02-01' = {
  name: 'staging'
  parent: zutaApp
}
```

This ensures that the staging slot is created alongside the web app in a single deployment. You can also do the same for the `ZutaFrontendApp` like this:

```
resource zutaFrontendApp 'Microsoft.Web/sites@2021-02-01' = {
  name: 'ZutaFrontendApp'
  location: 'eastus'
  properties: {
    serverFarmId: appServicePlan.id
    ... //other configurations
  }
}

resource stagingSlot 'Microsoft.Web/sites/slots@2021-02-01' = {
  name: 'staging'
  parent: zutaFrontendApp
}
```

Developing Serverless Applications with Azure Functions

To make Zuta scalable, we use Azure Functions for event-driven processing. Some use cases for Azure Functions in Zuta include:

Processing orders
: When a customer places an order, a function stores the order details in Cosmos DB.

Sending notifications
: When a payment is completed, another function triggers an email confirmation.

Stock management
: When stock levels fall below a certain threshold, a function notifies the admin.

To deploy an Azure Function that listens for new orders, first create the function app:

```
$ az functionapp create
    --resource-group ZutaResourceGroup
    --consumption-plan-location eastus
    --runtime python
    --functions-version 4
    --name ZutaOrderProcessor
```

Now, let's define a function that triggers whenever a new order is placed in Azure Storage Queue:

```
resource functionApp 'Microsoft.Web/sites@2021-02-01' = {
  name: 'ZutaOrderProcessor'
  location: 'eastus'
  kind: 'functionapp'
  properties: {
    serverFarmId: consumptionPlan.id
  }
}

resource queueTriggerFunction 'Microsoft.Web/sites/functions@2021-02-01' = {
  name: 'ProcessOrder'
```

```
        parent: functionApp
        properties: {
          config: {
            bindings: [
              {
                name: 'orderItem'
                type: 'queueTrigger'
                direction: 'in'
                queueName: 'order-queue'
                connection: 'AzureWebJobsStorage'
              }
            ]
          }
        }
      }
```

This is the infrastructure for the function that listens to the order queue and processes new orders automatically. Once you deploy the function code, you should have a working serverless service.

Using Azure Logic Apps for Workflow Automation

For Zuta's ecommerce platform, we use Azure Logic Apps to automate business processes that don't require custom code. A key workflow is order fulfillment, where we need to coordinate between order placement, inventory updates, and shipping notifications.

Let's create a Logic App (Consumption) with its required storage account. This logic app will handle the order fulfillment process:

```
$  az storage account create
        --name zutaorderlogicstr
        --resource-group ZutaResourceGroup
        --location eastus
        --sku Standard_LRS

$  az logicapp create
        --name ZutaOrderFulfillment
        --resource-group ZutaResourceGroup
        --storage-account zutaorderlogicstr
        --functions-version 4
        --runtime-version ~18
        --https-only true
```

Once the logic app is created, we define our workflow using an ARM template or through the Azure portal's designer. Here's what the workflow definition looks like in Bicep:

```
resource orderFulfillmentLogicApp 'Microsoft.Logic/workflows@2019-05-01' = {
  name: 'ZutaOrderFulfillment'
  location: 'eastus'
  properties: {
    state: 'Enabled'
    definition: {
      '$schema': 'https://schema.management.azure.com/providers/Microsoft.Logic/schemas/
                 '2016-06-01/workflowdefinition.json#'
```

```
contentVersion: '1.0.0.0'
parameters: {
  '$connections': {
    type: 'Object'
  }
}
triggers: {
  when_new_order_received: {
    type: 'ServiceBus'
    inputs: {
      topicName: 'orders'
      subscriptionName: 'fulfillment'
      connectionName: 'servicebus'
    }
  }
}
actions: {
  Process_Order: {
    type: 'Function'
    inputs: {
      functionName: 'ProcessOrder'
      method: 'POST'
      body: '@triggerBody()'
    }
  }
  Send_Email: {
    type: 'ApiConnection'
    inputs: {
      host: {
        connection: {
          name: '@parameters(\'$connections\')[\'outlook\'][\'connectionId\']'
        }
      }
      method: 'post'
      path: '/v2/Mail'
      body: {
        subject: 'New Order Processed',
        body: 'Your order has been processed successfully.'
      }
    }
  }
}
      }
    }
  }
```

The logic app we've created uses a storage account for internal operations and state management, and we've enabled HTTPS-only access for security. It's also configured to use Node.js 18 runtime, which is needed for some of our custom connectors and functions.

Developing APIs with Azure API Management

For API management in Zuta, we need to create a centralized gateway that handles all our API endpoints. This includes the product catalog API, order processing API, and user management API. API Management serves as a facade pattern implementation, providing a single entry point for all our microservices while handling cross-cutting concerns like security, monitoring, and rate limiting.

When choosing an API Management tier, we opt for the Developer SKU during our development phase. While this SKU doesn't provide the high availability of the Premium tier, it offers all the features we need for development and testing at a lower cost. As Zuta grows, we can seamlessly upgrade to Standard or Premium tiers without any API configuration changes.

If you are following through with these steps and creating resources, remember to delete the APIM resource after your test so you don't incur costs.

Let's start by creating our API Management instance:

```
az apim create
    --name ZutaAPIM
    --resource-group ZutaResourceGroup
    --publisher-name Zuta
    --publisher-email admin@zuta.com
    --sku-name Developer
    --location eastus
```

This command sets up our API gateway with basic configurations. The publisher name and email are required for managing developer communications and notifications about API changes. The location choice is crucial—we select `eastus` to minimize latency for our primary user base while ensuring compliance with data residency requirements.

Now, we need to import our APIs. For Zuta's product catalog API, we use OpenAPI (formerly Swagger) specifications. This approach provides several benefits: it automatically creates API documentation, enables API testing through the developer portal, and ensures our API definition serves as a single source of truth:

```
$  az apim api import
         --resource-group ZutaResourceGroup
         --service-name ZutaAPIM
         --path '/catalog'
         --display-name "Product Catalog API"
         --api-id catalog
         --api-type http
         --specification-url "https://zuta-webapp.azurewebsites.net/swagger/v1/swagger.json"
```

One of the critical aspects of API Management is implementing proper rate limiting. For Zuta's catalog API, we need to balance between providing good service to legitimate users while protecting our backend from potential DDoS attacks or abusive usage. We implement a rate limit of 100 calls per minute, which our analysis shows is sufficient for normal usage patterns while preventing abuse:

```
resource catalogApiPolicy 'Microsoft.ApiManagement/service/apis/policies@2021-08-01' = {
  parent: catalogApi
  name: 'policy'
  properties: {
    value: '''
      <policies>
        <inbound>
          <base />
          <rate-limit calls="100" renewal-period="60" />
          <validate-jwt header-name="Authorization" failed-validation-httpcode="401">
            <openid-config url="https://login.microsoftonline.com/tenant-id/v2.0/
                  ".well-known/openid-configuration" />
            <audiences>
              <audience>api://zuta-api</audience>
            </audiences>
          </validate-jwt>
        </inbound>
      </policies>
    '''
    format: 'xml'
  }
}
```

To organize our APIs effectively, we create products in APIM. Products in APIM are collections of APIs that we can publish together with specific terms of use and visibility settings. For Zuta, we want to create separate products for our internal services and external partner access:

```
$  az apim product create
         --resource-group ZutaResourceGroup
         --service-name ZutaAPIM
         --product-name "Zuta Internal APIs"
         --product-id zuta-internal
         --description "Internal APIs for Zuta microservices"
         --subscription-required true
         --state published

$  az apim product api add
         --resource-group ZutaResourceGroup
         --service-name ZutaAPIM
         --product-id zuta-internal
         --api-id catalog
```

One of the most critical aspects of our API Management setup is the implementation of proper versioning. For Zuta's rapidly evolving platform, we need to support multiple API versions while ensuring backward compatibility:

```
resource apiVersionSet 'Microsoft.ApiManagement/service/apiVersionSets@2021-08-01' = {
  parent: apiManagement
  name: 'catalog-versions'
  properties: {
    displayName: 'Product Catalog API Versions'
    versioningScheme: 'Segment'
    description: 'Version set for the product catalog API'
  }
}

resource catalogApiV1 'Microsoft.ApiManagement/service/apis@2021-08-01' = {
```

```
  parent: apiManagement
  name: 'catalog-v1'
  properties: {
    displayName: 'Product Catalog API v1'
    apiVersion: 'v1'
    apiVersionSetId: apiVersionSet.id
    path: 'catalog'
    protocols: [
      'https'
    ]
    subscriptionRequired: true
  }
}
```

Through these configurations, we've established a secure and well-organized API gateway that serves as the foundation for Zuta's microservices architecture.

Deploying Containerized Applications with Azure Kubernetes Service

For Zuta's containerized workloads, particularly our payment processing microservice, we'll use AKS. This gives us a managed Kubernetes platform that simplifies container orchestration while maintaining the flexibility we need for our microservices architecture.

First, let's set up our AKS cluster with the necessary configurations for our ecommerce platform:

```
$  az aks create
         --resource-group ZutaResourceGroup
         --name ZutaAKS
         --node-count 3
         --enable-managed-identity
         --enable-addons monitoring
         --generate-ssh-keys

$  az aks nodepool add
         --resource-group ZutaResourceGroup
         --cluster-name ZutaAKS
         --name paymentpool
         --node-count 2
         --labels workload=payment
```

The equivalent Bicep configuration shows our specific requirements:

```
resource aksCluster 'Microsoft.ContainerService/managedClusters@2023-07-02-preview' = {
  name: 'ZutaAKS'
  location: location
  identity: {
    type: 'SystemAssigned'
  }
  properties: {
    dnsPrefix: 'zuta-aks'
    enableRBAC: true
    agentPoolProfiles: [
      {
        name: 'systempool'
        count: 3
```

```
          vmSize: 'Standard_DS2_v2'
          mode: 'System'
        }
        {
          name: 'paymentpool'
          count: 2
          vmSize: 'Standard_DS3_v2'
          labels: {
            workload: 'payment'
          }
        }
      ]
      addonProfiles: {
        omsagent: {
          enabled: true
        }
      }
    }
  }
```

For payment processing service, we implement a secure deployment configuration:

```
apiVersion: apps/v1
kind: Deployment
metadata:
  name: payment-processor
  namespace: zuta-payments
spec:
  replicas: 3
  selector:
    matchLabels:
      app: payment
  template:
    metadata:
      labels:
        app: payment
    spec:
      nodeSelector:
        workload: payment
      containers:
      - name: payment
        image: zutaacr.azurecr.io/payment-processor:latest
        resources:
          requests:
            memory: "256Mi"
            cpu: "250m"
        env:
        - name: PAYMENT_API_KEY
          valueFrom:
            secretKeyRef:
              name: payment-secrets
              key: api-key
```

Now we can deploy this configuration:

```
az aks get-credentials -g ZutaResourceGroup -n ZutaAKS
kubectl create namespace zuta-payments
kubectl apply -f payment-deployment.yaml
```

This configuration provides Zuta with a secure and scalable environment for our payment processing microservice. The dedicated node pool ensures isolation of our payment workloads, while resource configurations help maintain stability and reliability.

Deploying a Storage Account

For Zuta's ecommerce platform, we need a reliable storage solution for our product images. Azure storage accounts provide a scalable and secure way to store these images, with features like CDN integration for faster global delivery. Let's set up the storage infrastructure that will handle our product image management.

First, let's create a storage account with the appropriate configurations for image storage:

```
$  az storage account create
         --name zutaproductimages
         --resource-group ZutaResourceGroup
         --location eastus
         --sku Standard_GRS
         --enable-hierarchical-namespace false
         --min-tls-version TLS1_2
         --allow-blob-public-access false

$  az storage container create
         --name products
         --account-name zutaproductimages
         --public-access blob
```

Here's the equivalent Bicep configuration that includes our security and performance requirements:

```
resource storageAccount 'Microsoft.Storage/storageAccounts@2023-01-01' = {
  name: 'zutaproductimages'
  location: location
  sku: {
    name: 'Standard_GRS'
  }
  kind: 'StorageV2'
  properties: {
    minimumTlsVersion: 'TLS1_2'
    allowBlobPublicAccess: false
    networkAcls: {
      defaultAction: 'Deny'
      virtualNetworkRules: [
        {
          id: subnet.id
          action: 'Allow'
        }
      ]
    }
  }
}

resource productContainer 'Microsoft.Storage/storageAccounts/blobServices/
      'containers@2023-01-01' = {
  name: '${storageAccount.name}/default/products'
```

```
    properties: {
      publicAccess: 'None'
    }
  }
```

Now, let's create an Azure function that handles image uploads for our products. This function will process incoming images and store them in our storage account:

```
public class ProductImageFunction
{
    [FunctionName("UploadProductImage")]
    public async Task<IActionResult> Run(
        [HttpTrigger(AuthorizationLevel.Function, "post")] HttpRequest req,
        [Blob("products/{rand-guid}.jpg", FileAccess.Write,
          Connection = "ZutaStorageConnection")] BlobClient blobClient,
        ILogger log)
    {
        try
        {
            var imageStream = req.Body;
            await blobClient.UploadAsync(imageStream, overwrite: true);

            return new OkObjectResult(new {
                imageUrl = blobClient.Uri.ToString()
            });
        }
        catch (Exception ex)
        {
            log.LogError($"Error uploading image: {ex.Message}");
            return new StatusCodeResult(500);
        }
    }
}
```

To ensure our images are delivered efficiently to users worldwide, we'll integrate our storage account with Azure CDN:

```
$  az cdn profile create
         --name ZutaCDN
         --resource-group ZutaResourceGroup
         --sku Standard_Microsoft

$  az cdn endpoint create
         --name zuta-images
         --profile-name ZutaCDN
         --resource-group ZutaResourceGroup
         --origin zutaproductimages.blob.core.windows.net
         --origin-host-header zutaproductimages.blob.core.windows.net
```

Whenever we need to reference this storage account in our functions or applications, we use the connection string stored in app settings:

```
$  az functionapp config appsettings set
         --name ZutaOrderProcessor
         --resource-group ZutaResourceGroup
         --settings "ZutaStorageConnection=DefaultEndpointsProtocol=https;
                    "AccountName=zutaproductimages;..."
```

This storage setup provides Zuta with a secure and scalable solution for managing product images. The use of geo-redundant storage (GRS) ensures our images are backed up across regions, while the integration with Azure CDN optimizes delivery performance for our global customer base. The function-based upload process provides a controlled and secure way to manage our product images, with built-in error handling and logging.

Deploying Cosmos DB for Zuta

For Zuta's ecommerce platform, we need a database solution that can handle both product catalogs and order information with high scalability and low latency. Azure Cosmos DB provides the perfect solution with its multimodel capabilities and global distribution features. Let's set up our database infrastructure to manage our product and order data.

First, let's create our Cosmos DB account with SQL API support, as this provides the most flexible querying capabilities for our ecommerce needs:

```
$  az cosmosdb create
        --name zuta-store
        --resource-group ZutaResourceGroup
        --locations regionName=eastus failoverPriority=0
        --default-consistency-level Session
        --enable-automatic-failover true
        --enable-free-tier false

$  az cosmosdb sql database create
        --account-name zuta-store
        --resource-group ZutaResourceGroup
        --name ZutaDB

$  az cosmosdb sql container create
        --account-name zuta-store
        --database-name ZutaDB
        --name Products
        --partition-key-path "/category"
        --resource-group ZutaResourceGroup
        --throughput 400

$  az cosmosdb sql container create
        --account-name zuta-store
        --database-name ZutaDB
        --name Orders
        --partition-key-path "/customerId"
        --resource-group ZutaResourceGroup
        --throughput 400
```

Here's the equivalent Bicep configuration that sets up our database with proper partitioning and indexing:

```
resource cosmosAccount 'Microsoft.DocumentDB/databaseAccounts@2023-04-15' = {
  name: 'zuta-store'
  location: location
  properties: {
```

```
    databaseAccountOfferType: 'Standard'
    enableAutomaticFailover: true
    consistencyPolicy: {
      defaultConsistencyLevel: 'Session'
    }
    locations: [
      {
        locationName: 'eastus'
        failoverPriority: 0
      }
    ]
  }
}

resource database 'Microsoft.DocumentDB/databaseAccounts/sqlDatabases@2023-04-15' = {
  parent: cosmosAccount
  name: 'ZutaDB'
  properties: {
    resource: {
      id: 'ZutaDB'
    }
  }
}

resource productsContainer 'Microsoft.DocumentDB/databaseAccounts/sqlDatabases/
containers@2023-04-15' = {
  parent: database
  name: 'Products'
  properties: {
    resource: {
      id: 'Products'
      partitionKey: {
        paths: [
          '/category'
        ]
        kind: 'Hash'
      }
      indexingPolicy: {
        indexingMode: 'consistent'
        includedPaths: [
          {
            path: '/*'
          }
        ]
        excludedPaths: [
          {
            path: '/"_etag"/?'
          }
        ]
      }
    }
    options: {
      throughput: 400
    }
  }
}
```

Earlier in the chapter, you saw how to deploy the function app for Zuta. Now, let's update its configuration to connect to Cosmos DB by setting the appropriate connection string. You can retrieve the Cosmos DB connection string and update your function app's settings using Azure CLI; for example:

```
# Retrieve the Cosmos DB connection string
COSMOS_CONN_STRING=$(az cosmosdb keys list
    --name zuta-store
    --resource-group ZutaResourceGroup
    --type connection-strings
    --query "connectionStrings[0].connectionString" -o tsv)

# Update the Function App configuration with the Cosmos DB connection string
az functionapp config appsettings set
    --name myFunctionApp
    --resource-group ZutaResourceGroup
    --settings CosmosDBConnection="$COSMOS_CONN_STRING"
```

Alternatively, if you prefer managing configuration with IaC using Bicep, and your function app is already deployed, you can reference it and update its settings as follows:

```
// Reference the existing Function App
resource functionApp 'Microsoft.Web/sites@2021-02-01' existing = {
  name: 'myFunctionApp'
}

// Reference the existing Cosmos DB account
resource cosmosAccount 'Microsoft.DocumentDB/databaseAccounts@2023-04-15' existing = {
  name: 'zuta-store'
}

// Retrieve the Cosmos DB connection string
var cosmosConnectionString = listConnectionStrings(
    cosmosAccount.id, '2021-04-15').connectionStrings[0].connectionString

// Update the Function App's app settings to include the Cosmos DB connection string
resource functionAppSettings 'Microsoft.Web/sites/config@2021-02-01' = {
  name: '${functionApp.name}/appsettings'
  properties: {
    CosmosDBConnection: cosmosConnectionString
  }
}
```

In both examples, the `CosmosDBConnection` setting is added to the function app's configuration, allowing your function code, such as the `UpdateProduct` function, to establish a connection with your Cosmos DB instance.

Now, let's create a function that interacts with our Cosmos DB to handle product updates:

```
public class ProductFunctions
{
    private readonly CosmosClient _cosmosClient;
    private readonly Container _container;
```

```
        public ProductFunctions(CosmosClient cosmosClient)
        {
            _cosmosClient = cosmosClient;
            _container = _cosmosClient.GetContainer("ZutaDB", "Products");
        }

        [FunctionName("UpdateProduct")]
        public async Task<IActionResult> UpdateProduct(
            [HttpTrigger(AuthorizationLevel.Function, "put", Route = "products/{id}")]
              HttpRequest req,
            string id,
            ILogger log)
        {
            try
            {
                string requestBody = await new StreamReader(req.Body).ReadToEndAsync();
                var product = JsonConvert.DeserializeObject<Product>(requestBody);

                await _container.UpsertItemAsync(product, new PartitionKey(product.Category));

                return new OkObjectResult(product);
            }
            catch (CosmosException ex) when (ex.StatusCode == HttpStatusCode.NotFound)
            {
                return new NotFoundResult();
            }
        }
    }
```

For optimal performance, we need to configure proper indexing and partitioning strategies. Here's a sample indexing policy for our Orders container:

```
{
  "indexingPolicy": {
    "indexingMode": "consistent",
    "includedPaths": [
      {
        "path": "/customerId/*"
      },
      {
        "path": "/orderDate/*"
      },
      {
        "path": "/status/*"
      }
    ],
    "excludedPaths": [
      {
        "path": "/shippingAddress/*"
      },
      {
        "path": "/_etag/?"
      }
    ],
    "compositeIndexes": [
      [
        {
          "path": "/customerId",
          "order": "ascending"
```

```
          },
          {
            "path": "/orderDate",
            "order": "descending"
          }
        ]
      ]
    }
  }
```

This Cosmos DB setup provides Zuta with a highly available, globally distributed database solution. The session consistency level offers a good balance between data consistency and performance, while our partitioning strategy ensures efficient data distribution and query performance. The automatic failover capability ensures business continuity, and the throughput settings can be adjusted as our business grows.

Continuous Integration and Continuous Deployment

For any modern application, especially an ecommerce platform like Zuta, manually deploying code changes is risky and time-consuming. This is where CI/CD comes in. Every time our developers push code changes for Zuta's product catalog or order processing system, we want these changes to be automatically tested, built, and deployed to our Azure environment.

Let's first set up a basic Azure pipeline for our product catalog API. We'll create this using YAML, which allows us to version control our pipeline alongside our code:

```
trigger:
  branches:
    include:
      - main
      - develop

variables:
  azureServiceConnection: 'zuta-serviceconnection'
  webAppName: 'zuta-catalog-api'

stages:
- stage: Build
  jobs:
  - job: BuildJob
    pool:
      vmImage: 'ubuntu-latest'
    steps:
    - task: DotNetCoreCLI@2
      inputs:
        command: build
        projects: 'src/Zuta.Catalog.API/*.csproj'
```

This pipeline configuration defines when the pipeline should run (on changes to `main` and `develop` branches) and sets up our basic build process. The key here is simplicity—we start with a straightforward build and can add complexity as needed.

For deployment, we want to implement a staged approach where changes go through development and staging before reaching production. Here's how we extend our pipeline:

```
- stage: Deploy
  jobs:
  - deployment: Deploy
    pool:
      vmImage: 'ubuntu-latest'
    environment: 'staging'
    strategy:
      runOnce:
        deploy:
          steps:
          - task: AzureWebApp@1
            inputs:
              azureSubscription: $(azureServiceConnection)
              appName: $(webAppName)
              package: '$(Pipeline.Workspace)/drop/**/*.zip'
```

For our Kubernetes deployments in the production environment, we implement a more sophisticated deployment strategy using GitHub Actions. This allows us to use the same repository for both our code and deployment workflows:

```
name: Deploy to AKS
on:
  push:
    branches: [ main ]
    paths:
      - 'services/payment/**'

jobs:
  deploy:
    runs-on: ubuntu-latest
    steps:
    - uses: azure/login@v1
      with:
        creds: ${{ secrets.AZURE_CREDENTIALS }}

    - name: Deploy to AKS
      uses: azure/aks-set-context@v1
      with:
        creds: ${{ secrets.AZURE_CREDENTIALS }}
        cluster-name: ZutaAKS
        resource-group: ZutaResourceGroup
```

This approach ensures that our payment processing service in AKS is updated automatically whenever changes are pushed to the main branch. The deployment only triggers when changes are made to the payment service code, preventing unnecessary deployments of other components.

The beauty of this setup is that it automates our entire deployment process while maintaining security and reliability. Each deployment goes through automated testing, and with features like deployment slots in Azure App Service, we can quickly roll back if issues are detected.

Monitoring and Debugging Your Live App

For a complex distributed application like Zuta, having proper monitoring in place is crucial. We need to track everything from user interactions in our web frontend to database performance in our backend. Let's start by setting up Application Insights for our main web application:

```
$ az monitor app-insights component create
        --app zuta-insights
        --location eastus
        --resource-group ZutaResourceGroup
        --application-type web
        --kind web

$  az webapp config appsettings set
        --name zuta-webapp
        --resource-group ZutaResourceGroup
        --settings "APPLICATIONINSIGHTS_CONNECTION_STRING=InstrumentationKey=your-key"
```

This basic setup is just the foundation. What makes it powerful is how you can use it to monitor real business scenarios. For instance, imagine if during a Black Friday sale you needed to track not just general performance metrics but specific business KPIs—like cart abandonment rates and checkout completion times. This can lead you to implement custom telemetry in our checkout process:

```
public class CheckoutController : ControllerBase
{
    private readonly TelemetryClient _telemetry;

    public async Task<IActionResult> ProcessCheckout(OrderRequest request)
    {
        var timer = System.Diagnostics.Stopwatch.StartNew();
        var properties = new Dictionary<string, string>
        {
            ["CartValue"] = request.TotalAmount.ToString(),
            ["ItemCount"] = request.Items.Count.ToString()
        };

        try
        {
            var result = await _orderService.ProcessOrderAsync(request);
            timer.Stop();

            _telemetry.TrackMetric("CheckoutDuration", timer.ElapsedMilliseconds);
            _telemetry.TrackEvent("CheckoutComplete", properties);

            return Ok(result);
        }
        catch (Exception ex)
        {
            _telemetry.TrackException(ex, properties);
            throw;
        }
    }
}
```

For Azure Functions handling payment processing, diagnostic settings can be configured to track performance and errors:

```
$ az monitor diagnostic-settings create
        --name zuta-function-diagnostics
        --resource zuta-functions
        --resource-group ZutaResourceGroup
        --logs '[{"category": "FunctionAppLogs","enabled": true}]'
        --workspace zuta-workspace
```

But logging is only useful if you know what to look for. You can develop specific queries that help you understand your system's behavior. For example, these Kusto queries help you identify potential issues before they affect customers:

```
let orderEvents = customEvents
  | where name == "OrderProcessing"
  | project timestamp, orderId = tostring(customDimensions.orderId),
     duration = todouble(customMeasurements.processingTime);

let systemMetrics = metrics
  | where name == "Processor Time"
  | project timestamp, cpu = avg;

orderEvents
  | join kind=inner systemMetrics on timestamp
  | where duration > 5000
  | project timestamp, orderId, duration, cpu
```

These queries will help identify several critical patterns. Different components of an ecommerce application require different monitoring approaches:

- Product catalogs need detailed performance monitoring due to constant access.
- Order processing systems require transaction tracking and completion rate monitoring.
- Payment systems need both performance and error monitoring with immediate alerting.

A central monitoring dashboard should combine these various metrics to provide a complete view of system health. This proactive approach to monitoring allows for early detection and resolution of issues before they impact users.

Security Best Practices for Your Live App

Securing an ecommerce platform requires a comprehensive approach to protect both customer data and business operations. For Zuta, this starts with proper secrets management. Rather than storing connection strings and API keys in configuration files, Azure Key Vault provides a centralized, secure solution for managing these sensitive values.

First, let's set up Key Vault and configure access using managed identities:

```
# Create Key Vault
$  az keyvault create
        --name zuta-vault
        --resource-group ZutaResourceGroup
        --location eastus
        --sku standard

# Enable managed identity for App Service
$  az webapp identity assign
        --name zuta-webapp
        --resource-group ZutaResourceGroup

# Grant the web app access to Key Vault secrets
$  az keyvault set-policy
        --name zuta-vault
        --object-id <managed-identity-object-id>
        --secret-permissions get list
```

For authentication and authorization, Azure Entra ID provides identity management. Here's how to configure the web application to require authenticated users from a specific tenant:

```
public void ConfigureServices(IServiceCollection services)
{
    services.AddAuthentication(JwtBearerDefaults.AuthenticationScheme)
        .AddMicrosoftIdentityWebApi(options => {
            Configuration.Bind("AzureAd", options);
            options.TokenValidationParameters.ValidateIssuer = true;
            options.TokenValidationParameters.ValidIssuer =
                $"https://sts.windows.net/{Configuration["AzureAd:TenantId"]}/";
        });

    services.AddAuthorization(options => {
        options.AddPolicy("RequireAdminRole", policy =>
            policy.RequireRole("Admin"));
    });
}
```

For a production ecommerce platform, proper RBAC is essential to maintain security and comply with the principle of least privilege. Different teams require different levels of access—developers need to deploy and debug applications, while operations teams need to monitor and manage resources.

Let's define comprehensive custom roles for different team members:

```
# Create role for developers working on the application
az role definition create --role-definition '{
    "Name": "Zuta Application Developer",
    "Description": "Role for developers working on Zuta",
    "Actions": [
        "Microsoft.KeyVault/vaults/secrets/read",
        "Microsoft.Web/sites/read",
        "Microsoft.Web/sites/write",
        "Microsoft.Insights/components/read",
        "Microsoft.DocumentDB/databaseAccounts/read",
        "Microsoft.Storage/storageAccounts/read"
    ],
    "NotActions": [
```

```
        "Microsoft.Web/sites/delete",
        "Microsoft.KeyVault/vaults/secrets/write"
    ],
    "AssignableScopes": [
   "/subscriptions/{subscription-id}/resourceGroups/ZutaResourceGroup"
    ]
}'

# Create role for DevOps engineers
az role definition create --role-definition '{
    "Name": "Zuta DevOps Engineer",
    "Description": "Role for DevOps engineers managing Zuta",
    "Actions": [
        "Microsoft.Web/sites/*",
        "Microsoft.KeyVault/vaults/*",
        "Microsoft.Insights/*",
        "Microsoft.DocumentDB/databaseAccounts/*",
        "Microsoft.Storage/storageAccounts/*"
    ],
    "NotActions": [
        "Microsoft.Web/sites/delete",
        "Microsoft.KeyVault/vaults/delete",
        "Microsoft.DocumentDB/databaseAccounts/delete"
    ],
    "AssignableScopes": [
        "/subscriptions/{subscription-id}/resourceGroups/ZutaResourceGroup"
    ]
}'
```

For managing team access to various Azure resources, specific built-in roles can be assigned alongside custom roles:

```
# Assign roles to DevOps team
$  az role assignment create
         --assignee "devops@zuta.com"
         --role "Zuta DevOps Engineer"
         --resource-group ZutaResourceGroup

# Assign reader roles to monitoring team
$  az role assignment create
         --assignee "monitoring@zuta.com"
         --role "Monitoring Reader"
         --resource-group ZutaResourceGroup
```

Security monitoring and governance can be enforced through Azure Policy. Here's how to implement compliance requirements:

```
# Require resource tagging
az policy definition create
    --name 'require-resource-tags'
    --rules '{
        "if": {
            "allOf": [{
                "field": "type",
                "equals": "Microsoft.Resources/subscriptions/resourceGroups"
            },
            {
                "anyOf": [{
                    "field": "tags['environment']",
```

```
                    "exists": "false"
                },
                {
                    "field": "tags['owner']",
                    "exists": "false"
                }]
            }]
        },
        "then": {
            "effect": "deny"
        }
    }'

# Assign the policy
az policy assignment create
    --name 'enforce-tagging'
    --policy-definition 'require-resource-tags'
    --scope /subscriptions/{subscription-id}/resourceGroups/ZutaResourceGroup
```

This security model provides several key advantages:

- Application developers have read access to necessary resources but cannot modify critical configurations.
- DevOps engineers can manage infrastructure but cannot delete critical services.
- Monitoring teams have read-only access to logs and metrics.
- All access is audited and can be reviewed through Azure Monitor.

Additionally, Azure Policy ensures all resources are properly tagged and configured according to organizational standards. This helps maintain consistency across the environment and simplifies resource management and cost allocation.

Regular security audits should review role assignments and policy compliance to ensure the platform maintains its security posture as the application evolves. This combination of custom RBAC roles and Azure Policy creates a robust security framework that maintains security while enabling development teams to work efficiently.

Emulators and Local Development

When developing a cloud native application like Zuta, testing against actual cloud services can be both expensive and time-consuming. Azure provides several emulators that allow developers to work locally while mimicking cloud service behaviors. Let's set up a complete local development environment.

For local storage development, the Azure Storage Emulator (or Azurite, its modern replacement) can be used to simulate blob storage for product images:

```
# Install Azurite using npm
npm install -g azurite
```

```
# Run Azurite for blob storage
azurite --silent --location data --debug data/debug.log
```

In the application code, switch between local and cloud storage using configuration:

```
public class StorageConfiguration
{
    private readonly IConfiguration _configuration;

    public string GetStorageConnection()
    {
        return _configuration["UseLocalStorage"] == "true"
            ? "UseDevelopmentStorage=true"
            : _configuration["AzureStorageConnection"];
    }
}
```

For Cosmos DB development, the local emulator (*https://oreil.ly/HnlGA*) provides a way to test database operations without incurring costs. Once the emulator is started, you can add the following connection settings to your development environment:

```
{
  "CosmosDb": {
    "UseLocalEmulator": true,
    "EmulatorConnectionString": "AccountEndpoint=https://localhost:8081/;
       AccountKey=
       C2y6yDjf5/R+ob0N8A7Cgv30VRDJIWEHLM+4QDU5DE2nQ9nDuVTqobD4b8mGGyPMbIZnqyMsEcaGQy67XIw/
       Jw==",
    "ProductsDatabase": "ZutaProducts",
    "OrdersDatabase": "ZutaOrders"
  }
}
```

For the Functions part of Zuta, the Azure Functions Core Tools enable local function development:

```
# Install Azure Functions Core Tools
npm install -g azure-functions-core-tools@4

# Create a local function project
func init ZutaFunctions --dotnet

# Run functions locally
func start
```

Development of the entire Zuta application locally can be orchestrated using Docker Compose. Create a *docker-compose.yml* file:

```
version: '3.8'
services:
  azurite:
    image: mcr.microsoft.com/azure-storage/azurite
    ports:
      - "10000:10000"
      - "10001:10001"
      - "10002:10002"

  cosmosdb:
    image: mcr.microsoft.com/cosmosdb/linux/azure-cosmos-emulator
```

```
    ports:
      - "8081:8081"
    environment:
      - AZURE_COSMOS_EMULATOR_PARTITION_COUNT=10
      - AZURE_COSMOS_EMULATOR_ENABLE_DATA_PERSISTENCE=true

  zuta-api:
    build:
      context: ./src/Zuta.Api
    environment:
      - ASPNETCORE_ENVIRONMENT=Development
      - UseLocalStorage=true
    ports:
      - "5000:80"
```

This setup allows developers to run the entire Zuta application stack locally, making development and testing faster and more efficient. Each service can be developed and tested independently, and integration tests can be run against the local emulators.

Testing Strategies on Azure

Testing is a crucial part of building Zuta. Without testing, we risk introducing bugs into production, which could lead to downtime, data loss, or security vulnerabilities. In Azure, testing goes beyond just writing unit tests. We need to test business logic, APIs, infrastructure, security, and performance to ensure our application is reliable under different conditions.

To achieve this, we implement different types of testing: unit testing, integration testing, and performance testing. Each type plays a specific role in validating the system's behavior before deployment. In this section, we will go deep into these testing strategies and tie them back to Zuta, showing how to test various components of the application.

Unit Testing for Azure Applications

Unit tests validate individual functions, methods, or components in isolation. In Zuta, we have a C# order processing service that verifies whether a user's payment is successful before confirming an order. This logic must be tested before deployment.

A unit test for this logic using xUnit would look like this:

```
using Xunit;

public class OrderServiceTests
{
    [Fact]
    public void ProcessOrder_ShouldReturnSuccess_WhenPaymentIsValid()
    {
        var orderService = new OrderService();
        var payment = new Payment { Amount = 100, Status = "Completed" };

        var result = orderService.ProcessOrder(payment);
```

```
            Assert.True(result.IsSuccess);
            Assert.Equal("Order Confirmed", result.Message);
        }
    }
```

This test creates an instance of the OrderService, simulates a valid payment, and verifies that the service correctly returns a confirmation message. If a developer changes the payment logic and breaks the function, this test will fail, preventing a faulty deployment. To automate this test in Azure DevOps, we add it to the build pipeline:

```
- task: DotNetCoreCLI@2
 displayName: 'Run Unit Tests'
 inputs:
   command: 'test'
   projects: '**/*.Tests.csproj'
   arguments: '--configuration Release'
```

Once committed, this pipeline ensures no untested changes make it to production.

Integration Testing with Azure Storage and Cosmos DB

While unit tests check small pieces of logic, integration tests validate interactions between multiple components. For Zuta, the backend processes customer orders and stores them in Azure Cosmos DB. We need an integration test to verify that an order is saved correctly in the database. The first step is to create a Cosmos DB instance using the `az cosmosdb create` command. After that, we write an integration test in C# to verify the order storage:

```
[Fact]
public async Task AddOrder_ShouldStoreDataInCosmosDB()
{
    var order = new {Id = "12345", Product = "Laptop", Quantity = 1};
    await _container.CreateItemAsync(order, new PartitionKey(order.Id));

    var retrievedOrder = await _container.ReadItemAsync<dynamic>(
        "12345", new PartitionKey("12345"));

    Assert.NotNull(retrievedOrder);
    Assert.Equal("Laptop", retrievedOrder.Resource.Product);
}
```

This test ensures that when an order is created, it is correctly stored and retrievable from Cosmos DB. Running this test in Azure Pipelines confirms that Zuta's database interactions are working before deployment.

Load and Performance Testing

Since Zuta will handle thousands of concurrent users, we need to test how well the system performs under heavy traffic. Azure Load Testing allows us to simulate high loads and measure system performance.

To run an Apache JMeter load test in Azure, we first create a Load Testing resource:

```
$ az load test create
    --resource-group ZutaResourceGroup
    --name ZutaLoadTest
    --test-plan test-plan.jmx
```

This command provisions the Azure Load Testing service, which acts as a centralized hub for running performance tests. Once created, this service allows us to upload test scripts, execute load tests, and analyze results.

Azure Load Testing relies on Apache JMeter to define test scenarios. JMeter allows us to simulate multiple users making requests to Zuta's API and analyze how the system responds. In our case, we want to simulate 500 users placing orders simultaneously to ensure our order-processing API can handle real-world traffic.

Before running the test, we must define a JMeter test plan (*test-plan.jmx*). This test plan instructs JMeter to send HTTP requests to Zuta's API. The simplified JMeter XML configuration for this test looks like this:

```
<TestPlan>
  <ThreadGroup>
    <stringProp name="ThreadGroup.num_threads">500</stringProp>
    <stringProp name="ThreadGroup.ramp_time">60</stringProp>
    <HTTPSamplerProxy>
      <stringProp name="HTTPSampler.domain">zuta-api.azure-api.net</stringProp>
      <stringProp name="HTTPSampler.path">/orders</stringProp>
      <stringProp name="HTTPSampler.method">POST</stringProp>
    </HTTPSamplerProxy>
  </ThreadGroup>
</TestPlan>
```

This configuration defines a Thread Group with 500 virtual users who gradually ramp up over 60 seconds. Each virtual user sends an `HTTP POST` request to the */orders* endpoint of Zuta's API, simulating customers placing orders.

Once the test plan is ready, we upload it to Azure Load Testing:

```
$ az load test file upload
    --resource-group ZutaResourceGroup
    --load-test-resource ZutaLoadTest
    --path test-plan.jmx
    --test-id OrderLoadTest
```

This command uploads our test script, allowing Azure Load Testing to execute it. With the test plan in place, we trigger the load test using the Azure REST API:

```
$ az rest
    --method post
    --uri "https://management.azure.com/subscriptions/{subscriptionId}/resourceGroups/
      "ZutaResourceGroup/providers/Microsoft.LoadTest/loadTests/ZutaLoadTest/
      "triggerTest?api-version=2023-04-01"
```

In the previous command, `{subscriptionId}` must be replaced with our Azure Subscription ID. This API call starts the test execution on Azure's infrastructure.

Alternatively, we can start the test manually in the Azure portal by:

- Navigating to Azure Load Testing
- Selecting `ZutaLoadTest`
- Clicking Run Test and specifying the test parameters

Once the test is running, we monitor performance metrics in real time to assess how Zuta handles traffic. Azure Load Testing provides detailed reports on failed requests, response times, and throughput.

To retrieve real-time test results from Azure CLI, we use:

```
$ az monitor metrics list
    --resource ZutaLoadTest
    --metrics "RequestsPerSecond" "FailedRequests" "ResponseTime"
```

This command fetches the number of requests per second, failed requests, and average response time from the test execution.

After the test completes, we analyze the results to determine whether Zuta's infrastructure is handling the load efficiently. The KPIs to evaluate are:

Response time
: The time taken for the API to process a request. If this exceeds 200 ms, optimizations are needed.

Failed requests
: The number of API requests that returned HTTP 500 (server error) or HTTP 429 (rate limit exceeded). A high failure rate indicates performance bottlenecks.

Throughput
: The number of requests processed per second. If Zuta processes fewer orders per second than expected, we may need to scale up resources.

If the test results indicate slow response times or failures, you should optimize Zuta's cloud architecture:

Scaling the backend
: If response times are too high, you can increase the number of instances in Azure App Service:

```
$ az appservice plan update
    --name ZutaAppPlan
    --resource-group ZutaResourceGroup
    --number-of-workers 5
```

This increases the compute power for handling concurrent requests.

Using Azure Front Door or Application Gateway

If Zuta's API struggles with too many requests, you can distribute traffic across multiple backend instances:

```
$ az network front-door create
    --resource-group ZutaResourceGroup
    --name ZutaFrontDoor
    --backend-address "zuta-api.azure-api.net"
```

Azure Front Door routes traffic to the most available backend instance, reducing latency.

Optimizing database queries

If Cosmos DB is slow, we adjust indexing strategies:

```
az cosmosdb sql container update
      --account-name ZutaCosmosDB
      --database-name OrderDB
      --name Orders
      --indexing-policy '{"includedPaths": [{"path": "/orderId/*"}]}'
```

This ensures that queries using `orderId` are indexed, improving retrieval speed.

This testing strategy prevents performance issues before they reach production, ensuring that Zuta delivers a fast, reliable, and seamless shopping experience to all users.

Summary

This chapter covered developer practices in Azure, using a hypothetical ecommerce app called Zuta to illustrate how to build, deploy, and manage cloud applications. We explored Azure development tools like Azure CLI, PowerShell, and SDKs, followed by deploying applications using Azure App Service and implementing serverless functions for event-driven processing. We introduced Azure Logic Apps for workflow automation and API Management for centralized API traffic control. For containerized applications, we leveraged AKS, while Azure Storage and Cosmos DB handled product images and transactional data. CI/CD were implemented using Azure DevOps and GitHub Actions to streamline development workflows. We emphasized monitoring with Azure Monitor and Application Insights and discussed security best practices like Azure Key Vault for secrets management, Entra ID for authentication, and Azure Policy for governance. Local development strategies using Azure emulators enabled efficient testing, while unit, integration, and load testing ensured reliability under high traffic. By applying these practices, developers can build scalable, secure, and efficient cloud native applications, reinforcing their readiness for the AZ-204 certification and real-world Azure development. In the next chapter, you will see how to put everything together as you prepare for the exam.

CHAPTER 14

Putting It All Together

As you prepare for this exam, it's important to remember that the AZ-204 certification is not just about memorizing facts or understanding individual Azure services in isolation. It's about demonstrating your ability to think critically, solve real-world problems, and apply your knowledge of Azure development in a practical, strategic way. This chapter is designed to help you transition from learning concepts to applying them effectively in the exam.

In this chapter, I'll break down the skills you need to succeed in scenario-based questions, including how to identify key requirements, evaluate trade-offs, and prioritize solutions. I'll also cover strategies for managing your time during the exam and maintaining focus under pressure. Additionally, we'll discuss the importance of maintaining a positive mindset, even when faced with challenging questions, and how to reflect on your performance after a practice exam to identify areas for improvement. By the end of this chapter, you'll have a clear roadmap for not only passing the exam but also building a strong foundation for your ongoing development in the Azure ecosystem. This is your opportunity to bring together everything you've learned and demonstrate your ability to think like a cloud developer in real-world scenarios.

Preparing for Azure Scenario-Based Questions

Scenario-based questions are a core part of the AZ-204 exam. Unlike straightforward multiple-choice questions that test your knowledge of specific Azure services or features, scenario-based questions present you with a detailed, real-world situation. These scenarios often describe a business problem or technical challenge, and you are asked to choose the best Azure solution or approach to address it. For example, you might be given a scenario where a company needs to process large amounts of data in real time, and you'll need to decide whether to use Azure Stream Analytics, Event Hubs, or another service. These questions are designed to test your ability to think critically, analyze requirements, and apply your knowledge of Azure in a practical, problem-solving context.

Why do scenario-based questions matter? They are a key way for Microsoft to assess whether you can translate theoretical knowledge into real-world solutions. In your day-to-day work as a cloud developer, you won't just be memorizing service names or features; you'll be solving problems. The AZ-204 exam reflects this by testing your ability to evaluate complex situations, weigh trade-offs, and make decisions that align with both technical and business goals. This is why scenario-based questions are so important: they simulate the kind of thinking you'll need to do on the job.

Key Skills for Scenario-Based Questions

To excel at scenario-based questions, you need to develop a specific set of skills. First, you must be able to identify business and technical requirements. This means reading the scenario carefully and understanding what the problem is, what the goals are, and what constraints exist. For example, a scenario might describe a company that needs to build a highly scalable web application with a limited budget. Your job is to identify the key requirements: scalability, cost-efficiency, and perhaps security if the application handles sensitive data.

Once you've identified the requirements, the next skill is evaluating trade-offs between Azure services. Azure has multiple services that can solve similar problems, but each has its strengths and weaknesses. For instance, if you need to store unstructured data, you might consider Azure Blob Storage, Azure Table Storage, or Cosmos DB. Blob Storage is cost effective for large files, Table Storage is great for simple NoSQL needs, and Cosmos DB offers global distribution and low latency but at a higher cost. You'll need to weigh these trade-offs based on the scenario's requirements.

You should also prioritize solutions based on constraints and goals. Not every solution will be perfect, and you'll often need to make compromises. For example, if a scenario emphasizes cost efficiency over performance, you might choose a less expensive service even if it's not the fastest option. Prioritization is about aligning your solution with the most critical requirements and making informed decisions.

Common Exam Scenarios

The AZ-204 exam often includes scenarios that require you to integrate multiple Azure services. For example, you might encounter a scenario where a company needs to build a serverless application that processes data from IoT devices, stores it in a database, and displays it on a dashboard. This could involve using Azure Functions for serverless compute, Event Hubs for data ingestion, Cosmos DB for storage, and Power BI for visualization. These scenarios test your ability to see the big picture and understand how different services work together.

Another common theme is designing solutions that satisfy the requirements of distributed systems. For instance, you might be asked to design a solution for a web application that experiences sudden spikes in traffic. In this case, you'd need to consider services like Azure App Service with autoscaling, Azure Load Balancer for distributing traffic, and Azure Cache for Redis to improve performance. The exam will test whether you can balance these factors to create a solution that meets the scenario's needs.

Security is also a frequent focus in scenario-based questions. You might be asked to design a solution that ensures secure access to resources, such as using Entra ID for authentication, Azure Key Vault for managing secrets, and network security groups to restrict access. These scenarios require you to think about security at every level, from identity management to data encryption.

Practice Strategies

To prepare for scenario-based questions, you need to practice. One of the best resources is Microsoft Learn, which has a practice assessment (*https://oreil.ly/rZNI_*) you can take to simulate the types of questions you'll encounter on the AZ-204 exam (Figure 14-1). These practice assessments are designed to mimic the format and difficulty of the actual exam, giving you a chance to test your knowledge and identify areas where you need improvement. For example, you might be presented with a scenario where you need to choose the best Azure service for a specific use case, such as selecting between Azure Functions and Logic Apps for a serverless workflow. By working through these practice questions, you'll get a feel for how scenarios are structured and how to approach them methodically.

The nice thing about the practice questions is that you can view the answers right away. That way, you can immediately understand where you went wrong and learn the correct approach. This instant feedback helps reinforce your knowledge and builds confidence for the actual exam. Figure 14-2 shows what this looks like when you take the practice test.

Reviewing sample questions is another key part of your preparation. Look for practice exams or question banks that focus on scenario-based questions. As you work through these questions, pay attention to the patterns and themes that emerge. For example, you might notice that scenarios involving real-time data processing often require you to choose between Event Hubs, Stream Analytics, and Azure Functions. By identifying these patterns, you can develop a mental framework for approaching similar questions on the exam. Additionally, reviewing sample questions helps you get comfortable with the exam's format and timing, which can reduce stress on test day.

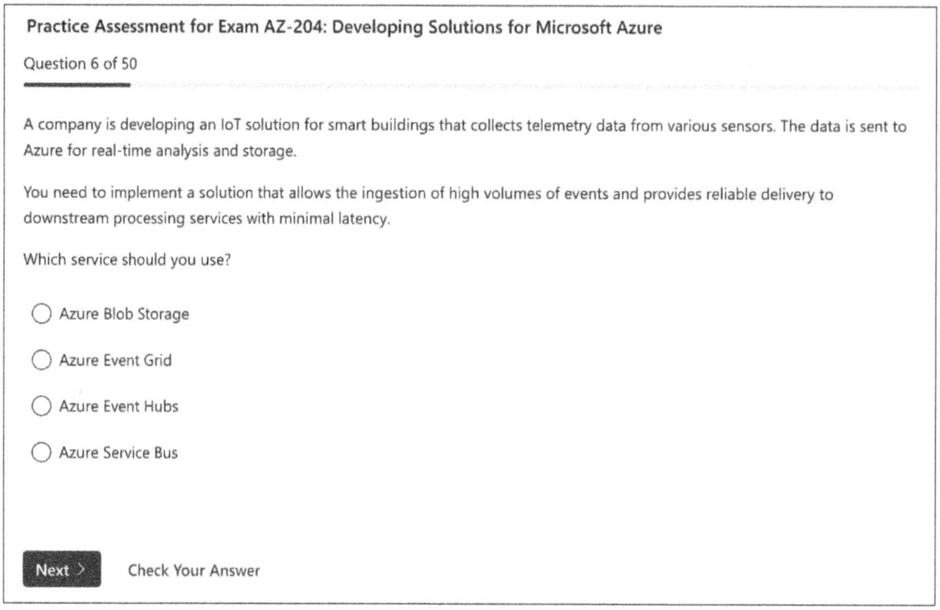

Practice Assessment for Exam AZ-204: Developing Solutions for Microsoft Azure

Question 6 of 50

A company is developing an IoT solution for smart buildings that collects telemetry data from various sensors. The data is sent to Azure for real-time analysis and storage.

You need to implement a solution that allows the ingestion of high volumes of events and provides reliable delivery to downstream processing services with minimal latency.

Which service should you use?

- ◯ Azure Blob Storage
- ◯ Azure Event Grid
- ◯ Azure Event Hubs
- ◯ Azure Service Bus

Next > Check Your Answer

Figure 14-1. Sample AZ-204 practice question

Practice Assessment for Exam AZ-204: Developing Solutions for Microsoft Azure

Question 6 of 50

A company is developing an IoT solution for smart buildings that collects telemetry data from various sensors. The data is sent to Azure for real-time analysis and storage.

You need to implement a solution that allows the ingestion of high volumes of events and provides reliable delivery to downstream processing services with minimal latency.

Which service should you use?

- ◯ Azure Blob Storage
- ◯ Azure Event Grid
- ◉ Azure Event Hubs

  ✓This answer is correct.
- ◯ Azure Service Bus

Azure Event Hubs is designed for high-throughput, real-time event streaming and is compatible with Apache Kafka, making it suitable for IoT scenarios. Azure Event Grid is more suited for event routing and serverless applications. Azure Service Bus is better for traditional enterprise messaging patterns, and Azure Blob Storage is not optimized for real-time event ingestion.

Explore Azure Event Grid - Training | Microsoft Learn

Discover Azure Event Hubs - Training | Microsoft Learn

Overview - Azure Event Grid | Microsoft Learn

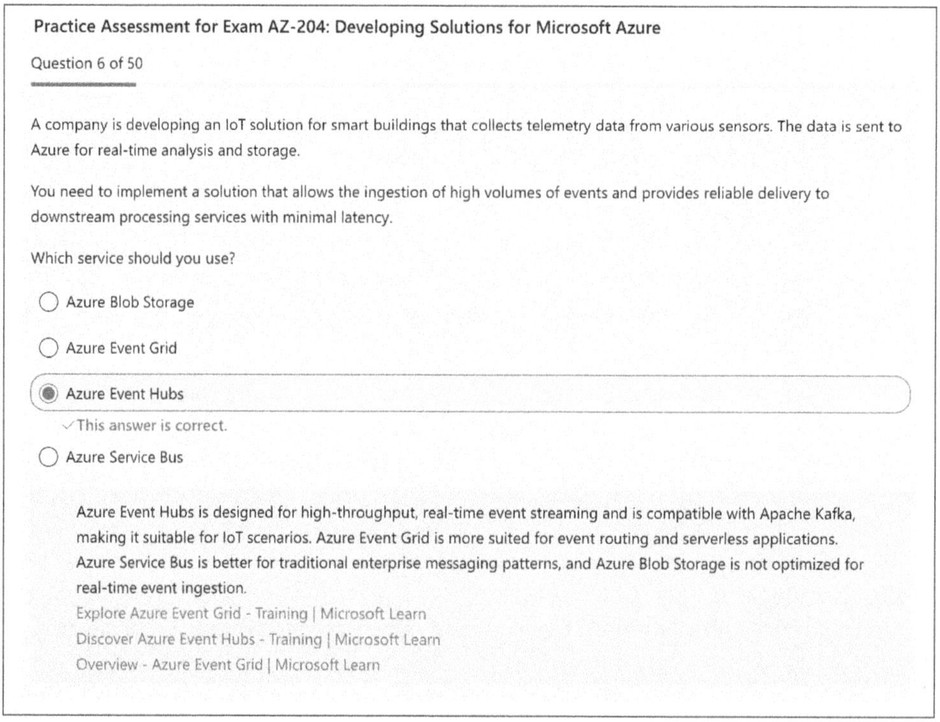

Figure 14-2. Sample AZ-204 practice question and answer

Finally, don't underestimate the value of community resources. Online forums, study groups, and social media communities are great places to discuss scenario-based questions and learn from others who have taken the exam. For example, you might find a discussion about a tricky scenario involving AKS and learn how others approached the problem. Engaging with the community can help you learn and see scenarios from different perspectives.

Strategic Approach to Exam Questions

When you're faced with an exam question, the first step is to read and interpret it effectively. This means taking the time to understand what the question is asking rather than rushing to pick an answer. Start by reading the question stem carefully, paying attention to every detail. For example, if the question describes a scenario where a company needs to process real-time data from IoT devices, make sure you note the specific requirements, such as low latency, fault-tolerant, or secure. These details are critical because they guide you toward the correct answer. Misreading or overlooking a key requirement can lead you to choose the wrong solution.

Another important skill is identifying keywords and requirements in the question stem. Keywords are the terms that define the problem or the constraints. For instance, if the question mentions serverless, you know that services like Azure Functions or Logic Apps are likely candidates. If the question emphasizes global distribution, you might think of Cosmos DB or Azure Traffic Manager. When you focus on these keywords, you can quickly narrow down the relevant Azure services and approaches.

Eliminating Incorrect Options

Once you've understood a multiple-choice question, the next step is to eliminate incorrect options. Start by ruling out options that clearly don't fit the scenario. For example, if the question is about real-time data processing and one of the options is Azure Table Storage, you can eliminate it because Table Storage is designed for simple NoSQL use cases, not real-time analytics. When you remove the obviously wrong answers, you reduce the number of choices and increase your chances of selecting the correct one.

Another technique is to avoid common traps and distractors. Exam questions often include options that sound correct but are subtly wrong. For instance, a question might ask about securing an application, and one of the options could be using Azure Firewall. While Azure Firewall is a valid security tool, it's primarily for network-level security, not application-level security. The correct answer might be Entra ID or Azure Key Vault, depending on the scenario. To avoid falling for these traps, always go back to the question and verify the option aligns with the specific requirements.

Prioritizing Solutions

After narrowing down the options, the final step is to choose the best Azure service or approach for the given scenario. This requires you to balance multiple factors, such as technical feasibility and the requirements. For example, if the scenario involves building a highly scalable web application, you might consider Azure App Service with autoscaling. However, if the scenario also emphasizes cost-efficiency, you might need to evaluate whether a less expensive option, like Azure VMs with manual scaling, could meet the requirements. The key is to prioritize the solution that best aligns with the scenario's primary goals.

Another aspect of prioritization is balancing technical feasibility with business requirements. Sometimes, the technically optimal solution might be too expensive or complex for the business's needs. For instance, using AKS might be the best technical choice for a microservices architecture, but if the company lacks the expertise to manage Kubernetes, a simpler solution like Azure App Service might be more practical. In these cases, you need to weigh the technical benefits against the business constraints and choose the solution that offers the best overall fit.

Maintaining a Positive Exam Mindset

Exams can be tough, and the pressure is understandable, especially when you're faced with challenging or unfamiliar questions. One of the most important skills you can develop is the ability to stay calm under pressure. When you feel stressed, your ability to think clearly and make good decisions can suffer. To manage stress during the exam, try deep breathing techniques. For example, take a slow breath in for four seconds, hold it for four seconds, and then exhale for four seconds. This simple exercise can help calm your nerves and refocus your mind. Another technique is to take short mental breaks. If you encounter a difficult question, pause for a moment, close your eyes, and reset your thoughts before moving forward.

Handling challenging or unfamiliar questions is another key part of staying calm. It's normal to come across questions that seem difficult at first glance. When this happens, don't panic. Start by breaking the question down into smaller parts. Identify the keywords and requirements and try to relate them to what you've studied. For example, if the question is about a service you're not entirely familiar with, think about similar services or concepts you know. Often, you can use your existing knowledge to make an educated guess. Remember, you don't have to get every question right to pass the exam. Focus on doing your best and moving forward.

Confidence plays a huge role in how well you perform on the exam. The best way to build confidence is through preparation and practice. The more you study and work through practice questions, the more familiar you'll become with the exam format and the types of questions you'll face. For example, if you've practiced multiple scenarios involving Azure Functions and Logic Apps, you'll feel much more confident when a similar question appears on the exam. Hands-on practice is especially important because it helps you understand how Azure services work in real-world situations. The more you practice, the less intimidating the exam will feel.

During the exam, it's easy to fall into mental traps that can undermine your performance. One common pitfall is self-doubt. You might start second-guessing your answers, especially if you're unsure about a question. While it's good to double-check your work, constantly doubting yourself can waste time and increase stress. To overcome self-doubt, trust your preparation. If you've studied thoroughly and practiced consistently, you're more than ready to tackle the exam. Remember, your first instinct is often correct, so avoid changing answers unless you're absolutely sure you made a mistake.

Time Management During the Exam

The duration of the exam is 100 minutes, so it's crucial to plan your time wisely to ensure you can answer all the questions without feeling rushed. Start by allocating time for different question types. For example, multiple-choice questions might take less time than scenario-based or interactive questions, which require more thought and analysis. A good rule of thumb is to spend about one to two minutes on straightforward multiple-choice questions and three to five minutes on more complex scenario-based questions. Drag-and-drop questions, which involve matching or ordering items, usually fall somewhere in between. By estimating how much time each question type might take, you can create a mental schedule for the exam.

Another important aspect of planning is setting milestones to track progress. For instance, you might aim to complete 10 questions in the first 15 minutes, or reach the halfway point by the 50-minute mark. These milestones help you stay on track and ensure you're not spending too much time on any one section. If you find yourself falling behind, you can adjust your pace accordingly. For example, if you've spent 10 minutes on a single question, it might be time to move on and come back to it later. Having a clear plan reduces stress and helps you stay focused throughout the exam.

Prioritizing Questions

Not all questions are created equal, and some will be easier for you to answer than others. A smart strategy is to tackle easier questions first. This helps you build momentum and gain confidence early in the exam. For example, if you come across a question about a topic you've studied extensively, like configuring an Azure App Service, answer it quickly and move on. This approach ensures you secure points for questions you know well, leaving more time for challenging ones later.

Avoiding Time Traps

One of the biggest challenges during the exam is recognizing when to move on from a challenging question. It's easy to get stuck on a difficult question, especially if you feel like you're close to figuring it out. However, spending too much time on one question can leave you scrambling to finish the rest of the exam. A good rule is to set a time limit for each question, say, three minutes, and stick to it. If you haven't made progress by then, move on and make a mental note to return to the question later. Remember, it's better to answer all the questions you know and come back to the tough ones later than to run out of time and leave questions unanswered.

Another time trap is overthinking. Sometimes, you might second-guess your answer or spend too much time analyzing every option. To avoid this, trust your preparation and go with your initial instinct. If you've studied well and practiced consistently, your first answer is often the correct one. Overthinking not only wastes time but can also lead to unnecessary stress and confusion.

Summary

As you get ready to take this exam, focus on applying your Azure development skills strategically. Scenario-based questions require analyzing business and technical requirements, evaluating trade-offs, and prioritizing solutions. Many scenarios involve integrating multiple Azure services, handling distributed systems, or ensuring security best practices. To prepare, practice with Microsoft Learn, review sample exams, and engage in study communities. During the exam, read questions carefully, identify key details, eliminate incorrect options, and manage your time wisely by tackling easier questions first and avoiding time traps.

Maintaining confidence and a positive mindset are essential. Stay calm, trust your preparation, and approach difficult questions methodically. Hands-on experience and familiarity with the exam format will help reinforce your knowledge too. And remember, the AZ-204 exam is just one step in your journey. The knowledge and problem-solving skills you've gained will serve you well in your career, helping you design and implement innovative solutions in the cloud. Keep practicing, stay curious, and continue learning. The Azure ecosystem is constantly evolving, and so should you. Good luck on your exam, and may this be the start of many achievements in your cloud development career.

Index

A

B

C

D

E

F

G

H

M

N

O

P

Q

R

S

T

U

V

W

Y

Z

About the Author

Adora Nwodo is a multi-award–winning engineering manager working at the intersection of cloud engineering and developer platforms. She's currently a Microsoft MVP and a mentor for computer science students at the University of Bristol. Previously, she was a software engineer at Microsoft, building mixed reality on the Azure cloud. Adora was recently featured on the Global 40 Under 40 list and has also been featured on major media platforms like Yahoo Finance, *Business Insider*, *The Guardian*, and more.

Colophon

The animal on the cover of *Microsoft Certified Azure Developer Associate (AZ-204) Study Guide* is a male indigo bunting (*Passerina cyanea*). Found throughout all of North America, these attractive songbirds can be heard singing from many forests, grasslands, cities, and suburbs.

While male indigo buntings are known for their deep blue plumage, interestingly, their feathers only turn blue during the summer season to attract mates. In the fall and winter seasons, their feathers are actually brown; female indigo buntings are brown all year long and do not change their feathers (with good reason, too—they're hidden away in dense thickets caring for their young). Indigo buntings are small birds, measuring 4.5–6 inches long with a wingspan of 7–9 inches; they can weigh between 0.40 and 0.75 ounces.

Males in particular are known for their bouncy, whistling songs, which they learn from other nearby males when they're young; their songs are used to mark territories and attract females. Indigo buntings like to dwell in wooded areas and grasslands but prefer to nest along roadsides. They feed on seeds, berries, and insects, and can sometimes be found foraging on lawns or yards with feeders.

Indigo buntings are abundant throughout their range and are considered a species of Least Concern in terms of their conservation status. However, intensive agriculture and urbanization do threaten their population.

Many of the animals on O'Reilly covers are endangered; all of them are important to the world.

The cover illustration is by José Marzan Jr., based on a based on an antique line engraving from *Shaw's Zoology*. The series design is by Edie Freedman, Ellie Volckhausen, and Karen Montgomery. The cover fonts are Gilroy Semibold and Guardian Sans. The text font is Adobe Minion Pro; the heading font is Adobe Myriad Condensed; and the code font is Dalton Maag's Ubuntu Mono.

www.ingramcontent.com/pod-product-compliance
Lightning Source LLC
Jackson TN
JSHW040021170825
89466JS00012B/66

* 9 7 8 1 0 9 8 1 7 3 4 9 4 *